Post-Conflict Security in South Sudan

Post-Conflict Security in South Sudan

From Liberal Peacebuilding to Demilitarization

Nyambura Wambugu

I.B. TAURIS
LONDON · NEW YORK · OXFORD · NEW DELHI · SYDNEY

I.B. TAURIS
Bloomsbury Publishing Plc
50 Bedford Square, London, WC1B 3DP, UK
1385 Broadway, New York, NY 10018, USA
29 Earlsfort Terrace, Dublin 2, Ireland

BLOOMSBURY, I.B. TAURIS and the I.B. Tauris logo
are trademarks of Bloomsbury Publishing Plc

First published 2019
Paperback edition first published 2021

Copyright © Nyambura Wambugu, 2019

Nyambura Wambugu has asserted her right under the Copyright,
Designs and Patents Act, 1988, to be identified as Author of this work.

For legal purposes the Acknowledgements on p. xii constitute
an extension of this copyright page.

Cover design: Rob Pinney
Cover image: A Sudan People's Liberation Army (SPLA) government soldier walks towards
the town of Malakal on 20 March 2014. (© AFP / Stringer)

All rights reserved. No part of this publication may be reproduced or
transmitted in any form or by any means, electronic or mechanical,
including photocopying, recording, or any information storage or retrieval
system, without prior permission in writing from the publishers.

Bloomsbury Publishing Plc does not have any control over, or responsibility for,
any third-party websites referred to or in this book. All internet addresses given
in this book were correct at the time of going to press. The author and publisher
regret any inconvenience caused if addresses have changed or sites have
ceased to exist, but can accept no responsibility for any such changes.

A catalogue record for this book is available from the British Library.

A catalog record for this book is available from the Library of Congress.

ISBN: HB: 978-1-7845-3694-7
PB: 978-0-7556-3598-6
ePDF: 978-1-7867-3587-4
eBook: 978-1-7867-2587-5

Typeset by Newgen KnowledgeWorks Pvt. Ltd., Chennai, India

To find out more about our authors and books visit
www.bloomsbury.com and sign up for our newsletters.

For Daniel Julius Kimani Nduati 1968–2014

Contents

List of Illustrations		x
Acknowledgements		xii
List of Appendices		xiii
List of Abbreviations and Acronyms		xiv
1	Introduction	1
	Research	4
	Arguments and structure	8
	Themes	9
	Liberal peacebuilding in South Sudan	11
	Exploring demilitarization literature	13
2	South Sudan	21
	Introduction	21
	Politics of state formation: past and present	23
	Towards the post-colonial state	25
	The legacy of slavery and the slave trade	28
	The identity complex in the Sudan	31
	The politics of identity in post-colonial Sudan	32
	Ethnic identities and conflict	34
	Conflict identities in South Sudan	36
	Conclusions	38
3	History of militarization	41
	Introduction	41
	Contextualizing militarization in South Sudan	41
	Pre-independence – before 1955	44
	Post-independence	46
	The First Civil War (1955–72)	46
	The Torit Mutiny	49
	The Second Civil War – The SPLA (1983–2005)	51
	The southern mutinies	52
	The Nasir Declaration	54

	The politics of oil and war	56
	Post-CPA militarization	58
	Juba Declaration of 8 January 2006	59
	Conclusion	62
4	Contextualizing security restructuring and reforms	65
	Introduction	65
	Security sector reforms (SSR) in South Sudan	68
	SSR and development	69
	Implementing DDR	76
	The challenges of DDR	78
	Conclusion	88
5	Realizing security restructuring and reforms	91
	Restructuring security	91
	Force reduction	94
	SPLA restructuring	97
	National Intelligence and Security Service in South Sudan's post-conflict security	100
	Reform by institutionalization	101
	The South Sudan Police Service	102
	From the shadows of the SPLA	104
	Beyond the empirical challenges: contextualizing the challenges to policing	105
	Need not dogma	108
	The legacy of war: societal constructions of security and the paradox of armed youth	112
	The cattle raider	115
	Conclusions	119
6	Restructuring governance	123
	Introduction	123
	Restructuring governance	124
	Building or rebuilding governance?	125
	Rethinking the restructuring of governance in South Sudan	129
	Building a party from the ashes of a rebel movement: from SPLA to SPLM	132
	SPLM dominance: undemocratic democracy?	137
	The elections	140

	A flawed election and resurgence of armed rebellions in South Sudan	144
	Elections and the re-emergence of war	147
	Democratizing governance	149
	Changing military structures and attitudes	151
	Illiteracy and democracy	152
	Institutions and restructuring governance in South Sudan	158
	Conclusion	160
7	Arms and livelihoods	163
	Introduction	163
	Social economic development and demilitarization	165
	A history of underdevelopment	168
	Taking stock – South Sudan's Development Plan	169
	This gun is our food – militarized livelihoods	171
	The long road back – demilitarizing livelihoods in South Sudan	174
	The gun for a hoe: agriculture as the answer?	177
	Realizing agriculture – the empirical	180
	Conclusion	184
8	Conclusion	187
	Beyond December 2013	188
	Contextualization of the South Sudan liberal peacebuilding experience	189
	Reviewing key themes	193
	Security	193
	Governance	195
	Arms and livelihoods	198
	Conclusion	200
Appendices		203
Notes		221
Bibliography		235
Index		261

Illustrations

Figures

1.1	President Salva Kiir Mayardit	6
1.2	Demilitarization through security, politics and social economic development	9
2.1	Timeline of Main political events in Sudan	22
3.1	Torit Memorial	50
5.1	Akwilino Lokwar Lopir herding cattle	116
5.2	Lokwar working as a guard	117
5.3	Attending school	117
5.4	Learning basic maths	117
5.5	Fetching clean water	118
5.6	Using skills from basic maths to run small business	118
6.1	Pre-2005 CPA travel permit	128
6.2	Post-CPA travel permit	128
6.3	Flyer – democracy public forum in Juba, South Sudan	132
6.4	Voting cards	156
7.1	South Sudan GDP shares in 2010	171
7.2	Residents of Mogos – Kapoeta East County 19 July 2011	172

Tables

5.1	SPLA divisions and locations	98
6.1	Focus Group 1 data extract	142
6.2	Focus Group 5 data extract	142
6.3	South Sudan's Governors	151
6.4	Focus Group 1 – Ikotos County	154
6.5	Focus Group 2 – Magwi County	154
6.6	Focus Group 3 – Budi County	154
6.7	Focus Group 4 – Lafon County	155
6.8	Focus Group 5 – Kapoeta South County	155

| 7.1 | World Bank – World development indicators 2012 | 170 |
| 7.2 | The agricultural sector in developing countries (1965–85) | 179 |

Maps

1	South Sudan in the Region	xvii
2	South Sudan in Africa	xviii
3	South Sudan: Administrative Divisions until 2015 – Ten States	xix
4	Map of Eastern Equatoria State's Eight Counties	xix
5	Map of South Sudan's New Administrative Boundaries – 28 States	xx
6	Areas key to the Sudan's modern history of militarization	43

Acknowledgements

This book is the work of a long process, one that began even before I did my undergraduate studies, after first coming into contact with South Sudan – then Southern Sudan – in 2002. Nevertheless, it would not have come to fruition without the support and assistance of many people in South Sudan and the UK.

I am eternally indebted to the Catholic Diocese of Torit for opening up the interiors of South Sudan to me. This book would have been impossible to complete without that support. To the Sudd Institute – your support and friendship has seen me this far. I am also grateful for the advice and guidance of Professor Edward Newman and Dr Alexander Beresford, without whom I doubt I would have completed this book.

To my family and friends, I don't even know where to begin. To friends, especially Abraham Awolich and Dr Henry Kippin, your friendship is invaluable. To my family, especially Iddah, Wakinas, Muriithi, Mwangi and Dan – I love you and thank God every day for you.

Finally, I would like to thank my parents, Wambugu Muriithi and Wanjiru Wambugu. When I think of the sacrifices you made to put me through school, the journey from Eastleigh to this point has been a long one. I can't find words strong enough to express how I feel, so all I'll say is, 'thank you'.

Appendices

A.1 New South Sudan Administrative Divisions – December 2015   203

A.2 Questionnaire – Perceptions of Demilitarization and DDR in South Sudan   204

A.3 Questionnaire – Restructuring Security   205

A.4 South Sudan Armed Rebellions: Date of Compilation February 2013   207

A.5 Archive document – staff list for SSRC in 2004   209

A.6 South Sudan National DDR Commission composition   210

A.7 Press Statement President Salva Kiir on 16 December 2013   211

A.8 South Sudanese reactions to 15 December 2013 – Dr Jok Madut Jok, Loyola Marymount University, California   213

A.9 South Sudanese reactions to 15 December 2013 – Prof. Samson Wassara, University of Juba   216

Abbreviations and Acronyms

ANC	African National Congress
ARCRSS	Agreement on the Resolution of the Conflict in the Republic of South Sudan
AU	African Union
BCSSAC	Bureau For Community Security and Small Arms Control
BICC	Bonn International Centre for Conversion
CAAFG	Children Associated With Armed Forces Groups
CANS	Civil Authority of New Sudan
CDOT	Catholic Diocese of Torit
CEO	Chief Operation Officer
COGS	Chief of General Staff
CoS	Council of State
CPA	Comprehensive Peace Agreement
DAC	Development Assistance Committee
DCOGS	Deputy Chief of General Staff
DDR	Disarmament Demobilisation and Reintegration
DFID	Department for International Development
DIGP	Deputy Inspector General of Police
DOT	Diocese of Torit (Catholic)
DPKO	Department of Peacekeeping Operations
DRC	Democratic Republic of Congo
EAPCCO	Eastern Africa Police Chiefs Cooperation Organisation
ECOWAS	Economic Community Of West African States
EES	Eastern Equatoria State
FAO	Food and Agriculture Organisation
FGD	Focus Group Discussions
GDP	Gross Domestic Product
GIZ	German Organisation for Technical Cooperation (formerly GTZ)
GNI	Gross National Income
GOS	Government of Sudan
GOSS	Government of South Sudan
HAC	Humanitarian Aid Commission
HDI	Human Development Index
HSBA	Human Security Baseline Assessment (For Sudan)
ICGLR	International Conference on the Great Lakes Region
IDDRP	Interim Disarmament, Demobilisation and Reintegration Programme

Abbreviations and Acronyms

IDDRS	Integrated Disarmament, Demobilisation and Reintegration Standards
IGAD	Intergovernmental Authority on Development
IGP	Inspector General of Police
INGO	International Non-Governmental Organisation
IR	International Relations
IRI	International Republican Institute
JEM	Justice and Equality Movement
JIU	Joint Integrated Unit
JMEC	Joint Monitoring and Evaluation Commission
JOC	Joint Operation Centres
KPA	Khartoum Peace Agreement
LRA	Lord's Resistance Army
NCP	National Congress Party
NDDRC	National Disarmament Demobilisation and Reintegration Commission
NDFSS	National Defence Forces of South Sudan
NDI	National Democratic Institute
NEC	National Elections Commission
NIF	National Islamic Front
NISS	National Intelligence and Security Service
NLA	National Legislative Assembly
NLC	National Liberation Council
OECD	Organisation for Economic Cooperation and Development
PKSOI	Peacekeeping and Stability Operations Institute
RSS	Republic of South Sudan
RUF	Revolutionary United Front
SAF	Sudan Armed Forces
SLA-AW	Sudan Liberation Army – Abdul Wahid
SLA-MM	Sudan Liberation Army – Minni Minawi
SNG	Special Needs Group
SPLA	Sudan People's Liberation Army
SPLM	Sudan People's Liberation Movement
SPLM/A	Sudan People's Liberation Movement/Army
SPLM-N	Sudan People's Liberation Movement-North
SRF	Sudan Recovery Fund
SRF	Sudan Revolutionary Front
SRRA	Sudan Relief and Rehabilitation Association
SSDDRC	South Sudan Disarmament Demobilisation and Reintegration Commission
SSDF	South Sudan Defence Forces
SSDM/A	South Sudan Democratic Movement/Army

SSDP	South Sudan Development Plan
SSLM/A	South Sudan Liberation Movement/Army
SSNBS	South Sudan National Bureau of Statistics
SSNDDRC	South Sudan National Disarmament Demobilisation and Reintegration Commission
SSPS	South Sudan Police Service
SSR	Security Sector Reform
SSRC	Southern Sudan Referendum Commission
SST	Security Sector Transformation
SSWS	South Sudan Wildlife Service
SuGDE	Sudanese Group for Democratic Elections
SuNDE	Sudanese Network for Democratic Elections
TGoNU	Transitional Government of National Unity
TMC	Transitional Military Council
UK	United Kingdom
UN	United Nations
UNDP	United Nations Development Programme
UNDPKO	United Nations Department of Peacekeeping Operations
UNISFA	United Nations Interim Security Force for Abyei
UNITA	National Union for the Total Independence of Angola
UNMIS	United Nations Mission in Sudan
UNMISS	United Nations Mission in South Sudan
USAID	United States Agency for International Development
USIP	United States Institute of Peace
VOA	Voice of America
WAAFG	Women Associated With Armed Forces Groups
WFP	World Food Programme

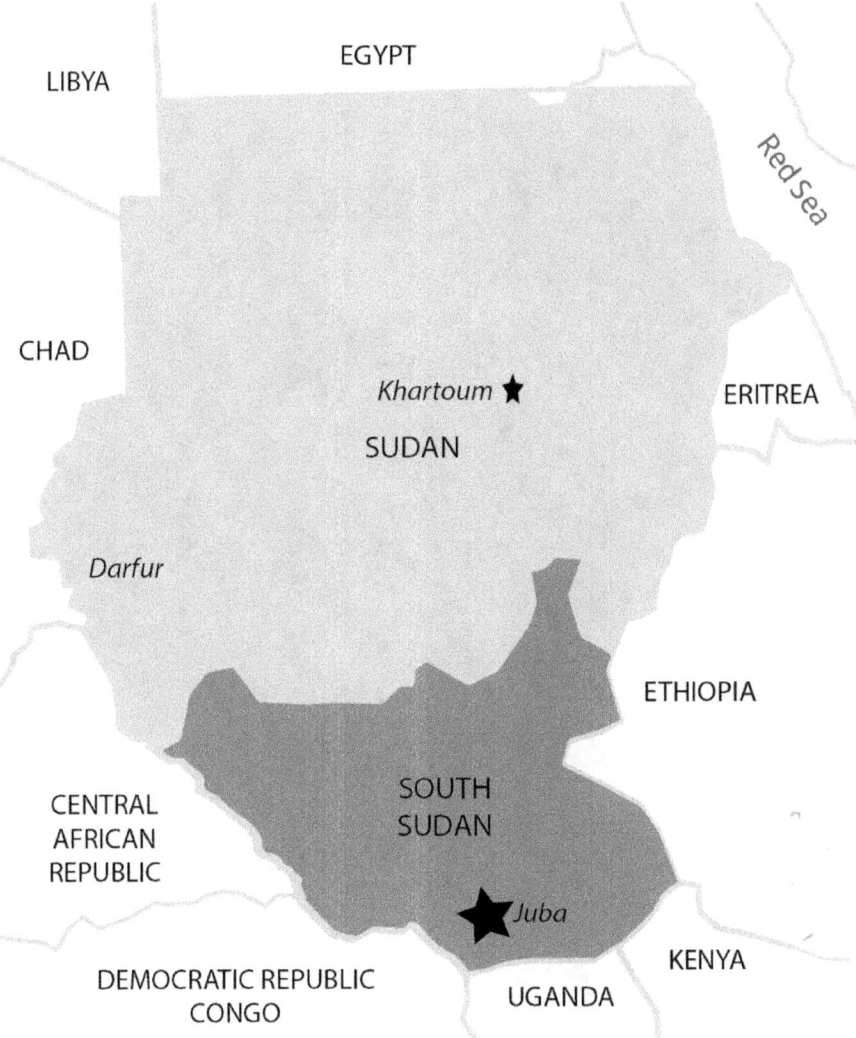

Map 1 South Sudan in the Region

Map 2 South Sudan in Africa

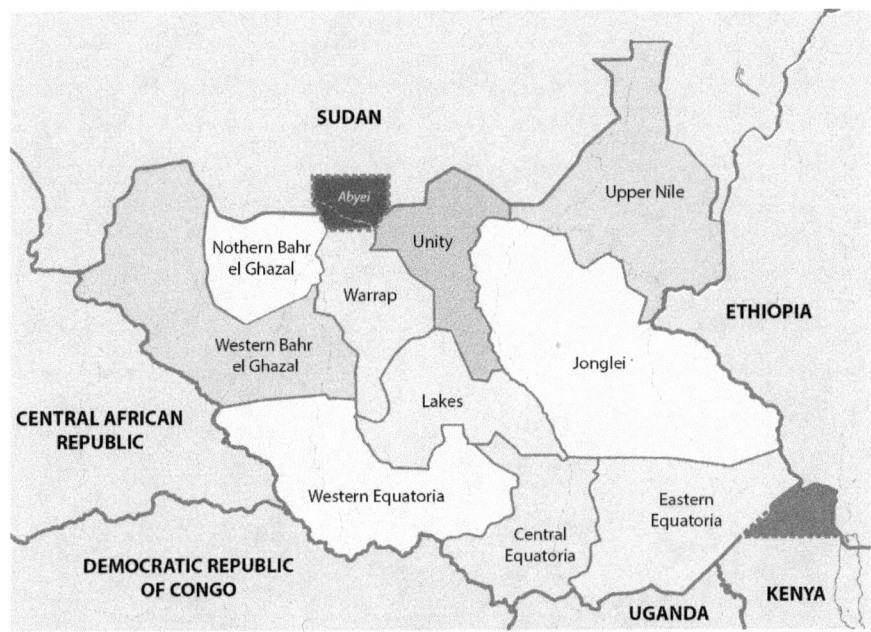

Map 3 South Sudan: Administrative Divisions until 2015 – Ten States

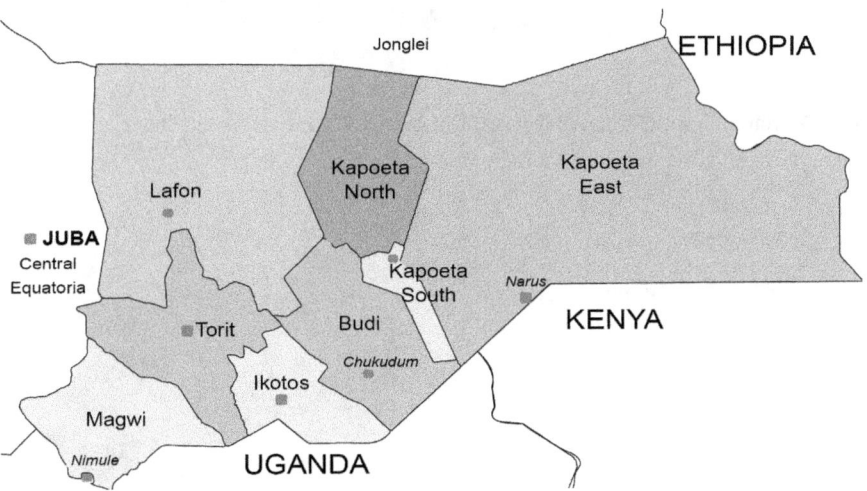

Map 4 Map of Eastern Equatoria State's Eight Counties

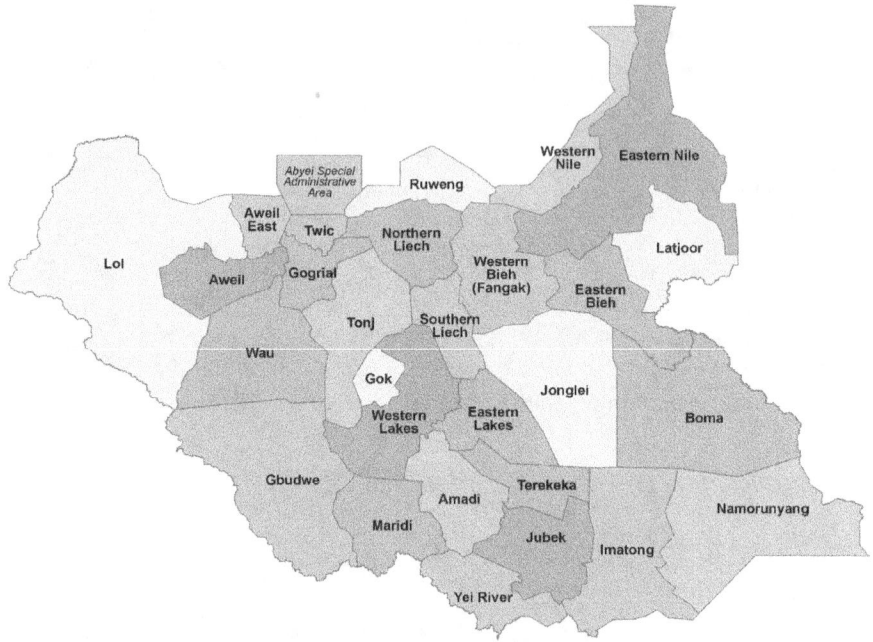

Map 5 Map of South Sudan's New Administrative Boundaries – 28 States

1

Introduction

On 9 January 2005, the Sudan Government and the southern rebel movement, the Sudan People's Liberation Army/Movement (SPLA/M) signed a peace agreement that ended the country's 21-year civil war. This set the country on a path to an internationally led post-conflict reconstruction based on liberal peacebuilding.[1] The protracted war between the south and north of Sudan was, at the time of the agreement, the longest running in Africa. The peace agreement known as the Comprehensive Peace Agreement (CPA) was based on a six-year transition period, after which the south would have a referendum to determine its fate, either to remain part of Sudan or secede into an independent state. On 9 January 2011, the referendum for the south's independence was held. Southerners voted overwhelming to secede from Sudan and, on 9 July 2011, the Republic of South Sudan came into being. However, 18 months later on 15 December 2013, the young country plunged into a new civil war in events that began as a power struggle within the ruling party, the SPLM.

The post-independence civil war that followed December 2013 raised many questions about not only South Sudan's journey to statehood, but also the circumstances under which this statehood was midwifed by the international community and the nature of its post-conflict security[2] structures. These questions fundamentally query what went wrong in the post-war reconstruction that followed the CPA in 2005 and in the formation of the new country, the Republic of South Sudan. The questions raised in this book thus extend not only to South Sudan's management of its affairs, but to the internationally led liberal peacebuilding intervention adopted in the country. Specifically, as to whether South Sudan's return to war just 18 months after its independence was an indictment of a liberal peace approach which prioritized democratic development and institutionalization, rule of law, human rights and market economy as the basis for the state security and peace.[3] As the country stumbles from one crisis to another and the rumbles of the post-December 2013 civil war continue, despite the signing of the August 2015 peace agreement, these questions are especially relevant.

The August 2015 agreement, known as the Agreement on the Resolution of the Conflict in the Republic of South Sudan (ARCRSS), like the CPA before it set South Sudan on the path to reconstruction. First, with the formation of a Transitional Government of National Unity (TGoNU) with a power-sharing formula between the Government of South Sudan and the armed opposition, the Sudan People's Liberation Army/Movement In Opposition (SPLA/M-IO)[4] as well as other interested parties. The ARCRSS was supposed to lead up to elections at the end of the transitional period. To a large extent, the new peace agreement mediated by the regional body the Intergovernmental Authority on Development (IGAD), with support from the international community, follows a similar pattern to the 2005 peace agreement, the overarching intention being the cessation of hostilities and the reconstruction of the South Sudanese state anchored in liberal democratic practices, resulting in a liberal peace.

However, despite the signing of the ARCRSS in August 2015, the country remained in a precarious state with uncertainty over its implementation. For the most part, until April 2016 the agreement could not be implemented nor the transitional government formed because the SPLA/M-IO leader Riek Machar had not returned to the capital Juba. The challenges of state reconstruction, peacebuilding, security sector reform and reconstructions faced by South Sudan did not, however, wane with the return of Machar and the SPLA/M-IO delegation to Juba and the formation of the transitional government. From its inception, the TGoNU was paralysed by suspicion and mistrust on both sides, lack of political will from the Government of South Sudan to implement the peace agreement and dire economic realities[5] resulting from the high cost of the post-December 2013 war (Luengo-Cabrera 2016).

The outbreak of fighting between Government and SPLA/M-IO forces in Juba in July 2016 in particular threatened to collapse the TGoNU and the August 2015 peace agreement upon which it was based. This fighting forced the departure of Riek Machar from Juba and his replacement with Taban Deng Gai as the new SPLA/M-IO nominated first vice president. The Joint Monitoring and Evaluation Commission (JMEC), set up to monitor and oversee the implementation of the August 2015 peace agreement, noted that the August 2015 peace deal in South Sudan was wounded but insisted it was not yet dead. Still, the fighting in July

2016 and the exit of Riek Machar from Juba significantly changed the stakes in South Sudan and further complicated the conflict and peace dynamics in the country.[6] Whereas the problem of security restructuring and reform preceded the December 2013 crisis and ensuing war, the damage inflicted on the country by the post-independence war was unprecedented.

The July 2016 fighting in Juba took the strain that the war exerted on South Sudan's social fabric to another level, further fracturing already fragile inter-community relations. The breakdown in community relations is likely to make the reconstruction efforts even more challenging. During the events which led to the post-December 2013 conflict, previously peaceful parts of South Sudan like the Equatoria also degenerated into conflict, further adding to the layers and dynamics of conflict in the country. The question of whether a liberal peacebuilding approach is appropriate for South Sudan's post-conflict reconstruction, both present and past, is thus not only timely, but necessary.

This book examines the various arguments and asks the fundamental questions by interrogating South Sudan's liberal peacebuilding-based post-conflict intervention. Specifically, the book focuses on the reconstruction of post-conflict security (Krause and Jütersonke 2005; Muggah 2009; Valters et al. 2014) as the prerequisite for the success of any broader reconstruction. While the formation of the TGoNU as stipulated in the August 2015 peace agreement set South Sudan on yet another phase of post-conflict reconstruction, this book concentrates on the previous post-conflict intervention period that followed the 2005 CPA. In particular, it interrogates the application of liberal peacebuilding in South Sudan, its failings and examines why the post-2005 intervention failed to result in the intended liberal peace.

While an approach based on liberal peacebuilding focuses on the promotion of democracy, market-based economic reforms and a range of other institutions associated with 'modern' states as a driving force for building peace (Newman 2009), an alternative approach that does not prioritize democratization and liberal institutionalization may offer a better chance of achieving stable post-conflict security and a subsequently lasting peace in South Sudan. Although reconstruction based on liberal peacebuilding remains the norm in post-conflict countries, this book makes a case for an alternative approach by exploring the concept of demilitarization and its applicability in South Sudan. This follows extensive fieldwork and research carried out in the country, investigating and examining the application of liberal peacebuilding-based post-conflict reconstruction strategies since the signing of the CPA in 2005.

Research

The research for this book was undertaken in Eastern Equatoria State with elite interviews in the capital Juba. The research took place over a period of three years, combining short research visits to South Sudan from 2009 and a final 18 months period of residence in the country between February 2012 and August 2013. Eastern Equatoria State borders Ethiopia, Kenya and Uganda in the south-east of South Sudan. The research site was chosen because of its history, firstly as the home of the Torit Mutiny which led to the First Civil War between the north and south of Sudan before independence in 1956 and as the home of the SPLA/M after its departure from Ethiopia in 1991 (Nyaba 1997). Eastern Equatoria was also viewed as an ideal research site for a study of demilitarization because of its diverse population and volatility.[7]

The research process adopted an ethnographic approach and used elite interviews in the capital Juba, focus group discussions in Eastern Equatoria and participant observations as its main tools of enquiry. A total of 167 people were interviewed including policymakers, government officials, security personnel in the army, police and intelligence services, international peacekeepers, diplomatic missions and humanitarian actors. Six focus group discussions were also held in Isoke, Chalokol, Kimotong, Mogos, Iboni and Juba with 63 participants in total. A further 18 months were spent in the capital Juba as a participant observer working as a BBC journalist.

This book draws from this fieldwork in its application of demilitarization to the reconstitution of post-conflict security in South Sudan and makes a contribution, not only to its theoretical underpinning, but to its empirical study as well. To this end, this book identifies the generic one-size-fits-all approach to liberal peacebuilding as its greatest shortcoming and presents that, in the case of South Sudan, liberal peacebuilding is at odds with local empirical realities. To effectively demonstrate this, the research that roots this book sought to answer four questions in particular:

1. Why has the application of prevailing post-conflict paradigms like liberal peacebuilding been challenging in South Sudan?
2. How does the evolution of South Sudan's post-conflict politics influence its demilitarization?
3. To what extent can demilitarization deliver societal post-conflict civil-military relations?
4. Is it possible to achieve this post-conflict societal transformation with an illiterate and non-urban population?

These questions especially cut across the different themes addressed in this book. With a focus on demilitarization, this is used and defined as a concept encompassing different elements, namely the restructuring and reforming of security, the restructuring of governance and the redressing of the country's social economic development. Demilitarization of conflict and society, it argues, is crucial to building sustainable peace in countries emerging from the scourge of civil war. As long-standing conflicts come to an end, a variety of approaches are adopted by national governments and international agencies aimed at supporting processes that facilitate this potentially volatile transition from formal peace to social peace (Porto et al. 2007). On the whole, it consolidates an approach based on post-conflict security by acknowledging the attainment of a secure and stable post-conflict security as the central goal of all post-conflict interventions. The book primarily argues that a stable and secure post-conflict security is a precondition for all other post-conflict interventions to succeed.

Nevertheless, the book also argues that the realization of a stable and secure post-conflict security is dependent on the management of post-conflict spaces like post-conflict social economic constructions, how security is restructured after conflict and how governance is organized. These three areas form the backbone of this book and provide the basis for a holistic approach to demilitarization by triangulating these three key post-conflict areas in South Sudan's ontological formations and individual empirical complexities. The presentation of demilitarization as an alternative post-conflict approach thus reinvigorates the engagement with demilitarization literature, which emerged briefly in post-conflict studies in the late 1990s but disappeared with the growth and development of liberal peacebuilding. This book thus removes demilitarization from the shadow of liberal peacebuilding and affirms it as a viable alternative in addressing the challenges of post-conflict security.

Although the space occupied by liberal peacebuilding as the prevailing post-conflict approach in South Sudan and other post-conflict countries is well-established in post-conflict reconstruction literature, its shortcomings are also equally prominent. In the case of South Sudan, the country's return to war after independence is one glaring example of these shortcomings. Events of the night of 15 December 2013 especially, raise significant questions for this book and its aspirations for 'demilitarizing South Sudan' and the championing of a post-conflict security approach to reconstruction. That South Sudanese citizens woke up to news of a coup on the morning of 16 December from a president in full military uniform, departing from his trademark dark suit and cowboy hat, also illustrates some of the challenges tackled in this book. The president, Salva Kiir Mayardit on the day stated that:

> Yesterday [15 December 2013] at about 6.30 pm, during the closing of the SPLM National Liberation Council (NLC) meeting, an unidentified person near Nyakuron Cultural Centre released gunshots in the air and escaped. This was followed later by an attack at the SPLA headquarters near Juba University by a group of soldiers allied to the former vice president Dr Riek Machar Teny and his group. These attacks continued until this morning (16 December 2013). However, I would like to inform you at the outset that your government is in full control of the security situation in Juba. The attackers fled and our forces are pursuing them. I promise you today that justice will prevail (Figure 1.1).

Apart from the weight of the presidential statement, the president's switch from civilian to military uniform illustrated some of the complexities that this book grapples with: specifically, the challenges involved in attempting the demilitarization of a country with a militarization of politics, a highly militarized society and a blurring of military and political lines. As such, this book presents that South Sudan's return to war in mid-December 2013 was broadly an illustration of the shortcomings of the prevailing post-conflict approaches

Figure 1.1 President Salva Kiir Mayardit.
Picture courtesy: Lomoyat: 16 December 2013.

in the country, which it argues were dismissive of its empirical complexities. After December 2013, South Sudan underwent an even deeper militarization of political and civil spaces.

As the country grappled with the ensuing post-December 2013 war, the facade of civilian oversight over the military and the military's role in the country's governance was long abandoned. Although this book broadly looks at the post-CPA intervention in South Sudan, its scope provides an exceptional opportunity in shaping the next post-conflict intervention in the country. The restructuring of security in the country's post-conflict environment must address the relationship between the civil and the military, which in a post-war setting is often a complex and entangled relationship. However, in the case of South Sudan, the restructuring of its civil–military relations must be sensitive to the extent of militarization in the country since the December 2013 conflict started. Specifically, that a restructuring of these relationships strictly based on the separation of the civil and the military may not always work for South Sudan.

A departure from Huntington's separation-based civil–military relations model (Huntington 1957) in the restructuring of South Sudan's civil and military relations is particularly recommended. Instead of separation as the model for remodelling South Sudan's relationships between its military and civil society, this book argues for a move towards a Schiff-based (2009) concordance theory and model of civil–military relations. Rebecca Schiff's concordance theory of civil–military relations, unlike separation, takes into account individual empirical complexities. As such, concordance is highly influential in the arguments and contextual framing of this book. Specifically, that for South Sudan to move beyond its current cycles and layers of conflicts, it must first engage in demilitarization. However, for this to truly have an effect that goes beyond the rhetoric and a surface vernacular of participation (Roberts 2010), it must involve local agency and not rely too much on the existing liberal peacebuilding approaches.

In particular, that a concordance between South Sudan's military, its elite and its citizenry based on its own unique realities as the basis for the redressing of post-conflict security with a focus on demilitarization is more likely to succeed than the current promise of liberal peacebuilding. Still, this research notes that redressing post-conflict security and minimizing the risks of returning to war would be more likely to succeed if local agency – the armed entities, the citizenry and the political elite – were in agreement on not only the kind of peace they see for themselves but, more importantly, on how that peace can be sustained.

Arguments and structure

The various arguments are presented in six chapters which provide a platform for further work and debate in developing a body of work that empirically examines the effectiveness of liberal peacebuilding as the default approach to post-conflict reconstruction. This introductory chapter examines the links between current contextual realities in South Sudan, key themes and introduces demilitarization as an alternative approach in post-conflict interventions. Chapter 2 introduces South Sudan and puts into context the key arguments. The chapter explores the history and politics of state formation and identity in the Sudan, the post-colonial state that emerged at independence in 1956 and their influence on South Sudan's current realities.

Chapter 3 expounds the context and the history of militarization in South Sudan by examining the various conflicts. It explains and assesses the various civil wars in South Sudan and, by so doing, exposes the magnitude of the challenges facing demilitarization in South Sudan. Chapters 4 and 5 both address the main thrust of the book, the restructuring of security in post-conflict South Sudan, focusing on the post-2005 period. They examine the interaction between the theories associated with post-conflict reconstitution of security and the realities of their application in South Sudan and draw conclusions. Chapter 4 examines the contextualization of security restructuring and reforms and specifically the application of two key concepts – SSR and DDR – in the design and approach of South Sudan's post-conflict restructuring and reforming of security from 2005. In particular, the chapter explores and examines their successes, challenges and shortcomings in the deconstruction of South Sudan's war security infrastructure.

Chapter 5 then builds on the debates in Chapter 4 by illustrating some of the empirical challenges involved in the realization of security restructuring and reforms beyond the broader theoretical rhetoric. This should involve tackling the immediate post-conflict activities of disarming, demobilizing and reintegrating of former fighters, the institutionalization of the post-war security infrastructure, including the legislative frameworks, and addressing the security legacy left by war. Chapter 6 examines the restructuring of governance and current debates on political consolidation, particularly the links between democratic elections, democratic institutions and democratic governance and their role in consolidating peace (Bastian and Luckham 2003: 2). The chapter engages with governance and related themes of democracy and elections and sets out to place them in the context of building political consolidation in a post-conflict country (de Zeeuw 2008). Chapter 7 explores the role of securing socio-economic development in a post-conflict country where arms and livelihoods are intrinsically linked. The chapter examines arms and livelihood dichotomies in South Sudan and addresses the reliance on the gun as not only a source of livelihood but also as a protector of livelihoods. The chapter argues that an alternative source of livelihoods not based on firearms is the final piece in the demilitarization puzzle in South Sudan.

Themes

To a large extent, the themes of security, governance and social economic development make up the basis of contemporary post-conflict engagements presented in the liberal peace thesis. However, instead of a post-conflict intervention that prescribes state-building, democratization and economic stabilization as the keys to post-conflict peacebuilding, a focus on demilitarization presents a process that has no blueprint. One that is totally reliant on the empirical reality of the country and, more specifically in the case of South Sudan, one that aims to reverse a legacy of militarization in a way that makes it possible for the processes of state-building to begin (Figure 1.2).

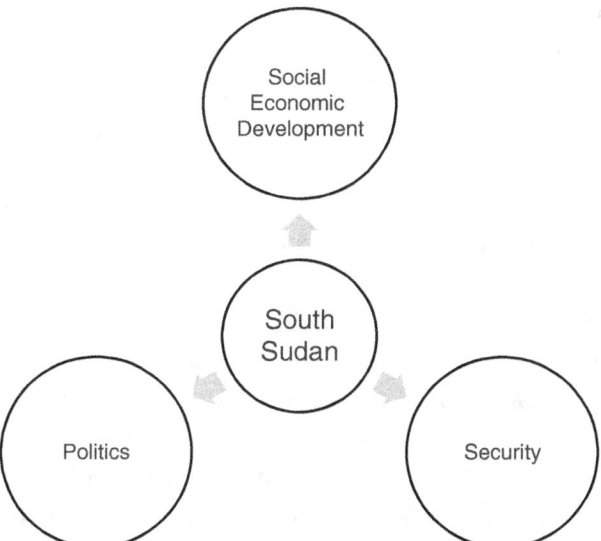

Figure 1.2 Demilitarization through security, politics and social economic development.

This book argues that these three are intrinsically linked to the aspirations of demilitarization. While the areas of security, politics and social economic development are all distinctly separate policy areas in South Sudan, they have been melted into a singular post-conflict transformation approach. This has edged the country's trajectory towards a Western-style liberal democracy but with a progression from the era of the Washington Consensus and neoliberalism pursuits to a more recent New York Consensus in pursuit of humanitarianism, humanitarian interventions and liberal peace which draws little distinction between political, economic or security matters, particularly in conflict or post-conflict spaces. Failing to allow political, economic and social processes to evolve independently, especially in post-conflict countries, is arguably counterproductive. The empirical evidence from South Sudan suggests that this forms the basis for a weak state and an even weaker statehood with an entrenched dependency culture.

With this in mind, this book presents that in South Sudan, there might be some reward in allowing political, economic and social processes to evolve independently and in a manner that suits the country, even when these may not result in democratization or a liberal state. Demilitarization as a post-conflict approach sets the tone for this by addressing issues of post-conflict restructuring of security, governance and the readdressing of livelihoods and social economic challenges in a highly militarized society as codependent but independent of each other. Political developments in South Sudan have resulted in armed conflicts, thus raising particularly difficult questions on the post-conflict intervention aimed at developing a multi-party political system and a liberal democratic state. This book examines political developments in the country by interrogating the restructuring of governance in the post-CPA period and beyond.

The other theme tackled here is development, which is used in relation to three discernible definitions as argued by Sumner and Tribe (2008). That is development as a long-term process of structural societal transformation, a short to medium-term outcome of desirable targets or a dominant 'discourse' of Western modernity. This book does not make any distinction and argues that in South Sudan, development is conceived to include all three definitions to varying degrees, depending on who is defining it and for what purpose. As such, this book also explores the power and influence that liberal peacebuilding interventions give to international development actors and questions their role in the broader arguments. It is the case that the development sector in South Sudan wields an unparalleled influence on the state which presents one of the paradoxes, not only in South Sudan but in contemporary liberal peacebuilding interventions more broadly.

At a time when the concept of security in contemporary society is much more multifaceted and complex (Buzan 2008: 8), this book on demilitarization tackles one of the most complex post-conflict security spaces in contemporary Africa, where traditional definitions of security have moved on from the state being the main referent (Stone 2009: 2). The epistemological challenge in defining security in any concrete and agreeable terms nevertheless go beyond this book, which is not an attempt at reinventing the arguments around definitions and constructions of security. The scope of security is simple and stays close to Barry Buzan's presentations of security and specifically his arguments that intertwine conceptual and empirical approaches to security. The relevance of Buzan's presentation to this book is especially in his arguments that 'security at the individual level is related to security at the level of the state and the international system' (Baldwin 1997: 7).

However, this still does not detract from the fact that 'understanding the concept of security remains a fundamentally different kind of intellectual exercise from specifying the conditions under which security may be attained' (Baldwin 1997: 8). This book's use of security therefore concerns itself with exploring the different conditions under which security in South Sudan can be attained, perhaps because after numerous attempts at defining security, it still remains an insufficiently explicated concept (Baldwin 1997: 24). This book thus interrogates the failings of the current approaches to South Sudan's post-conflict security and presents the different conditions under which security in South Sudan can be attained. The conditions central to South Sudan's attainment of a stable and secure post-conflict security form the key themes in this book. They essentially relate to themes that cut across this book, including key research questions pertaining to the security infrastructure, politics and social economic development in post-conflict South Sudan.

Liberal peacebuilding in South Sudan

The degeneration of South Sudan's post-conflict security to a post-independence civil war at the end of 2013 necessitates a keener look at liberal peacebuilding and its application in the country. As such, the unstable and insecure post-conflict security that has emerged in contemporary South Sudan compounds the assertions that the 'liberal peace project is in disarray, if not in crisis'

(Richmond 2009). Despite this, liberal peacebuilding influence on international interventions remains dominant.

Emerging in the post-Cold War interventions of the 1990s, liberal peacebuilding has evolved into an influential post-conflict framework embodying an anthology of post-conflict aspirations like peacebuilding, security, state-building, free market economics, governance and promotion of civil society. Empirical observations from the fieldwork illustrate an attempt at the realization of all these fronts in the internationally led post-conflict intervention in South Sudan. However, they also depict epistemological indifferences in contemporary post-conflict interventions in the country. Arguably, this is, in part, a result of the generic adoption and application of international liberal peace intervention in the country (Tadjbakhsh 2011).

Underwritten by an external military presence of international peacekeepers and legitimized by the pursuit of a liberal state and the trappings of democracy and development, the liberal peacebuilding effort in South Sudan evokes the same debates as those before it. This book presents that overwhelmingly, the idea of a 'liberal peace', with its European Enlightenment intellectual roots, has guided most of the peacebuilding programmes pursued by the United Nations and Western bilateral donors (Curtis 2012: 77). In South Sudan, this pursuit has been guilty of epistemological whitewashing (Richmond and Franks 2009) by overlooking the country's empirical complexities. This resonates with some of the critique of liberal peacebuilding that perceives a 'disconnect between the liberal governance packages promoted by international peacebuilders and the way in which politics is conducted locally in many countries emerging from conflict' (Curtis 2012: 78).

To a large extent, the international engagement in South Sudan post-2005 was especially guilty of overlooking the role of the South Sudanese in the country's post-conflict reconstruction, revalidating ongoing debates on the relationship between international engagement and peacebuilders and the 'locals'. Chapters 4 to 7 illustrate this. These chapters show that an international engagement that interacted and continues to interact with South Sudan from the premise of an incapable partner, while overlooking the role of the community receiving intervention, is perhaps one of the greatest tragedies of international liberal peacebuilding approaches. Emerging from nearly four decades of civil war and in the absence of a history of state-building, the UN, international agencies, multilateral and bilateral donors and regional bodies took the lead in South Sudan's peacebuilding and associate state-building processes. This raises a number of questions on the broader discussions of liberal peacebuilding, particularly: '. . . Is it possible to establish the conditions for legitimate and sustainable national governance through a period of benevolent foreign autocracy' (Paris and Sisk 2009: 8)?

This question is part of broader discussions on the legitimacy of liberal peacebuilding and state-building pursuits and bears particular relevance for South Sudan as one of the latest recipients of these pursuits. The local disquiet on the processes and pursuits of liberal peacebuilding encountered in this research suggests that liberal peacebuilding, despite the benefit of hindsight, has fallen into the same old critiques characterized by local complaints of international arrogance and heavy-handedness (Richmond 2009). At the height of the 2013–14 internal conflict, South Sudan's president accused the UN of running a parallel government in the country.[8] The perception of South Sudan by many international workers as corrupt, incapable, backward and in need of capacity building perhaps set the tone for their engagement with the 'locals'. These perceptions, however, are not limited to Western workers but are also held widely by regional workers from neighbouring countries.

The liberal peacebuilding approach in South Sudan based on these perceptions arguably contributed to the lack of a truly locally driven post-conflict solution for the country, specifically the lack of a locally driven reconstruction and recovery that allows local actors to frame their own requirements for a viable, just and durable peace, irrespective of liberal democracy and economic aspirations. Of similar interest is the examination of gaps between the stated objectives and actual outcomes of current post-conflict processes in the country (Paris and Sisk 2009: 311). This book thus expounds liberal peacebuilding by exploring an alternative in demilitarization and by exploring the links between the various overarching themes.

Exploring demilitarization literature

This book looks at the demilitarization of South Sudan at a critical time in the development of demilitarization literature. It comes at a time when demilitarization forms part of a broader debate on post-conflict security and the assertion that, above all, it must be context relevant. This evolution is not only aligned to the aspirations of this book in its attempt to put demilitarization at the centre of debates on post-conflict security, but it also allows for its development as a tool with which to contextualize security in a country coming out of conflict. This book also tackles demilitarization at a time when the ideals and perceptions of security have been evolving and morphing out of their traditional definitions (Coons 2012; Thomas 2001).

This is often referred to as the emergence of a new security. However, like most things defined as 'new', there are questions related to what exactly the new security entails. Perhaps this begins with the rethinking of security (Little, Smith 2006) especially in post-conflict countries and the growing influence of development politics over perceptions and construction of security. This is often referred to as the convergence of development and security and these new links have become particularly relevant in the construction of post-conflict security. In an era of post-conflict reconstruction and liberal peacebuilding, these have been informed by the need for public security, equal representation and distribution of resources as well as development as ways of consolidating peace. These form part of the growing liberal peace book that informs present-day constructions and perceptions of security.

This book, however, questions the utility of this liberal peace as the de facto post-conflict remedy and, in particular, with regards to addressing the issue of post-conflict security. In fact, it has not only changed the way in which security is perceived (Chuter 2011; Duffield 2001, 2007), but also how it's consumed. As such, its influence on what this book identifies as post-conflict demilitarization also cannot be ignored, especially within the current convergence of non-traditional security discourses (Coons 2012; Thomas 2001).

Demilitarization therefore draws on some of the broad themes presented by the liberal peace paradigm and reflects on the complexity of their implementation. In particular, this book explores the intricate relationship between everyday politics, prevailing social economic dimensions and security within the context of a post-conflict country against the critique of liberal peacebuilding. To begin with, the critique that '. . . failures in the liberal peace project are not because of the efficiency problems related to the technicalities of its workings, but in the problematic assumptions and contradictions within the model itself' (Tadjbakhsh 2011: 5), are closest to the critiques of this book. Specifically, that present post-conflict engagements in South Sudan are too generic, often met with complaints of 'being thought out elsewhere' by local officials and failing to converge the aspirations of the international intervention with the expectation of the recipient communities.

It is, however, with this critical view of liberal peacebuilding that this book presents demilitarization as a viable tool in the reconstitution of post-conflict security. A reconstitution that entails the engagement of a community in redrawing the terms of engagement that govern their security at the end of a conflict is crucial for sustainable peace. Demilitarization offers a framework with which to redraw and redress the premise of post-conflict security while taking into consideration context, culture and traditions of the society in question (Schiff 2009).

There is no single definition of demilitarization (Stearns 2013), rather an overlay of literature with some reference to demilitarization being a concept, a phenomenon, and even a process. Alden (1995), for instance, writes of demilitarization as a process riddled with political, military and humanitarian obstacles which mirror some of the empirical observations in this book. On the other hand, Lamb (1997) perceives demilitarization as a concept with deep historical roots, although he also repeatedly refers to demilitarization as a phenomenon. Lamb (1999), however, takes these arguments further, presenting demilitarization 'as a multi-dimensional phenomenon, relative and amorphous in nature, which is shaped by context, stimuli and historical experience'. In more recent literature, Stearns (2013) reaffirms these arguments and presents that although demilitarization as a term can be validly applied, there is no single definition of the term.

This book perceives demilitarization within similar contexts and especially highlights the synergies between different perceptions and constructions of demilitarizations reflected across the literature. Some of these synergies include the reaffirmation of the links between militarism and demilitarization. On this, Lamb, for example, argues that demilitarization is not a static phenomenon, but rather a process (Lamb 1999: 3) that's vital in addressing militarism and militarization harnessed during the war but also in the deconstruction of that militarism after the war. As such, this book reaffirms the links between demilitarization and militarism; a link that in South Sudan has significant influence over the success or failure of the construction of the country's post-conflict security. More recent literature on demilitarization like Stearns (2013) further highlights these links and the broad, conceptual understanding of demilitarization as an exercise in reversing the onset of militarism and militarization (Stearns 2013: 2). Subsequently, it is the case that demilitarization is often derived from conceptual debates over militarism.

This link particularly helps to trace demilitarization beyond its post-World War II existence. Lamb (1997), for instance, traces demilitarization as far back as 1860 and argues that although 'the term demilitarisation had not been formulated yet, much of the debate on war centred around when and under what circumstances militarism could be seen to exist, but also when and under what circumstances it would disappear' (Lamb 1997). Although today's definitions and perceptions of demilitarization have moved on to reflect modern political realities (Lamb 1999), they are not too far removed from early perceptions. Indeed Stearns (2013) argues that the most successful exercises of demilitarization were in the pre-Cold War periods.

In particular, he cites the demilitarization of India by the Indian emperor Ashoka in 269 BC as one of the early examples of demilitarization in the world (Stearns 2013: 7). Indeed, despite the attention paid to demilitarization in the twentieth century, the exercise goes back centuries. Stearns (2013), for example, offers a number of examples of this and presents that demilitarization was a common exercise with victors often reducing the military prowess of their rivals. A society that successfully invades another, whether in recent history or the more remote past, typically works to reduce the local military apparatus [. . .] and one of the results of Russia's loss in the Crimean War, in the 1850s, was that it forced the demilitarization of the Aland Islands in the Baltic Sea (Stearns 2013: 4).

The history of demilitarization is thus extensive and extensively reaffirms the links between militarism and demilitarization and arguments that, for the most part, demilitarization often revolves around big militaristic events, be it in the most recent history or the more distant past. Such events would include: the world wars, the Cold War, the end of a period marked with coups and military governments like in South America and the end of a period marked by civil wars like in sub-Saharan Africa. Subsequently, demilitarization is reasserted as the reversal of decades of militarization through the sustained reduction in the size and influence of the military sector in state and society and the reallocation of military resources to civilian purposes (Lamb 1999). From this, it is evident that demilitarization has held considerably different meanings over time. In the period following the world wars, for instance, demilitarization became the realization of the decommissioning of large armies and war machinery. In the post-Cold War period, demilitarization embodied the reduction of military spending, hardware and military governments. This particular period in the 1990s also accounts for most of the literature on demilitarization and, in particular, Lamb's work provided a base for the development of demilitarization literature. This book's particular adoption of demilitarization as a concept with different dimensions is especially similar to the works of not only Lamb (1997, 1999) but also Hutchful (1998) and Cock (1997) who also define demilitarization as a multi-dimensional process.

This book particularly takes on Eboe Hutchful's view of demilitarization and, as argued in a conference paper on the future of demilitarization in Africa (Hutchful 1998), that 'demilitarisation is not the product of specific actions alone, but rather is a qualitative process that should be examined in terms of its totality' (Hutchful 1998: 4). While Hutchful's writings are dated, his arguments cannot be discounted as the premise of this book will show. Indeed this book looks at demilitarization in South Sudan qualitatively, in its totality and taking into consideration the country's individual circumstances represented in what Hutchful argues to be the different phases of demilitarization, namely:

- Downsizing military budgets;
- Demobilizing and reintegrating soldiers and former combatants;
- Redefining the role of the military, with particular emphasis on collateral functions, such as national development and peacekeeping;
- Restructuring security-related institutions in order to facilitate civil and parliamentary control and to initiate a process of reconciliation between armed forces and civil society; and
- Reformulating security paradigms and structures, favouring collective security measures that emphasize the importance of regional stability and acknowledge Africa's autonomous capacity to deal with conflict issues.

This idea of demilitarization not only forms the basis for the construction of demilitarization as used in this book, but it also represents different dynamics that continue to inform perceptions of security in post-conflict countries. In fact, the parameters set by Hutchful are particularly close to those concerns with modern liberal peacebuilding. That notwithstanding, it is perhaps the conclusions of the 1998 Arusha Conference on demilitarization that most resonate with this research that 'the degree of demilitarisation is dependent on, among other things, the size of the country, the levels of conflict, the military's role in society and the extent of political consensus' (Hutchful 1998: 5). These conclusions mirror the key argument in this book: that demilitarization is case-specific and should take into account a country's socio-economic, cultural and political peculiarities; that the restructuring and reconstitution of post-conflict security should be a reflection of a concordance between the players, that is the military, the elite and the citizenry (Schiff 2009) rather than the international community's projection of the ideal; and that this is particularly important with the onslaught of indiscriminate international liberal peacebuilding in countries coming out of conflict.

This book, therefore, not only reframes Hutchful's conception of demilitarization but arguably moves it forward, especially as most of the literature on demilitarization is from the 1990s. This also raises a few questions, in particular why demilitarization literature has failed to move beyond its late

1990s inception and what implication this has on this particular research based on the premise of demilitarization. Arguably, the demise of demilitarization from mainstream conceptions of security coincides with the rise of the liberal peace. Demilitarization, therefore, was part of the first generation of post-conflict literature, but its aspirations were overrun by a liberal evolution in post-conflict reconstruction. After the 1990s, challenges to security shifted from inter-state conflicts to intra-state conflicts. Although the post-Cold War conflicts of the 1990s informed the inception of demilitarization, they also played a significant part in the development of liberal peacebuilding. Nevertheless, the complexity and brutality of these wars in the Balkans, Zaire, Sierra Leone, Liberia, Rwanda, Burundi and Somalia also underwrote the 'need for a broader approach to security underscored by emerging experiences in the global south and the Balkans' (Schnabel and Ehrhart 2005: 22).

This broad approach has, however, seen a convergence of conflicting and sometimes competing processes, attempting to rewrite the parameters of post-conflict engagements under a broadly accepted international liberal peacebuilding framework. As such, the emergence of new security dichotomies and, in particular, the emergence of the liberal peacebuilding nexus has moved debates on post-conflict security away from demilitarization. Nevertheless, with the growing disparity between theory and practice of present-day post-war reconstructions, a rethink of the current trajectory of post-conflict reconstructions, especially of security, is overdue.

This thus begins with a revaluation of demilitarization within the context of present debates, which have moved from those driven by Cold War hangovers of the 1990s to those more in line with present-day liberal constructions. This phase of demilitarization perhaps begins with Isima's (2004) articulation of demilitarization as 'the need for a drastic reduction of the political influence of the military and security agencies of the state'. A departure from his predecessors' concerns over military hardware and troop numbers, this departure perhaps indicates different political periods. Nevertheless, the influence of the preceding literature – Cock (1997), Lamb (1997, 1999), Hutchful (1998), Alden, Thomas and Mazrui, as well as Luckham – is not lost on Isima (2004) who uses demilitarization to mean the reduction of the power and influence of the armed forces in domestic politics. However, Isima (2004) also draws the literature together and moves it towards current liberal peacebuilding debates. In particular, he draws from the works of Chachiua (2000) and Clark (2001) who argue that demilitarization's existence is twofold: that is demilitarization of the state and state security institutions, and demilitarization of society – distinctions that hold significant relevance to this book, which seeks to develop demilitarization by reconciling the paradoxes around it. This book goes on to test the notion of demilitarization as a dual process and, as such, questions the prevailing wisdom around liberal peacebuilding.

Perceptions of demilitarization as a multi-track process are nonetheless not new as both Clark (2001) and Harris (2003) also perceive demilitarization to exist on two levels. Clark (2001), for instance, perceives demilitarization to exist as surface demilitarization and deep demilitarization. 'Surface demilitarisation is concerned with the disbanding of forces, surrendering arms and implementing ceasefire agreements and deep demilitarisation is addressing the roots of militarisation and undoing the legacy of war and militarisation as part of an effort to reconstruct society on a different basis' (Clark 2001: 1). Here, the top-down, institutional approach and the prerequisite reform and restructuring of security forces correspond with surface demilitarization, while deep demilitarization aligns with a bottom-up process initiated at the community level (Clark 2001: 6). These dynamics are also addressed by Chachiua (2000) who characterizes them as quantitative demilitarization and qualitative demilitarization. Quantitative demilitarization is concerned with the process of withdrawing tangible military instruments such as defence expenditure, force level, arms procurement and military intervention in politics while qualitative demilitarization tackles the non-tangible side of demilitarization, which reverses militaristic ideologies and values as well as de-emphasizing violence as a means of resolving conflict (Chachiua 2000: 2; Harris 2003; Isima 2004). It is this qualitative demilitarization that this book is most concerned with and arguably results in the failure of post-conflict security consolidation, often resulting in a return to violence.

As such, this book asserts that to deal with the non-tangible aspects of demilitarization, the process must be holistic, involving not only the 'institutional' demilitarization concerned with structural demilitarization but also qualitative and societal demilitarization. The book argues that to achieve this, the onset of demilitarization must depart from current post-conflict peacebuilding blueprints and rethink the whole process, especially its engagement with prevailing structures of security and the attempt to reconstitute them from a war service to a viable post-conflict status.

2

South Sudan

The Southern Sudan is remote – the world's periphery. It is isolated in terms of communications. It is hard to find people who have been there and the indigenous people do not travel. It belongs to 'nobody'. The Southern Sudan is legally part of the Sudan governed by Khartoum, but in practical terms this is mostly an empty claim. Khartoum's jurisdiction and control covered the main cities and five miles outside when I visited the area in July 1970. Many educated Southern Sudanese believe that the bond to Khartoum is a legacy of the slave trade and that it has no other foundation than that.

Reinton 1971: 241

Introduction

The new Republic of South Sudan, which attained its independence on 9 July 2011, is the focus of this book. However, as a new country, its history is, of course, tied to that of the Republic of the Sudan, from which it seceded. Although the split of the Republic of the Sudan resulted in the creation of one independent country, in reality it resulted in the creation of two countries: the Republic of South Sudan and the Republic of Sudan. The fact that the Republic of Sudan retained the sovereignty of the Republic of the Sudan often overrides the fact that with the secession of South Sudan, the country that existed before, up to 8 July 2011, ceased to exist and in its place two new countries emerged on 9 July 2011. As such, the history of the Republic of the Sudan, from hereon referred to as the Sudan, has a lot to bear on the two new republics of South Sudan and Sudan.

A detailed look at the history of the Sudan and the countries that emerged out of it on 9 July 2011 is the first step to unpacking and disentangling the processes and politics of state formation in the Sudan. It examines their influence on the post-colonial state that emerged in the Sudan after independence and points at identity as one of the defining factors in the construction of the Sudanese post-colonial state. Here, specific attention is paid to conflicting Arab and African identities referred to by the renowned South Sudanese scholar, Francis Deng, as the 'War of Visions'. In assessing these conflicts, one can draw conclusions on their influence, not only on the politics but on the social, economic and cultural gestations in the post-colonial state that was Africa's largest country.

Although Sudan's history goes back centuries, this book concentrates on the most recent history in periods represented in the timeline (Figure 2.1). Although this is an overtly compact representation of Sudan's political history, it provides a snapshot of the political processes that have shaped its contemporary political realities. The periods articulated in the timeline are thus some of the most influential in the coming together and formation of the post-colonial state and, by extension, the contemporary Sudanese states.

Events in this timeline, although not exhaustive, are nevertheless markers of specific periods in the historical construction and political institutionalization of the Sudan (Idris 2005). More specifically, they are benchmarks in the complex process of state formation.

Figure 2.1 Timeline of Main political events in Sudan.

Politics of state formation: Past and present

At independence in 1956, the Sudan was Africa's largest country. However, the story of Sudan's post-independence existence is one that was echoed across the continent by other countries. By 1973, more than half of Africa was under military rule and the Sudan was no exception. Some of the complexities of the Sudanese post-independence state discussed here notwithstanding, the country's experiences of state-building draw parallels to other African states. This is particularly the case in the pattern of rapid passage from constitutions modelled upon the French Republic or Westminster democratic models, through one-party states, to military dictatorships which became a striking feature of state formation in post-independence Africa (Southall 1974: 157).

A full understanding of post-conflict security in South Sudan thus begins, not with the emergence of the post-independence state, but by identifying and understanding the underlying legacies of the colonial state (Young 2004: 25). The silent incorporation of the colonial state legacies into the post-colonial state was of significant influence on the post-independence state formations. Study of neocolonialism that emerged in the post-colonial period provided greater insights on this. In the Sudan, like in other post-colonial states, the colonial legacies were passed on essentially in the structures and the formal language of state apparatus to be found in the laws and the legal codes of the post-independence constitutions (Mamdani 2005).

Going back to the colonial state is thus a valid place to start the quest for a better understanding of not only the contemporary Sudanese states, but also the post-colonial state from which they are derived. As the time elapsed since African independence now begins to appropriate the time period during which African subjects experienced a consolidated colonial regime, new historical experience reshapes social memory and begins to obscure the colonial past (Young 2004: 48). Yet, it is still the case that although most of Africa has moved beyond its post-colonial label, the colonial experiences that came to define its post-independence existence are not altogether erased. Rather, they have been rewoven into the new political fabric of the contemporary African state in a process informed by changing internal and external experiences within the context of new local and international paradigms. As such, today, contemporary African states have evolved beyond their post-colonial limitations and they continue to draw from these experiences.

However, for a country that missed most of the post-colonial political and socio-economic experiences of the post-colonial state as a result of protracted civil wars, there are questions as to what the future holds for South Sudan. More specifically, can newly independent South Sudan fast-forward past the post-colonial experiences that have shaped the contemporary African state? At a time when most of the current African states struggle between the hindsight of yesterday and the promise of the future, can the realities of the post-colonial state and the aspirations of the developmental state be reconciled with changing international paradigms, most notably, paradigms that have shifted from the Washington Consensus and the neoliberalism it entailed to those relevant to contemporary Africa. South Sudan's journey into statehood in 2011, therefore, had the benefit of hindsight and the opportunity to learn from the political, economic, social and cultural experiences and mistakes of other post-independence African states. The question therefore remains, did South Sudan embrace this benefit of hindsight and what impact did this have on the formation of the current South Sudanese state?

Some of these answers are perhaps to be found in the experiences and the politics of the post-colonial state in the Sudan. The politics of the post-independence Sudan are nevertheless those of a post-colonial state in crisis. For the most part, the politics of the Sudan in the 1950s and 1960s can be defined as falling into two categories: one democratic front which was the umbrella for the Sudanese Communist Party and the Muslim Brotherhood (Deng 1995: 18), the result of which was a post-colonial state besieged by coups (Berridge 2015) and countercoups, in conflict with itself, and in desperate search for a national identity, especially with the rise of political radical Islam. At the centre of the post-independence state in the Sudan, however, was the First Civil War 'The Anyanya 1', addressed in more detail in the next chapter on militarization.

Arguably the civil wars in the Sudan are a direct result of the centralization of the Sudanese post-colonial state. Although centralization of power is a hallmark of the post-colonial state in Africa, in the Sudan this centralization manifested itself in radical ideology and marginalization of the periphery outside the two cities of Khartoum and Omdurman. The control of the country's peripheries by the centre through regional and local governments is one of the legacies of the Sudanese post-colonial state. However, maintaining control and loyalty, despite institutional insufficiencies and economic underdevelopment, has a price. It is this marginalization and underdevelopment that has arguably continued to fan conflicts in the Sudan.

Beyond the civil war, though, the post-colonial state in the Sudan has been one of mixed fortunes and realities. In the contemporary politics of both Sudans' histories, underdevelopment continues to play a significant part in the formation of the modern political spheres. However, it is also within Sudan's historical contexts going back to the pre-imperialist state, the creation of the imperialist state and the subsequent Sudanese post-colonial state that the idea of the state in the Sudan often runs into trouble (Woodward 1990). In part, this can be attributed to a history of ambiguity in Sudan's colonial experiences in which the Sudan was never formally a British colony (Woodward 1990), but rather the land between British interests in East Africa and Egypt through which the Nile flowed, linking the two (Oduho and Deng 1963). This is evident in the British engagement with the Sudan in the form of a condominium with Egypt, something that was unique to Sudan in the British Empire.

Towards the post-colonial state

The ambiguous imperial status of the Sudan as a condominium and the limited resources for governing a vast and 'poor' country, arguably set the ground for the weak state that emerged at independence. This, coupled with contesting Afro-Arab identities, not only influenced but also shaped the process of state formation in what was Africa's largest country, covering nearly 1 million sq. miles at 967,500 sq. miles. From the onset, the post-colonial state in the Sudan was almost wholly defined by radicalized politics and the pursuit and imposition of a single vision of nation through the policy of Arabisation and Islamisation (Idris 2005). The pursuit of a single vision of Islamic and Arab nationhood has been the basis of the radicalization of the post-colonial state in the Sudan and has subsequently festered the crisis of identity that has become the bedrock of political instability and recurring conflicts in the country (Bassil 2013).

The conflicts in the Sudan from the east, the south and more recently the west in Darfur, are a result of the different manifestations of the post-colonial state. However, despite the differences over time in Sudan's conflicts, they all stem from similar grievances which can be traced to the politicization of identity and religion. More specific to these conflicts is the domination of the central Nile valley elite of Khartoum over the rest of the country. This is part of the legacy of the Khartoum-based colonial administration and more broadly the colonial state in Africa. Although the experiences of most of the post-colonial states in Africa are similar, Sudan's experiences present some level of uniqueness. While the post-colonial state negotiated between national identities and the dream of pan-Africanism embodied by most of the continent's post-colonial leaders like Kwame Nkrumah, Ahmed Sékou Touré and Julius Nyerere among others, Sudan's struggle was more profound.

Within a complex history that amalgamated different cultures through centuries, Sudan's post-colonial experiences differed from the rest of the continent. At the fore were questions as to the very nature of the country. What was Sudan? Or as al-Tayeb Salah, a prominent Sudanese Nubian writer puts it, 'Who are we?' These questions not only contributed to the ignition of Sudan's First Civil War, they are at the heart of the Sudanese post-colonial struggle of belonging. Was Sudan African or Middle Eastern as part of the Arab North Africa?

It is in the persistence of the debates on Arabism and Africanism, all of which have multiple meanings in the Sudanese context, that the dominant Khartoum Arab elite emerged in the formulation of the post-colonial state in the Sudan. However, although Sudan's move to the Arab League was an institutional expression of a post-colonial state leaning towards the Middle East, the raging civil war between the north and the south pointed to a social contradiction on the matter. According to Francis Deng, it is this period that moved issues of identity in the north and south of Sudan from the realm of benign self-perception to the politically contested stage of national symbolism with all the associated implications that shaped power and wealth-sharing as well as other national values (Deng 1995: 4).

Still, this was not unique to Sudan as an identity and the centralized state that emerged in the Sudan after independence is part of a broader legacy of the post-colonial states in Africa. However, unlike most of post-colonial Africa, the state that emerged at independence in the Sudan predated the colonial experience. While most of post-colonial African states came into existence on the basis of the colonial borders of the 1884–5 Berlin Conference, Sudan's borders at independence were older than the colonial borders of the Berlin Conference as outlined by Peter Woodward:

> Unlike in most of the rest of Africa, the creation of a British-ruled state in Sudan was not the country's first experience of statehood within roughly those borders. The Turco-Egyptian invasion of 1820 had not only carved out approximately the same area to govern, but the colonial rulers had also been defeated and succeeded by the Mahdists who had themselves inherited the same structural characteristics [...] just as the British were to do in their turn. (Woodward 1990: 13)

As such, the processes and the journey to Sudanese statehood precede even the colonial state. Indeed it is arguable that ancient states in the Sudan even preceded the Turco-Egyptian state. 'Sudan's position in the trading networks of Africa and the Middle East encouraged a series of state developments, from the Meroitic period following the decline of ancient Egypt down through the Nuba kingdoms of the Middle Ages and later into the Funj state' (Woodward 1990: 19). What influence then have these early experiences of statehood had on the creation of the Sudanese post-colonial state?

The ancient Sudan was for thousands of years a recipient of the benefits of external influences. There is, as such, a tendency in the modern Sudan for the glorification of the history of statehood associated with the legacies of the riverine kingdoms of the Nile, especially the ancient kingdoms of Nubia, Kush and Funj (Deng 1995: 37). In addressing the complexities of Sudan's post-colonial statehood, Francis Deng concludes that while the glorification of the ancient states of the Sudan is part of the wider nation-building process, it also tends to cloud the complexities, diversities and variations associated with these historical experiences (Deng 1995: 37).

However, despite the experiences of the ancient riverine states in the Sudan, it was not until Mohammed Ali's invasion of Sudan in 1820 and the Turco-Egyptian state that followed that the present state of the Sudan started to take shape. Although the social influences of the Turco-Egyptian period in the Sudan are discussed elsewhere in this chapter, their impact on the preceding Sudanese states has been daunting. The Mahdist state that overthrew the Turco-Egyptian state and the colonial states largely kept the same structures. It was not until the independence of Egypt in 1922 that the colonial state in Sudan emerged from the shadows of the Turco-Egyptian structures and influences.

The independence of Egypt in 1922 opened up the Sudan to the first experiences as a colonial state. Until then, the status of the Sudan as part of the Anglo-Egyptian Condominium had allowed for an ambiguous colonial period. However, this also came with new complexities for the Sudan, complexities that were to re-emerge in negotiations on the nature of the post-colonial state in the Sudan. The most prominent feature of this period, however, was the social organization of the Sudan that was to pass on to the post-independence state. The independence of Egypt not only forced a rethink of the colonial state but more specifically the hierarchical form of social organization. This exposed contradictions between externally imposed hierarchical social organization and indigenous egalitarian social organization which was common in the struggle between colonialism and anti-colonialism in Africa (Reinton 1971: 241).

The removal of Egyptian military officials and civil servants from the Sudan was the first phase of the social and institutional organization of the Sudan after Egypt's independence in 1922. The removal of the Egyptian 'Ma'mur'[1] and their replacement with the British civilian administrators in what came to be known as the Sudan Political Service in 1924, marked yet another significant shift in the construction of the Sudanese colonial state not directly linked to Egypt.

The rest of the colonial period in the Sudan between 1924 and its independence in 1956 was more or less a negotiation in the establishment of the post-colonial state. However, in these negotiations, there were questions in particular on the nature of the state that would emerge in Sudan after independence. For most northerners, the periods preceding the colonial state, and particularly the Turco-Egyptian period and the Mahdist state, had created in the Sudan a sense of a superior Arab Islamic identity permitted by Islam and the assimilations of Arab culture. As such, negotiations of the post-independence state in the Sudan were dominated by the re-emergence of the African Arab debates. Here, an underdeveloped south with a largely uneducated population was widely viewed by the emerging northern elite as inferior. The south was thus, from the beginning, at odds to compete for equal representation in the post-colonial state, fuelling fears of northern domination and with this came the spark that ignited the First Civil War.

This has been the paradox of Sudanese post-independence existence. It is the complexity and politicization of identity that continue to haunt the Sudan today, even as two separate states. Indeed, post-South Sudan's independence, the issues and complexes of identity in the Sudan did not wane but rather reinvented themselves and re-emerged in the contemporary politics of the two Sudans. But what makes identity politics in the two Sudans so explosive and able to transcend differences over time in changing social, economic and political dispensations? The answers to this question and perhaps the wider question of identity in the Sudan lie in the legacy of slavery and the slave trade from which contemporary Sudanese identities have evolved.

The legacy of slavery and the slave trade

To many scholars of African identities, the colonial states played a significant role in the shaping of contemporary African identities and the various ways that they are manifested in today's African societies. To a large extent, the impact of the colonial legacy on identities in Africa can be summed up by the various narratives of the natives or the settlers as laid out in the works of Mamdani

(1996, 1998, 2001), Ahluwalia (2001) and Ndlovu-Gatsheni (2013). Specifically Ndlovu-Gatsheni (2013) argues that:

> What is known about identities prior to colonisation is that they were very fluid, permeated by a complex process of assimilation, incorporation, conquest of weaker groups by powerful ones, inter- and intra-marriage alliances, fragmentation and constant movements. Identities that crystallised from this complex milieu were social and moral in character rather than solid and political. (Ndlovu-Gatsheni 2013: 197)

Although this presentation and conceptualization of African identities is conventional in studies of African identities, in the Sudan, differences emerge. Here, the main influence on modern Sudanese identities seems to be less with the country's experiences of European colonialism, but more the legacy of slavery and the slave trade in the Sudan over thousands of years (Leopold 2003, 2006). In the Sudan, slavery and the slave trade as a phenomenon predates the colonial state and, to some extent, outlived it (Jok 2001). The Abeed or Abid is a common phrase in the Sudan meaning slave and used more derogatorily to address southerners (Deng 1995). The legacy of the slave trade has undoubtedly had a significant influence on constructions of Sudanese identities. The question that emerges from this though is: How have constructions of identity based on a legacy of slavery influenced the shaping of the state in Sudan? More importantly, how has the identification based on this legacy affected or influenced people's participation in the political, economic, social and cultural aspects in the country (Deng 1995)?

Due to limitations in political, social, economic and cultural participation, the politicization of identities in the Sudan, but also more widely in the post-colonial state in Africa, has emerged. This has been, more often than not, in the form of violent conflict. To look at identity, though, there is perhaps the need to define it and for the purpose of this book, identity is used in close relation to Francis Deng's definition. That is: the way individuals and groups define themselves and are defined by others on the basis of race, ethnicity, religion, language and culture. More innately clan, lineage and family are often a part in the construction of identities (Deng 1995). Despite deep-rooted ethnic or tribal historical legacies, ultimately the question of identity in the Sudan goes back to discussions of slavery. The centrality of the historical legacy of slavery and colonialism in the crisis of the post-colonial state in the Sudan can therefore not be ignored (Idris 2005). These legacies, however, go beyond the Sudan to include North Africa and the Sahel. On the whole, the complexity of slavery in these regions and especially in the Sudan is an amalgamation of centuries of the practice. Here though, modern-day slavery remains and continues to exist within the changing dynamics of the Sudanese state.

However, the articulation of distinctions based on race, ethnicity and religion made by Arab slave-takers have remained the same in the Sudan. These continue to inform the basis on which modern Sudanese identities are based, including perceptions of black southerners as infidels, indisputably inferior and therefore 'natural' slaves (Jok 2001). These distinctions have survived for decades and have fuelled various forms of oppression of the black south. It is embedded in the Bilad al-Sudan or 'the nation of the blacks' reference to the south and distinction of the South of Sudan as the traditional source of slaves for Arab traders from the central Nile valley and beyond (Jok 2001).

While slavery has long been subject to international condemnation and largely invisible in the contemporary world, in the Sudan[2] the practice of slavery has remained endemic.[3] More specifically, slavery has evolved into a complex system that keeps up with economic and social political changes in the Sudan.[4] 'The post-colonial Sudanese civil wars especially changed the face of slavery with the capture of countless women and children from the south who were then sold into slavery in the north, with many becoming concubines, domestic servants, farm labourers, or even soldiers trained to fight against the south where they came from (Deng 1995; Jok 2001). As such, although the legacy of slavery in the Sudan goes back thousands of years (Jok 2011), its present-day manifestations continue to be the backbone of the complex web of overlapping identities in the Sudan. Post-South Sudanese independence, questions remain as to how these have changed.

This is part of the legacy of the Bilad al-Sudan (the land of the blacks) and the presentation of the Arab 'superior' which shaped the post-colonial Sudanese state, although its politics goes back beyond the 1820 Turco-Egyptian invasion. However, it was with Mohammed Ali's invasion of Sudan that the modern Sudanese social strata emerged, with the slaves being at the bottom and the king and his courtiers at the top. The Turco-Egyptian expansionist drive and Mohammed Ali's penetration of the Sudan in search of slaves and gold further entrenched the social divisions in the Sudan and the sole identification of southerners as Abeed. The Islamisation of the Sudan and the use of Islam as a buyout of the slavery further added to the complexity of the slavery legacy in the Sudan. The Turco-Egyptian rule profoundly changed the social, religious and political character of the Sudan and it is from these experiences that the 'Arab' as superior and the master of the Abeed was made (Woodward 1990: 23).

The impact of this legacy on the central political discourse in the country has been resounding as has the presentation of Sudan's post-independence wars as conflicts between the Arab north and the black south. Nevertheless, Sudan's identity complexes should be understood, not only contextually, but also more broadly, specifically as part of a complex and ongoing debate on African identities, politics and the state.

The identity complex in the Sudan

The identity complex in the post-colonial Sudan should ultimately be understood as twofold. In one sense, Northern Sudanese 'Arabs' vehemently resisting any attempt by the non-Arab population to identify the country with black Africa (Deng 1995: 3). In another sense, in the South Sudanese assertion of Africanness as a counter-identity to Arabism which has seen Africanism acquire a dimension that has racial, cultural and national connotations (Deng 1995). As such, the issue of identity in post-colonial Sudan could be summed up as a tug of war in which 'the more the north asserted its Arabness, the more the south asserted its Africanness as a counter-identity' (Deng 1995: 4).

This brings us back to the question, 'Who then is Sudanese and what is being Sudanese?' Although these are simple questions, they have not only defined the political and social interactions in the Sudan, they have also been the fuel that has kept alight many conflicts in the country. On the heels of the CPA, Robert Collins (2005) in the work 'In Search for the Sudanese' argues that: 'This new man, the Sudanese, is neither African nor Arab; he is Sudanese in which the individuality of many ethnicities has been melted into a race of men belonging to two worlds but to neither' (Collins 2005: 74).

Although Collins' position is shared by many scholars and Sudan pundits – the position of one state – many nationalities is one that has consistently failed to translate into a political reality. While the reasons for this are valid, not least the difficulty of overcoming a weighty history of constructed identities based on prejudices, the prejudices that exist in the Sudan, and which are made vivid in the country's post-colonial state, are indeed deep-rooted and historically embedded; part of a cycle that has been passed on through generations presented in various monographs of the north-south interaction based on a 1947 Report to the Fabian Colonial Bureau (Oduho and Deng 1963) which noted that:

> Educated Sudanese regarded the south as Egypt regarded them. The south, like Northern Sudan to Egypt, was a source of cheap labour and servants. This is an outline of a structure that developed over decades. Egypt was the centre for ruling the Sudan, a political gate to the largest country in Africa. The slave trade in the Sudan was largely organised through Cairo as an expression of the social structure already outlined, a social structure based upon immense economic inequalities as relevant at the time, before Burton and Speke explored the Nile, as they are today. (Oduho and Deng 1963: 17)
>
> A study of southern immigrants in Omdurman concludes with the fact that most northerners know the southerners as former slaves and thus become reluctant to interact with them on an equal basis. (Rehfisch 1964: 103)
>
> Northerners do not seek unskilled labour jobs with building contractors since many southerners have been doing this work, and the northerners do not wish to work with them. (Reinton 1971: 242)

It is from this premise that most of the interactions between the north and south that have resulted in the revolving door of conflict are based. However, while the issues of identity are not new in discussions of the post-colonial state in Africa, in the Sudan these discussions have evolved beyond the presentations of identity as wholly ethnic. Nevertheless, grasping perceptions of identity, not only in the Sudan but also in the new countries, the Republics of Sudan and South Sudan, broadly begins the process of unravelling the political, social, economic and cultural processes that have evolved around it and which are central to the Sudanese post-colonial state. However, despite the conflicting Arab-African dimensions in the Sudanese experiences of identity, there are still similarities to be drawn with other experiences in the post-colonial African state.

The politics of identity in post-colonial Sudan

Post-colonial identities in Africa are not only broad but remain largely contested. Linked to colonial experience, identity in the post-colonial African state has been an important ingredient in the evolution of the politics of the post-colonial state. Even with the evolution of the post-colonial state into the various forms of the contemporary state in Africa, identity has remained a particularly complex issue despite being the subject of numerous papers, books and countless academic inquiries. The study of identity in Africa is thus part of a complex analysis of causality in which no single set of factors is determinant or can be analysed in isolation from others (Berman 2010: 4). It is by and large an amalgamation of tradition, culture and historical influences, including the colonial state and the onset of modern religion, specifically Christianity and Islam.

The issue of identities, and especially African identities, remains a complex subject to tackle. Debates are especially polarized between those who perceive African identities from a traditional concept, based on cultural identities which are marked by a number of factors including 'race', ethnicity, gender and class among others (Clarke 2008: 510), and those who perceive identity as a construction based on shared political, social and economic truths, irrespective of culture otherwise referred to as 'constructed identities'. Nonetheless, although these two groups are representative of at least the main arguments surrounding African identities, they are by no means exhaustive. Still, although they point at core arguments, they do little to resolve them.

Discussions on ethnic identities and constructed identities do raise some relevant questions for South Sudan, especially with the first cracks in the new state taking ethnic dimensions. Understanding manifestations of identity in the south and especially the influence of ethnicity on the country's new political dispensation is thus an essential part of understanding part of the state formation processes. The influence of ethnicity on southern politics can be traced beyond the Second Civil War, although it was in the SPLA/M war that the manifestation of politicized ethnicity witnessed in contemporary South Sudan began to emerge. Despite the presentation by Deng (1995) of the north–south civil wars as a clash of 'civilizations', African vs. Arab and a contest of will between modern religions in Islam and Christianity, the worst of the fighting was between southern factions following the 1991 SPLA/M split. The degeneration of the southern rebel movement, the SPLA/M, along ethnic lines arguably entrenched the ethnic aspects of political rivalries and it is from these splits that contemporary splits in South Sudan's politics continue to be drawn.

As such, understanding the influence of identity or perceptions of identity in the politics of the Sudan and especially in the south is of great importance to unravelling the links between identity and militarism in the Sudans. This in turn has direct consequences for demilitarization which in South Sudan is especially important in view of the interlocking influences of ethnic identity and violent conflicts. Despite conventional perceptions of identities in the Sudan as a divide between Arab and African, post-South Sudan's independence empirical evidence points to a blur in the distinction between them in both Sudans. Any illusions of resolving Sudan's identity complexes with the north and south split have long been overridden by the new wave of conflicts loosely driven by issues of identity in the two countries.

The conflicts in Sudan's Blue Nile and South Kordofan states, as well as South Sudan's endemic inter-communal fighting, thus raise the same questions about ethnicity, tribes and identity that besieged the African post-colonial state. Still, over 50 years since the first wave of independent African states, ethnicity and tribalism continue to be used interchangeably and easily and are casually woven into discussions of identity in the post-colonial state. Despite presumed strides in untangling ethnicity and the patronage systems it commands in African politics, recent political developments in South Sudan evoke doubt on presumed progress in reducing the negative impacts of ethnicity.

Ethnic identities and conflict

The links between conflict and ethnicity in Africa is one of the oldest conundrums of post-independence Africa. Although the influence of ethnicity might not always be obvious, it can also not be denied. However, although competing ethnicities are often pitted as the driving factor in African conflicts, this view runs into trouble in regards to Somalia where, despite seemingly ethnic hegemony, issues of identity manifesting in warlordism have been the driving factor behind the country's long and evolving civil war (Davies 2014; Esteban et al. 2012; Kusow 2004; Woodward 2003). Despite the perceived ethnic and cultural hegemony of Somalia, the complexities of Somali identities highlight the premise of constructed identity in the clanism that has dominated Somali conflicts since the overthrow of President Siad Barre in 1991. As an example, Somalia reaffirms the case that every identity includes and excludes and establishes mechanisms for attaining this (Schöpflin 2001).

Arguably, Somalia's sense of identity is one that has been constructed over a long time and is derived from the almost seemingly homogenous nature of the country. Not surprisingly, there are those who argue that the Somali sense of identity is one that is influenced by different narratives and exclusions (Kusow 2003). Somalia has thus found its own way to include and exclude. Somalia as an example, however, exemplifies the complexities surrounding identity in Africa and their ability to not only ignite conflicts but to sustain them as well. It also brings us back to the same old question: why do identities have the power to start conflicts and what makes identities, especially in Africa, so explosive?

The answer perhaps lies, not in the conflicts themselves, but in the patriarchal political societies that emerged in post-independence Africa. Arguably, it is in the highly centralized post-colonial African states and the strongman politics they embodied that ethnic conflicts became political conflicts. Strongman politics in Africa entrenched not only patriarchy, but also the degeneration of institutionalism and constitutionalism at the expense of personal rule. How then this drives African conflicts and the relationship between ethnicity and conflict in Africa is nevertheless complex. It is perhaps best explained by Marina Ottaway in a 1999 essay on ethnicity and politics in Africa in which she explains:

> Most African leaders manipulated ethnicity in order to keep themselves in power. Some did it in a rather benign way, forging alliances with leaders of many ethnic groups or co-opting potential ethnic opponents into their governments. This did not make for democracy, but it often made for peace and stability, keeping the country together and preventing open conflict from emerging. (Ottaway 1999: 304)

Whereas co-opting ethnic opponents into government played a part in the politicization of ethnicity in Africa, it is perhaps the reliance on ethnic groupings by the ruling class to consolidate their power that has arguably been most detrimental. This allowed for the creation of ethnic-based patriarchal systems that oversaw unfair distribution of national wealth, rewarding ethnic groups seen to be loyal to the status quo and often marginalizing others. The sense of injustice begotten from ethnic patriarchy and marginalization has been at the core of most conflicts in Africa (Clapham 1998) and is the link between ethnicity and conflict. The endeavour to attain state power that has spurred on rebellions, insurgencies and guerrilla movements in the continent is thus arguably driven by the desire to reverse these injustices.

However, although marginalization based on ethnicity remains the most visible element of political patronage, how ethnicity manifests itself in Africa has evolved over the years. This modern-day manifestation of ethnicity was particularly evident in Kenya in December 2007 and January 2008. Here, a disputed presidential election fought along tribal lines brought the country, perceived to be a stable democracy, to the verge of a civil war. Arguably, Kenya's experience is a reflection of the enduring influence of ethnicity in African politics and its unrelenting ability to ignite civil wars and evolve to changing political times (Cheeseman 2008; Cheeseman et al. 2014; Lynch et al. 2014).

On the other hand, there are other motivations for conflict in Africa which have little to do with identity. These, Boas and Dunn (2007) argue, include; 'Ideology, grievances against the central government, regional and social marginalisation, elite desires to capture state power, the crisis of the post-colonial state and the extreme politicisation of autochthony debates' (Boas and Dunn

2007). These particularly ring true for South Sudan and together help to explain the post-independence ethno-political conflicts in the country that culminated in the 15 December coup attempt. Still, although Boas and Dunn's presentations of the links between identity and conflicts in Africa point to diverse motivations for conflict, many independent of ethnicity, the influence of ethnicity is always lurking in the background.

However, despite this, Boas and Dunn's points on other motivations of conflict and their separation from ethnicity make a significant contribution to the identity thesis. They particularly do this by providing an argument that validates the debate around constructed identities. As pointed out earlier in this chapter, despite their growing relevance, constructed identities in Africa are often overshadowed by ethnic identities. The role of constructed identities is not only relevant in accessing and understanding conflicts in Africa but more so in sustaining the wars. It is most plausible that ethnic identity is more likely to evoke blind loyalty in starting conflicts and that the ethnic dimension in conflicts is perhaps more compelling in influencing one's decision to voluntarily join a rebellion by tapping into the primal sense of self-preservation. Nevertheless, it is also the case that constructed identities and particularly those constructed around the war, or around causes of the war, also help sustain these conflicts. This is particularly true of countries that have experienced long periods of war or that have had regular conflicts.

This is the conundrum that besets South Sudan. Dismantling the bonds of comradeship and animosities built and constructed over decades of war, but also dismantling the mistrust and suspicion also constructed over decades of the civil war. Letting go of the legacies, both positive and negative, of the civil war and deconstructing the influences of the civil war is one of the greatest challenges in South Sudan's demilitarization. Taking into consideration the influence of identities, ethnic or constructed, in starting civil wars, it is as important a consideration as tackling demilitarization.

Conflict identities in South Sudan

Encompassing the influence of identity in post-conflict planning is especially relevant for the demilitarization process and the fragile nature of most peace agreements in the continent is testament to this. More important is acknowledging African identities as a complex mix of traditional presentations of identity, particularly in the 'ethnic', and the evolution of these identities over time. This especially means moving ethnicity and discussions of identity from the realm of sweeping generalizations associated with the greed thesis (Boas and Dunn 2007). It also means moving discussions of ethnic politics from the same page as discussions on barbarism and unsophisticated backwardness perceived to drive populations to savagery (Clapham 1996, 1998).

This not only sets the stage for a more comprehensive understanding of African identities and their influence on the composition of the political in a given state, it also moves debates beyond the sweeping generalizations that continue to impinge on African identities today. A better understanding of these conflicts, and the influence of identity on them, perhaps presents the best chance of averting what has become a cycle of evolving ethnically induced political violence in twenty-first-century Africa. In the negatives that have come to characterize the African state – the degeneration of the post-colonial state, the rise of military rule and African strongmen in post-independence Africa and the subsequent cycles of civil wars – ethnicity remains at the centre. This is especially true in view of recent conflicts in South Sudan, Chad, Central African Republic, DRC and even Mali. Although ethnic identities still play a part in triggering conflicts, constructed identity cannot altogether be ignored as recent conflicts in Central African Republic centre on Muslim-Christian dichotomies.

The post-colonial crisis of identity in the Sudan has unravelled in the years since South Sudan's independence and presents new challenges while repeating patterns of the past in an age widely seen as post-colonial. The new conflicts in the two Sudans also point to divergences in modern understanding of Sudanese identities beyond the Arab-African synergy that was definitive of the politics and conflicts in the Sudanese post-colonial state. This might be traced back to the fact that the Arab-African manifestations of identity in the Sudan are part of a larger story; a story that the post-conflict reconstruction thesis that this book engages with is part of. On the whole, it is a story that highlights changing relationships between the different populace in the country and their evolving interaction with the different processes of state formation and state development in the country beyond the remnants of the founding Turco-Egyptian state.

The secession of South Sudan is arguably just one of the more recent processes of state formation in the Sudan. Still, the demise of the old Sudan and the creation of two new Sudans from the previous north-south divides profoundly changed the dynamics of north-south identity. Often seen as the Arab-African dichotomy, South Sudan's independence changed not only north-south interactions, but also their interaction with the outside world and especially the region. However, despite the chance offered by South Sudan's independence for the two Sudans to cut the new parameters of identity, empirical evidence indicates that old habits die hard. To a large extent, the issue of identity has continued to define politics, not only in the new South Sudan but also in Sudan. Still, the independence of South Sudan may have forced a rethink of the prevailing definitions and approaches to identity in the country. Nonetheless, the rebellions in South Kordofan and Blue Nile in the Republic of Sudan and the recurrence of inter-communal fighting in South Sudan is indicative of a pattern of repeating old mistakes.

Independence has by no means wiped out thousands of years of shared cultural, social and political links upon which the Sudanese identity is constructed. Empirical observations into South Sudan especially point to the use of Arabic as a new constructed identity, although perhaps used more to exclude than to include. The use of Arabic as a qualifier of 'Sudaneseness' in post-independence South Sudan and as a tool of exclusion is in itself ironic. The use of Arabic in everyday interactions by security services and government officials as a tool for distinguishing between South Sudanese and 'foreigners', mainly Eastern African labourers and traders, is not only peculiar but points to a larger quandary of the 'Arab identity' in post-independence South Sudan. Such instances and empirical interactions that point to a blurring of African-Arab identities in South Sudan, however, point to a more complex reality that shows that Sudan's north-south divide is not a purely Arab-African divide.

As such, the secession of South Sudan from the Sudan has not put to rest the Arab-African debates in the two Sudans but rather intensified them as the two countries, the Republics of Sudan and South Sudan, now strive to redefine themselves beyond the presumed north-south / Arab-African presentations in the contemporary history of the Sudan. The Arabic legacy in post-independence South Sudan is, however, just one part of a complex amalgamation of cultures and traditions to be found in contemporary Southern Sudan. Like in the Sudan before it, the politics of identity have also not vanished in the new independent South Sudan. In fact it can be argued that independence has again exacerbated issues of identity viewed largely through ethnicity in the emerging patriarchal South Sudanese state.

Conclusions

The webs of conflicts, violent social patterns and dysfunctional governments in many parts of Africa make the state a far less dominating, agenda-setting actor than in the first post-independence decades (Young 2004: 24). For South

Sudan, which attained independence more than 50 years after the first wave of independent African countries, the state faces unprecedented challenges. More specifically, South Sudan's Achilles heel seems to be the challenge of achieving post-conflict statehood in a highly militarized society where the balance of power remains with the military and former rebel army. South Sudan's present experiences are rooted in a long and shared history with Sudan as part of the Sudan. As a case study, this long history forms an important part in understanding the country's experiences. Despite independence, South Sudan started its existence not from a vacuum, but from a history that dates back thousands of years. In the narratives that culminate in the illustrative history of ancient Sudan are ancestral links between today's southern tribes and Sudan's ancient kingdoms of the central Nile valley.[5]

While the complex history from which South Sudan was born bears significant influence on the country's present status and interactions, it is its assertion into statehood that perhaps bears most significance to its demilitarization. Although the country's long wars, the Anyanya war from 1955 to 1972 and the SPLA/M war from 1983 to 2005, make it an ideal case in a post-conflict study, its assertion into statehood amidst high levels of militarization adds new dimensions to the exercise. South Sudan as a case study thus helps contextualize the challenges to demilitarization by reflecting the country's prevailing political and security realities. South Sudan's post-conflict development is therefore an ongoing interaction with demilitarization and its different elements. This demilitarization has been parallel to the country's development and political milestones since the end of the Second Civil War in 2005. Some of these milestones – the six-year interim period, Sudan's first national elections, the referendum on independence – are addressed in greater detail in this book.

This chapter's compact look into the case study thus not only sheds light into the country but provides the contextual detail needed in understanding the specifications and approaches to demilitarization associated with the case study. This goes back to a key theme of this book, in a bespoke approach to demilitarization and post-conflict reconstruction. As this chapter indicates, every conflict is different, every country unique, as is every attempt at demilitarization. It is these differences in history, culture and traditions that should inform demilitarization and other post-conflict engagements if they are to succeed.

This detracts from conventional approaches to post-conflict interventions criticized for being generic. The importance of an individual approach to demilitarization nevertheless comes to fruition while faced with some complexities associated with demilitarization and the present international liberal peace engagement in the country. Although an assessment on South Sudan's post-conflict standing can be interpreted as a very public and distinctive failure of 'state' or the liberal peacebuilding experiment in the country, most of these challenges can arguably be traced back to the generic one-size-fits-all international neoliberal approach to post-conflict reconstruction. Taking into account the various challenges to the post-colonial state in Sudan, it comes as no surprise that the country may have missed most of the post-colonial political and economic makers that shaped the contemporary African state. These include the onset of globalization, the third wave democratization, the emergence of the developmental state associated with the nationalist politics of post-independence Africa and the global paradigm shifts of the 1980s that gave rise to neoliberal politics and the Washington Consensus that came with it.

3

History of militarization

It has always struck me that, from the very beginning of my existence – even before I was born – my life has always been deeply confronted with violence, injustice and conflict.
                     Bishop Paride Taban, Catholic Diocese of Torit – South Sudan

Introduction

This quote sums up many of the narratives, both personal and collective, encountered during the research that informs this book. In this chapter it is argued that war in the Sudan initially militarized the country and that therefore, in order to successfully address *d*emilitarization, militarization itself, including its extent and deep ramifications, must be fully understood.

In this way, this chapter not only explores militarization in the Sudan but the country's history as well.

Contextualizing militarization in South Sudan

Stavrianakis and Selby (2012) particularly make a significant contribution to the conceptual literature on militarization. They particularly argue that the concept and subject of militarization have not received significant attention in recent debates, especially on the place of militarization in contemporary studies.[1] This book offers not only an update of the existing literature on militarization and militarism, but a revision: offering a new conceptualization of militarization and militarism and its changing faces in contemporary political spaces. However, while the contextualization offered by Stavrianakis and Selby (2012) is more aimed at compounding the place of militarization and militarism in contemporary IR studies, there is also an acknowledgement that the study of militarization and militarism is interdisciplinary. Indeed Stavrianakis and Selby (2012) argue that the study of militarism sits at the crossroads between international politics, security studies and international relations theory (Stavrianakis and Selby 2012). More broadly, however, this most recent work on militarization bears significant relevance to this study of demilitarization, especially as the empirical realities in South Sudan dictate that it is not plausible to address the country's demilitarization without looking at its militarization.

In South Sudan, understanding the country's militarization is arguably the first step in an attempt to understand the cultivation of the military culture that has normalized the production of organised violence in the country. Still, this exercise is not exactly straightforward with the multidisciplinary constructions of militarization and militarism touched on by Stavrianakis and Selby (2012). With this in mind, this book presents that the literature on militarization is indeed extensive and arguably primarily exists in two forms: that concerned with militarization and that which looks at militarism. However, the distinction between the two is not always clear, and in some instances, like in Stavrianakis and Selby (2012), the two are used synonymously. Despite this, the scope in the study of the two is not only wide and diverse but it also cuts across different periods in political history (Wendt and Barnett 1993). Some of the other most recent work on militarization and militarism comes from Eichler (2012) in which she states:

> There are many competing definitions of militarism and militarisation. I do not use militarism to imply the dominance of the military over the state or society, but rather define militarism as an ideology that promotes a central role for the military and its personnel in state and society. This role is shaped by particular social-historic and political economic contexts. Militarism might inform state policies such as increases to military budgets, special social policy towards military professionals, or universal conscription. War necessarily relies on militarism as it privileges a military solution over other, non-violent solutions.
>
> The terms militarism and militarisation are sometimes used interchangeably. I differentiate between militarism as an ideology (or a set of ideas), and militarisation as a process. I define militarisation as any process that helps establish and reinforce a central role for the military in state and society. Thus militarisation (and the adjective militarised) will be used to underscore the socially and politically constructed nature of military's importance. Politicians, society and individuals become militarised when their beliefs and actions

support a central role for the military. Militarisation is thus achieved when militarism is not questioned but accepted as normal and necessary. (Eichler 2012: 4)

Eichler (2012) not only sums up the various debates on militarism and militarization but also offers the closest definition to the one aspired to by this chapter. While Eichler makes a clear distinction between ideology and process of militarization, this book uses militarization to include both ideas and processes. This, however, is more by default than by design, because after two civil wars spanning nearly four decades, ideas and processes or militarism and militarization have been amalgamated. This presents a number of challenges, not least the difficulty of placing South Sudan's militarization within a certain typology. However, despite these challenges, Wendt and Barnett's (1993)

Map 6 Areas key to the Sudan's modern history of militarization.

arguments on third-world militarization are perhaps the closest reflection of South Sudan and show the fluidity of the militarization thesis in the new country.

In particular, they compare militarization in the Third World with militarization in the West by exploring the similarities but also stressing their differences. In so doing they present two different forms of militarization; firstly, capital-intensive militarization which is conventional or 'technocratic'. Here, military capability is based primarily on physical and human 'capital' that is largely advanced weapons systems and highly skilled soldiers. On the other hand, it can be based on a labour-intensive military based on unconventional 'people's armies' in which capability is based more on 'labour' or force size. This can be inclusive of the mass mobilization of militias (Wendt and Barnett 1993). Militarization in the Sudan over the different periods can thus be classified as neither capital- nor labour-intensive but rather a combination of the two.

The history of conflict in the Sudan, especially in the post-independence period, shows a combination of conventional warfare with modern weaponry (capital-intensive militarization) and the recruitment of local militia (labour-intensive militarization) by both protagonists. Wendt and Barnett call this the 'alternative defence, relying on the mass mobilization of militias' which has been a common feature of war in the Sudan. In the Sudan civil wars, the militia of both the SPLA/M and GOS added a different dynamic to the war and the militarization narrative in the country and will be addressed later in this chapter. This again goes to point at the difficulty of placing South Sudan's militarization within a specific scope of the existing literature. Nevertheless, it does help to narrow the field as somewhere between militarization as presented by Wendt and Barnett (1993) and by Eichler (2012). As such, this chapter will use militarization generally within these scopes to refer to the central role played by the military in both state and society in South Sudan in a way that places it at the centre of everyday life in the country and also the unspoken military's influence over policies and politics.

Pre-independence – before 1955

Political dominance achieved by military conquest is a common feature in history and perhaps more so in Sudan than in other African countries. Historically, where great kingdoms and empires existed, great military power did too. This was true from the chiefdoms of the Americas, warring African kingdoms, the kingdoms of Europe and the Middle East, or indeed the Far East (Hunwick

1999; Vansina 1956, 1962). Evidence of its military might has been found in ancient artefacts and is perhaps best symbolized by Apedemak, the Nubian lion-headed warrior god (Haynes 1992). The history of the Sudan is therefore difficult to remove from the legacies of military conquests that characterized the Nile riverine basin that for centuries have been at the fault line of competing ideologies. The northern Nile basin attracted the interest of not only traders but also Arab and early Islamic expansionist ambition and European exploration curiosity (Holt and Daly 1988: 23).

Such interactions along the Nile date as far back as AD 639 after the conquering of Egypt by the Muslim Arabs between 639 and 641 which brought to the border of the Nubian a militant power (Holt and Daly 2000: 13). This arguably changed the trajectory of the region making military conquest a de facto social economic determinant in the Sudan which carried on through to Turco-Egyptian rule (Collins 2005; Hill 1965). The use of military prowess was nevertheless not a preserve of the northern kingdoms alone, as evidence points to a sophisticated system in the south as well. 'The Shilluk, for example, today occupy a comparatively small area on the western bank of the White Nile, but previously their range was much more extensive. This can be attributed to a decline in their military power, especially with the coming of firearms and steamers which empowered their northern neighbours' (Holt and Daly 2000).

This history could arguably have little or nothing to do with the narratives of militarization in present-day Sudan or South Sudan; however, they could also be the key to explaining and understanding that militarization. Current conflicts in the two Sudans are drenched in centuries of history, most of which goes back to the legacy of military invasions and slave trading established by the Turks and Egyptians.[2] This was continued by the Mahdists[3] and included a battle for religious superiority (Holt 1961: 14). All these have had a profound effect on the psyche of the Sudan and form the basis of most conflicts and bad relations between the riverine Arab tribes in the north and the African tribes in the south. These were particularly plundered by the Khalifa army in search of slaves, gold, ivory and ebony among the tribes of the Nuba Mountains and Funj (Holt 1961: 13) who suffered the same fate as those in the south.

The more recent history of the Sudan also presents with narratives that perhaps continue to bear relevance to present-day militarization of the now two Sudans. This again raises questions as to the effect of Sudan's history and especially the Condominium era (1899–1955) on present-day conflicts in the country. Arguably, the Condominium not only set the foundations for the administration and system of government adopted at independence, it also divided the Sudan administratively between a north and south. This simple decision not only shaped the politics of post-independence Sudan in 1956 but has continued to be at the centre of the complex relationships between the African and Arab cultures of the Sudan (Collins 2005). It is these relationships that have directly informed the two post-independence civil wars.

Post-independence

The First Civil War (1955–72)

Sudan's history may be riddled with narratives of war and militarization but it is perhaps the post-independence period and the two civil wars from 1955 that have left the greatest mark. According to the memoirs from that time, there was little militarization during the early days of the First Civil War and it was not until the 1960s that the then rebel movement, the Anyanya 1, started crossing into the Congo, then Zaire, to sell ivory and trade it for weapons (Eisman 2011: 40). Until this point the people in the Equatoria used bows and arrows to defend themselves. In particular, Eisman (2011: 47) narrates how in 1965 the people of Lowoi had come down from the mountain with spears and arrows to protest the arrest of their priest by the Anyanya. This is a particularly important piece in South Sudan's militarization puzzle. Exploring how communities in Lowoi moved from bows and arrows in 1965 to semi-automatic weapons by the end of the Second Civil War in 2005 is perhaps the key to understanding militarzsation in South Sudan. The answer, however, is perhaps to be found in the modern history of Sudan which has been mostly one of alternating civilian and military rule.

> This began with democracy at independence in 1956, followed by the military takeover of 1958 under General Ibrahim Abboud, who was forced out of power in 1965 by a popular uprising. The civilian rule that followed Abboud's demise was in turn overthrown in 1969 by the military under the leadership of Gaafar Mohamed Numeiri, who was subsequently forced out of power in 1985 by his minister of defence, General Abdel Rahman Seward Dahab, and the civilian rule that followed Numeiri's overthrow was ousted in 1989 by yet another military coup, engineered by the National Islamic Front, using General Omar al-Bashir, who is still in power today. (Francis Deng in Collins 2008)

These assertions by Francis Deng offer a snapshot of Sudan's post-independence militarization and especially the assertion of the military into politics in the coups and countercoups. However, amidst all this was an ongoing war in the south. There are questions, therefore, as to whether the civil wars in the south went on for as long as they did as a result of weak central governments in Khartoum (Johnson 2003). Nevertheless, despite the coups, the biggest contributors to the militarization thesis in the Sudan and especially the south are the two civil wars (Lokosang 2010: 17). The First Civil War with the Torit Mutiny on 18 August 1955 was in effect the first step from Lowoi in 1965 to 2005. Like most of Sudan's wars, this one was also fuelled by 'socio-economic grievances derived from culturally and regionally imposed political marginalisation' (Ylönen 2005).

Nevertheless, this marginalization had a different face then and was mainly seen in terms of unequal distribution of resources and government positions at independence.[4] There was widespread fear among Southern Sudanese that the social political landscape in independent Sudan would be dominated by northerners. This fear stemmed from a history of a difficult relationship between Sudan's predominantly Arab north and African south. This dynamic, however complex, can be summed up as one that has evolved over time, with the north absorbing the interactions from the outside world and especially Islam, and the south separated from the north by the Sudd, escaping most of that influence.

It is this relationship that informs the bulk of the militarization narrative in the Sudan, from the beginning of Arab migration to the Nile basin to the present day, in particular the quest for a Muslim, quasi-Arab identity for north Sudan, vis-à-vis the struggle to retain a traditional African identity for the tribes of South Sudan.[5] This struggle informed the fear of Arab indoctrination by South Sudanese at independence (1956) by the few educated southerners. They feared that with the entire administrative infrastructure in the north, the south faced not only indoctrination but also exclusion along lines seeking to preserve the status quo (Nyaba 1997: 15). Of these times, Bishop Paride Taban of the Catholic Diocese of Torit, then a seminarian, writes:

> We could foretell that independence would mean more freedom only for those who would attain, enjoy and use power but not necessarily a better time for the Sudanese. Arabs had always felt superior and they had very often looked down on us, our culture and our identity; so there was no equality between us. Even the remuneration would make a difference. Northerners and Anglo-Egyptians working in civil administration or companies in the south would get a 'southern allowance' as if they were working in a foreign country. (Eisman 2011: 29)

Although the status quo in Sudan was that of a superior Arab north and an inferior African south derived from a complex history of social political interaction over many centuries, its modern-day assertions can be traced back to the Condominium.[6] During this period, British concerns over growing Egyptian influence in the Sudan and the spread of Islam led to the introduction of the Closed District Order, officially separating the south from the north (Breidlid 2010, 2014; Lokosang 2010: 12). The order, among other things, barred Northern Sudanese from entering or working in the south. It also gradually replaced Arab administrators and expelled Arab merchants to discourage the spread of Islam.

This closed-door policy also severed economic ties with the north and arguably set the stage for the delinking of the two Sudans that culminated in the south's secession in 2011. It also marked the beginning of the exclusion and neglect of Southern Sudan. Lack of resources and manpower by the British colonial administration also meant that the south got a sketchy colonial administration with little social economic input. As such, British colonial rule subjected southern tribes to isolation, excluding them from a share in Sudan's development budget and from pre-independence planning for the Sudan (Collins 2008; Lokosang 2010).

During this period, there were, for example, no efforts to educate the population in the south apart from the scattered schools established by Christian missionaries (Nyaba 1997). This was in total contrast to the north of the country which benefited highly from not only having the colonial administrative centre based in Khartoum, but also from its ties and proximity to the Arab world. Egypt in particular played a significant role as the joint colonial administrators of Sudan, providing educational opportunities, healthcare and an infrastructure for the north which the south lacked (Lokosang 2010). These inequalities are at the heart of narratives that have fuelled Sudan's civil wars, beginning with the First Civil War. Sentiments of inequality are not especially hard to find in the Sudan's history, but in preparing for independence they became more pronounced, especially with the end of the closed-door order.

In the period preceding Sudan's independence, a decision was made at the Sudan Administrative Conference (SAC) of 1946 (Ylönen 2005) to revoke the closed-door order and unite the two Sudans. This decision set in motion a number of events that ultimately led to the First Civil War. First, the end of the Closed District Order saw British officials in the south replaced mainly by Northern Sudanese in a new policy of Sudanising the administration. However, by 1954, of the eight hundred administrative posts that had been 'Sudanised', only six junior level positions were filled by southerners (Nyaba 1997; Ylönen 2005: 10).

> When they started Sudanisation, even those of us who had gone to school with the missionaries knew there was no place for us; the Arabs didn't want us.[7]

This was perceived by many southerners as a deliberate effort to exclude them from the post-colonial administration of their territories (Collins 2005: 203; Ylönen 2005). The subsequent adoption of Arabic as the official administrative language in the south increased the fear among southerners of a return to northern political and socio-economic domination. This fear was actualized by the gunning down of southern workers demonstrating their dismissal and replacement by northerners in the Zande Scheme in July 1955. This event – the shooting of southern workers by the army and police – is viewed by many southerners as the event that began the war, sowing the seed of discontent from which the Torit Mutiny was to rise, and with it the First Civil War.

The Torit Mutiny

The mutiny in Torit was significant because the town had always been an important military post, including serving at the base for the King's African Rifles (KAR) during World War II (Eisman 2011: 28). This mutiny, therefore, although it claimed only 261 Northern Sudanese and 27 Southern Sudanese lives before Northern Sudanese troops took back control and established government control in Equatoria (Collins 2005: 204), changed the interaction between the north and south. The mutiny forced a reshuffle of the government with the most able southerners transferred to the south and those in the Equatoria demoted or transferred north. Most of the mutineers were rounded up, tried, executed and buried in mass graves to be found outside the present-day town of Torit (Figure 3.1).

Those who escaped arrest gave rise to the rebellion that became the South Sudan Liberation Movement (SSLM) or the Anyanya, meaning 'snake', under the leadership of Joseph Lagu. The rebellion in the south, however, did not take off immediately after the Torit Mutiny, sparked off by junior soldiers, but rather after, when the few educated South Sudanese started fearing that they were being targeted by the government (Eisman 2011; Nyaba 1997). It is only then that South Sudanese intellectuals and politicians joined the southern rebellion to form an organised armed resistance (Eisman 2011; Lokosang 2010: 27).

Although the southern rebellion was initially a small and uncoordinated one, this soon changed and by the early 1960s its activities extended to recruitment, training, and raiding government police posts in the south in order to acquire

Figure 3.1 Torit Memorial.
Source: Nyambura Wambugu – taken November 2010.

arms. In response, the government tackled the rebellion by throwing all resources from a struggling national economy at it. This culminated in a Soviet arms deal in 1968 which resulted in a gradual flow of heavy military equipment into the country.

> By the mid-1960s it became government policy to cut Anyanya support by attacking civilians and destroying infrastructure thought to be supporting it. This, however, only created further anti-north sentiments among the southerners. After Numeiri took power in the 1969 coup, he launched a campaign against the Anyanya with the newly acquired Soviet military hardware, further escalating the destruction and population displacement in the south. (Ylönen 2005: 16)

The mutiny of the Southern Equatoria Corps (SEC) on 18 August 1955 in Torit, following rumours that they would be disarmed and transferred to the north (Ylönen 2005), can therefore be viewed as the beginning of the militarization of modern-day Sudan. The acquisition of arms by both sides also set the country on the road that accounts for the change from Lowoi in 1965, when villagers protected themselves with bows and arrows, to the society that has normalized the presence of firearms in the community and uses the AK-47 with the casualness and ease of the walking stick.[8] The escalation of fighting in the south was to continue until the 1972 Addis Ababa peace settlement ended the major hostilities. However, by the signing of the Addis Ababa Agreement, Southern Sudan's first post-independence militarization had gone full circle and set the stage for the Second Civil War which followed eleven years on.

The Second Civil War – The SPLA (1983–2005)

The Second Civil War in the Sudan started after the collapse of the Addis Ababa Agreement and set off the country's second phase of militarization, the aftermath of which both South Sudan and Sudan are still grappling with today. 'The accord which ended the war was intended also as a political formula to establish the basis for addressing three intertwined national problems: political instability, lack of social economic development and the disunity created by conflicting aspirations based on political, cultural, racial and, most importantly, the religious heterogeneity of the Sudan' (Wakoson 1993). To achieve this, the agreement guaranteed the south regional autonomy within one united Sudan. 'A southern regional government known as the High Executive Council exercising executive powers, an independent public service commission and a southern people's regional assembly with legislative powers were established in the southern capital Juba' (Nyaba 1997: 19).

However, despite the promise of peace, the years of the peace accord were eventful ones and ultimately led to the Second Civil War eleven years after the signing of the Addis Ababa Agreement. During this time, the Sudan embarked on ambitious agricultural and infrastructural projects that pushed up the country's national debt leading to eventual economic collapse (Collins 2005: 45). As such, the 1970s was a period in which the Sudan was marred by riots and protests (Nyaba 1997) driven by economic despair. The discovery of oil in Bentiu in 1978, however, offered the country and President Numeiri a way out of the economic slump (Collins 2005: 44; Nyaba 1997). But the protests, riots and attempted coups in Khartoum had made President Numeiri weary. In an attempt to consolidate his position, Numeiri sought new allies, turning to the religious conservatives who, in exchange for their support, advocated an Islamic state which contradicted the Addis Ababa Agreement (Nyaba 1997).

On 23 May 1983, President Numeiri abrogated the Addis Ababa Agreement by unilaterally redividing the Southern Region into the previous separate regions of Bahr el Ghazal, Upper Nile and Equatoria. In September he scrapped the Sudan civil and penal code which had governed the country since the Condominium and brought in the 'September Laws'. The September Laws adopted Sharia as the supreme law of the land and effectively turned Sudan into an Islamic state. The September Laws were, for many southern people, the last straw. Adoption of Sharia law for all Sudanese, regardless of their religious affiliation, was the last nail in the coffin of the Addis Ababa Agreement. Anticipating trouble in the southern garrisons, Numeiri attempted to transfer them to the north and with that pushed underlying discontent among the troops into a full-blown mutiny (Collins 2005: 50). The mutiny of the 104 and 105 battalions of the Sudanese Army in the southern towns of Bor, Ayod and Pibor led by Majors Kerubino Kuanyin Bol and William Nyuon Bany are seen as the beginning of Sudan's Second Civil War. It is from this point that South Sudan's second militarization begins.

The southern mutinies

Although the mutiny of the 104 and 105 battalions was the turning point that saw the complete breakdown of the Addis Ababa Agreement, it was not the first sign that the peace agreement was in trouble. A few years earlier a small group of southerners, mainly consisting of former fighters from the first Anyanya war, had regrouped as the Anyanya 2 and started attacking government installations. The formation of the SPLA in 1983 after the southern mutinies, therefore, found the units of Anyanya 2 already operating against the Sudanese Army in the south (Nyaba 1997: 45). Anyanya 2 attacks were, however, small in scale and didn't cause Khartoum much concern. As such, the mutinies after September 1983 were perceived in the same light with President Numeiri choosing to send a southern colonel, John Garang (also known as Dr John Garang de Mabior), to deal with the mutiny while he remained preoccupied with actualizing the September Laws (Collins 2005: 52). However, instead of crushing the rebellion, the colonel joined it, took charge and fled to Ethiopia to form the SPLA (Sudan People's Liberation Army).

This begins the narrative of South Sudan's second rebellion that, from the beginning, took a military inclination. The military direction taken by the SPLA was arguably a result of many circumstances. One, there was a lack of political activity in Southern Sudan in the form of political parties or political affiliations, other than those that were carved along tribal allegiances at the time (Nyaba 1997). Two, the SPLA arguably came into being mainly as a reaction to changing policies in Khartoum. As such, the SPLA, unlike many of the African rebellions, was not deeply rooted in any political ideology and neither did it have any credible political leadership (Nyaba 1997: 27). Three, the SPLA's main supporter at the time was Ethiopia's ruling military junta, the Derg, under the leadership of Mengistu Haile Mariam. Mengistu had long-running disputes with Numeiri due to Khartoum's long-standing support for the Eritrean war of independence from Ethiopia. However, of the three factors, it is perhaps the Derg's influence that had the most influence on the trajectory the SPLA took.

At the same time, the mutineers in 1983 were also profoundly different from their counterparts who had fled Torit in August 1955. They were not only part of the Sudan Army, they were well-trained and well-armed (Collins 2005: 52). This was the starting point for the rebel movement that was to dominate life in the south for the next two decades. After its inception, the SPLA grew, mainly due to the support received from Mengistu and the refuge he provided in western Ethiopia. However, Mengistu was more in favour of support for military officials as opposed to politicians whom 'he generally viewed as selfish enemies of the people who could sell out the liberation struggle at any time' (Nyaba 1997). This, it has been argued, is how Col John Garang came to the leadership of the new movement because of his educational background – a doctorate from the USA coupled with his military credentials made him an obvious choice to head the SPLA (Collins 2005; Nyaba 1997).

The SPLA, therefore, began its rebellion with a deeply rooted military identity. From the onset, politicians in the movement were marginalized in favour of those like John Garang who had military credentials (Lokosang 2010; Nyaba 1997). They not only found themselves sidelined, but also without any influence in the activities of the SPLA at a time when the new movement was recruiting, training and arming the new rebel army (Nyaba 1997). It is such events earlier on in the movement that cemented the dominant role of the army in the southern rebellion. The autocratic leadership style adopted by Garang also left little room for the democratically inclined within the movement, both in theory and practice. Ethiopia's support to the SPLA, as it grew in strength and numbers, gave it enormous firepower that brought it several impressive victories (Nyaba 1997). However, apart from the odd victories, the war in Sudan remained at a stalemate, especially against a backdrop of changing national politics in which Numeiri was ousted from power in 1985.

The Departure of Numeiri from the political scene also changed perceptions of the 'southern problem' in Khartoum. After Numeiri, a 15-man Transitional Military Council (TMC) took over running the country alongside a civilian cabinet under Dr Dafallah al-Ghazouly. The fall of Numeiri offered reconciliation in the Sudan with Dafallah and his cabinet eager to reach out to the SPLA/M.

However, the movement, which had earlier declared itself not a separatist movement but a revolutionary movement whose aim was to liberate the whole of the Sudan from Numeiri, refused to engage (Collins 2005: 59). Garang argued that the TMC was composed of previous Numeiri generals and, as such, nothing had really changed. For its part, the TMC turned to a military solution for the 'southern problem' and started employing divide and rule tactics in the south by sponsoring elements of Anyanya 2 (Collins 2005: 62) still operating in the countryside against the SPLA/M. The result was an unsuccessful military campaign on both sides (LeRiche and Arnold 2012).

The Nasir Declaration

The deadlock in the war was mirrored by the deadlock in Sudan's politics in Khartoum. Nonetheless, this period[9] was one of massive militarization in the south. The SPLA attracted more recruits while the Sudan Army was supplying southern tribes with arms exploiting old ethnic rivalries to sabotage the SPLA/M efforts. This, however, did little to unlock the war stalemate; the coup d'état on 30 June 1989, though, was to change the nature of the conflict entirely. At the time of the 1989 coup, there was also growing discontent within the southern movement, particularly in the context of changing national politics and following years of unsuccessful military campaigns. The feeling that the movement was in need of a new vision and political guidance was widespread, including within the top hierarchy.[10] The rank, nevertheless, remained intolerant to criticism or political indifferences. Suggestions of reforming the movement to give it a more concrete political dimension were met with a heavy-handed response (Nyaba 1997; Rone et al. 1994). There was growing frustration among those politically inclined within the movement who felt the armed struggle was not the only way forward, against those who defended the movement's military structure and status quo (Akol 2011).

The discontent within the SPLA/M grew as politics within the movement became more localized and tribal, mainly between the tribes of the Upper Nile and Bahr el Ghazal regions. From its inception, the SPLA had been perceived by most southerners as a predominantly Dinka movement (Collins 2005). The Anyanya 2 who had remained outside the SPLA were perceived to be more of a Nuer outfit (Collins 2005; Nyaba 1997; Rone et al. 1994: 25) and the Equatorians who had borne the brunt of the First Civil War were reluctant to join either side. Although these cracks within the movement were visible from time to time, the SPLA was able to quell any efforts at dissent (Collins 2005). This was, however, to change on 28 August 1991 when, in a radio message from the town of Nasir, the SPLA's second in command, Commander Riek Machar, addressed all units of the SPLA announcing that the leader John Garang had been overthrown. With hindsight, this move was not entirely a surprise as relations and tribal tensions within the movement's top leadership had escalated through the years (Akol 2011). As such, Riek Machar was joined by other commanders in the Upper Nile region – Dr Lam Akol, Gordon Koang Chol and the SPLA barracks in Ayod, Waat, Adwong, Adok, Ler and Akobo in what came to be known as the Nasir Declaration (Rone et al. 1994: 26).

However, the announcement did not have the intended effect as most of the SPLA remained loyal to John Garang, splitting the SPLA into two groups. The Nasir Declaration thus marked the beginning of yet another chapter in southern militarization and one of the bloodiest periods in Southern Sudan's history as the SPLA degenerated into tribal factions. These factions, however, had enormous fighting power because at the time of this announcement, the SPLA had an estimated 120,000 soldiers (Nyaba 1997). It had at this point also succeeded in capturing all the southern states in Sudan with the exception of a few garrison towns of Juba and Yei and rural Bahr el Ghazal, as well as small parts of Upper Nile south of the Sabot river near the border with the north (Nyaba 1997). After the split, the two groups turned this fighting power against each other and began massacring civilian population perceived to support the other.

This episode is particularly important in the construction of South Sudan's militarization narrative as both sides of the split armed and recruited civilians into their ranks. It is remnants of these civilian recruits that continue to make up the many militia in South Sudan. It is also during this period that the youth took up arms to protect their communities against the feuding factions. Notably, this period saw the inception of the 'White Army' in the coming together of Nuer youth to protect their homeland. The White Army remains active in the Upper Nile and Jonglei states and has contributed to continued conflict and insecurity in the region, including the fighting in Jonglei State in early 2012 (Arnold and Alden 2007). In the most recent December 2013 conflict, the White Army formed the bulk of former Vice President Riek Machar's fighters.

During the split, the arming of the civilian population also became a double-edged sword. While the civilians helped the SPLA fight the Sudan Army, they also severely weakened the SPLA's capacity to exert control over local communities through the use of force. This, together with the infighting, severely weakened the SPLA and changed the dynamics of power in the wider north–south conflict which had taken a back seat after the SPLA split. At this point, the new National

Islamic Front (NIF) government in Khartoum also changed its approach to the 'southern problem' and used the SPLA split to reinforce its hold on the south and recaptured some strategic towns. Khartoum achieved this by coercing Riek Machar's SPLA-United, which, despite having control of the northern parts of Southern Sudan bordering the north, was in desperate need of military support. As such, in exchange for weapons and military supplies, Machar allowed Khartoum safe passage to John Garang's controlled areas. This passage allowed the Sudanese government army to capture some SPLA towns like Pochalla (April 1992), Kapoeta (June 1992) and Torit, among others (Nyaba 1997: 75).

This also opened yet another chapter of civilian militarization, this time driven by the government in Khartoum. The Sudan Army, taking advantage of growing resentment against the SPLA by local communities caught in the middle of the internal fighting, started arming local communities to 'defend' themselves against the SPLA. This was particularly evident in Eastern Equatoria, especially with the Toposa and Pari community.[11] This arming of civilians was the greatest legacy of the north–south war in the Sudan. This period in Sudan's history was also marked by a changing of the guard in Khartoum with the 30 June 1989 military coup, which brought the Muslim Brotherhood-backed National Islamic Front (NIF) and Brigadier General Omar Hassan Ahmad al-Bashir to power. This significantly changed the way the Sudan was governed and how the north–south war was conducted. On the one hand, the NIF galvanized the Islamisation project started by President Numeiri's September (Sharia) Laws of 1983 and also aggressively pursued a military victory against the SPLA in the south. On the other hand, it embarked on the first real consulted efforts to explore Sudan's oil commercially.

The politics of oil and war

On a micro-level, the NIF continued to arm civilian populations by creating local militias, including arming southern communities as mentioned above. Similarly, the NIF also heavily armed 'northern Arab' tribes along the north-south border to carry out a programme that came to be known as depopulisation for oil,[12] which also saw a return to slave raiding in Southern Sudan. On a macro-level, the militarization of Sudan also increased with the Sudanese state embarking on extended arms acquisitions to fight the SPLA and to sustain militia proxies. However, whether this tactic worked or not is open to debate, but what is clear is the effect of this arming of civilians on the militarization narrative of the Sudan.

The impact of this period was thus felt not only in the Sudan but also in the region. While on the domestic macro-level it escalated the north-south war, on the micro-level it was responsible for the deterioration of community relations. Regionally, this militarization spilled over into neighbouring countries with the increased proliferation of small arms. The sudden accessibility of firearms only served to escalate already existing community conflicts to unmanageable levels. On this Jok (2001) argues: 'When the second civil conflict broke out in 1983, traditional agreements disintegrated and relations turned into almost irreconcilable hostilities [...] these conflicts would have remained sporadic and manageable, as they had been for many generations, had the government of Sudan not decided to manipulate them for its political designs' (Jok 2001).

The arming of civilians did, however, not end with the SPLA split or the governments. The falling out of Riek Machar and Dr Lam Akol and the subsequent split of SPLA-United became another major source of civilian armament. With the disintegration of SPLM-United, its different army units fell under the command of different commanders who, desperate to make a living, turned into thugs for hire in the oil-rich Greater Upper Nile region (ICG 2002). Subsequently, Riek Machar moved to Khartoum and made official his collaboration with the Government of Sudan (GOS) with the signing of the 'political charter', a framework for peace between the GOS and the SPLA-United on 10 April 1996. The political charter was presented by Riek Machar and the NIF as a basis for peace negotiations and as a step forward in Sudan finding peace from within. However, those opposed to the charter saw it as an effort by the National Islamic Front to evade peace negotiations that had already been set up under the auspices of the Intergovernmental Authority on Development (IGAD).[13]

IGAD had already produced a framework for peace negotiations between the SPLA and the Government of Sudan by presenting some basic principles known as the Declaration of Principles in 1994. These principles were to govern the peace process by focusing the negotiations on the contentious issues that had fuelled the conflict and been seen as hard to resolve (Waihenya 2006). The IGAD principles, however, included two issues omitted in the 1996 political charter: the issues of the separation of religion and state and self-determination for Southern Sudan. Nevertheless, Machar's political charter is perhaps more criticized for undermining the IGAD process by opening a parallel peace process than for its omission of the self-determination and religion and state issues.

Machar's political charter resulted in the signing of the Khartoum Peace Agreement (KPA) between SPLA-United and the National Islamic Front

(NIF) in Khartoum. Although sometimes ridiculed, Machar's signing of the political charter and the subsequent Khartoum Peace Agreement forced the NIF Islamist government to adopt a democratic constitution, even if arguably only on paper (Nyaba 1997). In the KPA, Southern Sudan was given self-determination only in theory. The agreement made Riek Machar an assistant to President Bashir and president of the Southern Sudan Coordinating Council as well as commander of the GOS forces in the south. On paper, the KPA was the best deal ever presented to Southern Sudan (ICG 2002) and the 2005 Comprehensive Peace Agreement is arguably a revised version of Machar's 1997 Khartoum Peace Agreement.

However, despite Machar's KPA, fighting between what was now called the SPLA proper or SPLA-Torit and the different splinter groups of SPLA-United continued. The militarization of local communities also continued, mainly through the normalization of conflict and violence in communities that had learned to integrate the war into the reality of their day-to-day lives. Although there was a general consensus that a reconciliation of the two SPLA factions was necessary to resolve the wider Sudan conflict (Nyaba 1997), reconciliation between the two SPLA factions remained elusive. However, in January 2002 in Nairobi, Kenya, an agreement between Machar and Garang was reached. This marked a new beginning for the SPLA reconciliation and reinvigorated the stalled IGAD peace talks which had dragged on since 1994. However, as the negotiations between the SPLA and the Government of Sudan continued and peace looked more likely, both sides intensified their military campaigns in what both sides called the 'final push', an attempt to gain as much military advantage as possible before meeting at the negotiating table with the hope of using the military gains as negotiating leverage. As such, 2002 and 2003 saw an increase in military activities in Southern Sudan with the remilitarization and the rearming of an already highly militarized society. Subsequently, as the civil war drew to a close, the surge of military activity in the south also brought with it an increase in military supplies, leaving the countryside littered with weapons that provided the springboard for most of the militarization witnessed after the signing of the peace agreement in 2005.

Post-CPA militarization

At the end of the peace negotiations in Naivasha, there were already concerns that the peace deal between the Government of Sudan and the southern rebels, the

SPLA/M, could be jeopardized by other rebel factions that were not part of the peace deal (Rands 2010; Young 2006). Until the CPA, there were several armed groups still operating in the south – a fallout of the SPLA/M woes in the 1990s. Ever since the leadership struggles within the Sudan People's Liberation Army (SPLA) in 1991, homelands had also provided the major battlefield for escalating military confrontations among South Sudanese themselves (Human Rights Watch 1999; Jok and Hutchinson 2002: 6; Johnson 1998; Jok and Hutchinson 1999; Nyaba 1997). The formal end of hostilities between Khartoum and the southern rebels, however, did not address the other conflicts that mushroomed after 1991 which had trapped Southern Sudanese civilian populations in a rising tide of ethnicized, south-on-south military violence (Hutchinson 2001). As such, exactly one year after the signing of the CPA, the government of Southern Sudan formulated the Juba Declaration as the first step towards addressing other armed groups apart from the SPLA operating in the south.

Juba Declaration of 8 January 2006

The main aim of the Juba Declaration was to prevent renewed conflict between the SPLA and the South Sudan Defence Forces (SSDF). The SSDF came about in 1997 with the signing of the Khartoum Peace Agreement between the Government of Sudan and SPLM/A-United, SSIM, EDF and other groups (now known collectively as SSDF) (Young 2006: 18). The integration of the SSDF into the SPLA is therefore a significant part of South Sudan's reform and restructuring of post-CPA security and will be addressed in more detail in Chapter 5. It is, however, from this integration as part of the Juba Declaration that most of the post-CPA militarization has emerged, particularly from SSDF groups and leaders resisting integration as a result of fallout in the leadership. Before the start of the SSDF–SPLA negotiations in Juba, there were concerns within the SSDF rank about the final status of the South Sudanese Army in view of an SSDF–SPLA agreement. To address these concerns, SSDF Gen Gordon Koang unsuccessfully sought consultation between the leader Paulino Matip and the 502 SSDF officers.[14] The refusal by Paulino Matip to engage, strained relations with his top generals and set in motion what was the beginning of South Sudan's post-CPA militarization. Despite this, the Juba Declaration negotiated by Matip and President Salva Kiir was a success as it attempted to resolve the issue of armed militias in the south and integrated various groups to either the SPLA or the Sudan Armed Forces (SAF) as illustrated by the UN monitoring of forces below.

However, despite the promise of peace that should have come with the SPLA and SSDF agreement, the subsequent disintegration of the SSDF created a new insecurity in the country, reaching levels that had not previously existed. After the signing of the Juba Declaration, over 250 SSDF officers rebelled against the SSDF integration into the SPLA and nominated Gen Koang as their leader. As of 31 March 2006, Gordon Koang's SSDF was controlling 75 per cent of the Greater Upper Nile, 10 per cent of Greater Bahr el Ghazal and 15 per cent of Greater Equatoria.[15] The ramifications of this particular episode have come to define South Sudan's post-CPA militarization and turned regions like Upper Nile into battlefields between Matip, now integrated into the SPLA as the deputy commander-in-chief of South Sudan, and Koang's SSDF.

After the Juba Declaration, the SSDF commanders who did not join the SPLA have contributed significantly to rearming the rural populations and their kin as their main support base. The disintegration of the SSDF was nevertheless not a surprise, especially because it was never one unit to begin with. The fallout after the signing of the Juba Declaration, though, renewed old rivalries resulting in a mushrooming of new militias, particularly across the greater Upper Nile region. However, apart from the militarization resulting from the SSDF fallout, the other significant post-CPA militarization came about following the April 2010 election. The post-election insurrections, as they are commonly known, were mainly a result of disgruntled commanders, some from the SSDF Juba Declaration fallout, who felt cheated in the April 2010 national elections addressed in Chapter 6 and Appendix 4.

The Government in Juba responded to the upsurge in militia activity by offering amnesty to not only the post-election insurrections but also to all the other militias, including the post-Juba Declaration ones. Many militia leaders have hid the call for amnesty and negotiated themselves into higher military ranks within the SPLA. However, continued 'security incidents in Upper Nile State had also demonstrated that these former commanders had increasingly little influence over the more youthful leaders in the field' (Rands 2010: 19). Similarly, despite the perceived success of amnesty in resolving most of South Sudan's post-CPA militia upsurge, the insurrections have had a profound effect on the country's militarization. They have, for instance, not only rearmed civilian populations but also passed on military skills to a generation that had little to no memory of the war, especially the militarization after the 1991 SPLA split. More importantly, the militia has redefined militarization in the south and changed its dynamics by rebelling against the southern SPLA/M-led government as opposed to Khartoum.

One rebellion that has completely rewritten the militarization narrative in South Sudan is that of David Yau Yau in Pibor County in Jonglei State. What may have started as a small post-election insurrection soon snowballed into an armed conflict that had taken on ethnic dimensions, not only encompassing the Murle as a community, but all their neighbours as well. Although the dynamics of the David Yau Yau rebellion are often seen through the Jonglei lenses, especially in relation to the Lou Nuer and, to some extent, the Dinka Bor, this particular insurrection had an effect beyond Jonglei. Informant interviews with members of the Eastern Equatoria leadership, for example, point to a new militarization of communities bordering the Pibor 'to contain' the rebellion within the Murle borders. This presents the biggest challenge to internal militarization in post-CPA South Sudan and it also runs parallel to the narratives of externally driven militarization resulting from conflicts over the border areas.

However, even with internal strife, fragile relations between Sudan and South Sudan over their border also resulted in a new form of militarization in the region. There had been evidence of military build-up along the border and especially around disputed regions like Abyei since the signing of the CPA.[16] Relations between the two countries also hit an all-time low in April 2012 when the countries edged towards all-out war. This incident not only pointed to advanced state militarization on both sides, but also compounded South Sudan's militarization as one that stems from internal fragmentation and external aggression. The border issue had also primarily been responsible for failures to implement most of the CPA provisions that required a scaling down of both the SPLA and SAF, especially as many on both sides saw and treated the CPA as nothing more than a ceasefire (Rands 2010). This not only explained the deep-rooted mistrust on both sides but also the pursuit of what can be described as an arms race in the post-CPA period contrary to the aspirations of the peace agreement. Events of April 2012, however, marked a turning point and forced the intervention of the African Union and the UN Security Council in resolution 2046.[17]

The UN Security Council resolution 2046 obliged both sides to amicably find a solution to not only border disputes, but all other outstanding and unresolved issues. Nevertheless, the possibility of war between the two countries constantly looms in the background and has resulted in a new militarization in South Sudan's border areas. A heavy SPLA deployment at the borders, the arming of border communities and a reluctance to completely disarm civilian populations viewed as an army in waiting are key to this and are addressed further in the following chapters.

Conclusion

In the case of South Sudan, the reality of militarization is that of complex, multifaceted and interlinked processes. These, over time, have produced a militarization puzzle of interconnected processes that ultimately must align in order for a holistic representation of militarization to emerge. This brings together ongoing parallel processes of militarization in South Sudan as well as those that preceded them, beginning from early civilizations and the pre-independence period before the First Civil War in 1955. Although this period may appear to have few direct links to present-day militarization in South Sudan, it does set the stage for events that ignited two civil wars spanning nearly four decades. The narratives established in this period are not only embedded in the country's history but shaped the political, religious and cultural complexes that have beset the Sudan for decades. This is addressed in the second part of this chapter looking at the period after the beginning of the First Civil War, the independence in 1956 and through the Second Civil War. This period was the most destructive in South Sudan and thus contributed the most to its militarization, notably by leaving a trail of light weapons littered across the south.

The proliferation of small arms in South Sudan as a result of the civil wars opened the door for the latest and most recent militarization in the country after the signing of the CPA. The chapter especially identifies internal militia insurrections in the south and conflicts over the indistinct border as the two principal drivers of South Sudan's post-CPA militarization. In looking at militarization in South Sudan through three specific periods in its history, it is clear that although history has played a significant part in South Sudan's militarization, most of the post-CPA militarization is a direct result of its modern-day political attributions rather than history. This is true for not only South Sudan but also in Sudan where SPLA units in the Blue Nile and South Kordofan's Nuba mountains known as SPLM-North (SPLM-N) restarted fighting with Khartoum after the secession of the south. This conflict has not only played into the border conflicts between Sudan and South Sudan, but has also had a profound effect on their most recent militarization.

The rebellions in Blue Nile and the Nuba mountains, although in Sudan, have also had a direct impact on the militarization narrative in the south. The SPLM-N under the leadership of Malik Agar have become a direct cause of conflict between Sudan and South Sudan. Khartoum accused South Sudan of supporting and arming the SPLM-N and, in retaliation, provided arms to militias and rebels in the south (Blanchard 2012). However, Juba denies supporting the SPLM-N just as Khartoum denies supporting rebels in the south, especially David Yau Yau in Pibor. Despite these denials, the issue of supporting each other's rebels has become a hindrance to resolving many of the outstanding differences as demanded by UN resolution 2046. The African Union has appointed an envoy to investigate these accusations. Resolution of South Sudan's support for the SPLM-N will be the first step towards not only defusing tensions between the two countries, but also towards stopping recent militarization. It is against this backdrop that this book begins to tackle the issue of demilitarizing South Sudan.

The 2013–14 crisis has, however, added to the militarization complex in South Sudan. The rebellion that followed events of December 2013 is arguably a culmination of all the different levels of militarization in the country.[18] While this new militarization of South Sudan, especially in the Upper Nile region, presents a significant challenge to the country's demilitarization, this book argues that it is in fact a direct result of the country and the international liberal peacebuilding efforts in the country failing to demilitarize after the end of the Second Civil War. Indeed, this book argues that the new militarization in South Sudan is nothing more than a regrouping of existing rebellions and armed groups in Upper Nile under the leadership of the former vice president Riek Machar, who was also leader of the Nasir Declaration. That the new rebellion and most recent phase of militarization in South Sudan is draped in history, both past and modern, is undeniable. Similarly, that as a country emerging from a history of militarization and militarism, the importance of demilitarization as the most significant of all other ongoing processes cannot be overstated. This book argues especially strongly that like in the post-CPA period, which embraced the liberal peacebuilding and state-building process, if the country does not focus on demilitarization as part of a holistic post-conflict approach off the back of the current 2013–14 crisis, it is unlikely that South Sudan will be able to shake off its history of militarization.

4

Contextualizing security restructuring and reforms

Introduction

The deconstruction of the war security infrastructure is a cornerstone of demilitarization in post-conflict South Sudan. The next two chapters engage with debates surrounding South Sudan's post-conflict restructuring of security as part of this deconstruction and the attempts at institutionalizing this restructuring and subsequent reforms. They specifically explore and examine the successes, challenges and shortcomings in the design and approach of South Sudan's post-conflict restructuring and reforming of security following the 2005 peace agreement. However, following South Sudan's return to conflict in December 2013, the arguments here also offer the benefit of hindsight to South Sudan's next phase of reconstruction with the formation of the Transitional Government of National Unity (TGoNU) in April 2016. These chapters on the restructuring and reconstitution of security structures and applications specifically argue that the approach to post-conflict restructuring and reforming of security should be two-faceted. On the one hand, dealing with the structural, policy and institutional restructuring of security immediately after the cessation of hostilities, and on the other, examining what the restructuring of post-conflict security looks like in real terms at the micro-level.

However, the empirical reality of South Sudan moves beyond this two-faceted approach and instead presents a four-phased approach to the demilitarization narrative in the country. First, by tackling the immediate post-conflict activities of the disarming, demobilizing and reintegrating of former fighters; then the institutional building of the post-war security infrastructure, including the legislative frameworks; then shifting the focus to those who join the national army and security services and their retraining to finally addressing the security legacy left by war. These four areas of focus broadly interact with the broader arguments in this book and are especially potent in highlighting the gaps between the theory and practice of post-conflict security. It is in addressing these four areas that the restructuring and reforming of security in South Sudan as presented in this book departs from the overarching liberal peacebuilding thesis.

Also of equal significance is the assertion that the redressing of post-conflict security in South Sudan cannot be successfully achieved solely from a position of theoretical underpinning. This is widely reflected in various conversations with international and regional agency, but more so in conversations with local agency, especially politicians, policymakers and ordinary citizens. In interviews, these local actors often reiterated that 'in South Sudan everyone is a soldier – the police, the fire brigade and even the wildlife police were all SPLA, but because not everybody can remain in the army, we need some to become police and even traffic'.[1] These assertions reinforced empirical observations during the extended periods of fieldwork in South Sudan and the conclusions that indeed the SPLA epitomized both past and contemporary approaches and perceptions of security in the country; that, as such, the restructuring and reforming of security in the country must begin with the SPLA, the former rebel army, and all its splinters and affiliates. While restructuring and reforming the SPLA represents a 'tangible' institutional and structural reform in the restructuring of post-conflict security, the greatest challenge in South Sudan remained that of denting and diminishing the influence of the SPLA on the country's wider security sector, politics and society. Still, the importance placed on the restructuring and reform of the SPLA cannot be overstated and remains of paramount importance in the success of the overall reform and restructuring of security in the country, mainly following the December 2013 crisis.

This is an especially important part in the institutionalization of security and part of the four-point approach to the restructuring and reforming of security in South Sudan. However, the complexity of professionalizing the SPLA increased immensely following South Sudan's post-independence war. Still, as a dominant security partner in South Sudan, professionalizing the SPLA would have real implications for the country's entire security sector. Arguably, it was in the attempt to professionalize the SPLA that the formulation of a national security strategy and legal framework emerged, subsequently resulting in the restructuring and reform of civilian security structures like the South Sudan Police Service (SSPS). However, despite some gains and successes in the professionalization and institutionalization of the SPLA after the 2005

CPA, like with most interventions in South Sudan, the devil remained in the detail.

At the core of South Sudan's restructuring of security was also the fact that the current South Sudanese state had its beginnings in a regional government set-up emanating from the semi-autonomous regional government of Southern Sudan. This was a direct result of the 2005 CPA and borrowed heavily from the SPLA/M in terms of structure, outlook and in practice (Metelits 2004). The challenges emanating from this reality are embodied in the astronomical challenges which must be addressed and accounted for beyond the formal processes if the structuring and reform of security is to succeed. This represents a significant challenge to the restructuring and reforming of security as do acknowledgements that the contemporary South Sudanese state that emerged from the relics of a two decades-long civil war morphed not from design, but by default.

This was because the SPLA/M was the only functioning southern institution[2] at the end of the war in 2005, and also the only negotiating partner in the peace agreement. It is also the case that South Sudan's empirical underpinning is behind some of the challenges faced by the prevailing liberal peacebuilding-based attempts at post-conflict reconstruction in the country.

In examining and exploring the disparities between the internationally formulated liberal peacebuilding programmes in South Sudan against the country's actual needs at the most basic level, it is possible to identify and redress some of the failings of liberal peacebuilding. That this contributed to the country's return to war and the speed with which a political conflict turned into a military one. In particular, it also reaffirms the perceived critique of liberal peacebuilding and the very idea of a liberal peace as a limited peace for a limited minority (Roberts 2010). More specifically, that liberal peacebuilding provides the kind of peace it believes people should have rather than the kind of peace people might seek for themselves if their stakeholder status meant something more than participating in someone else's idea of peacebuilding (Roberts 2012: 367). In the case of South Sudan, as is often the case, this led to the creation of a post-independence paradigm that was geared towards protecting the state by prioritizing security while it excluded, relegated, and abandoned the broader scope of societies (Roberts 2012: 367). More specifically that:

> As monopoly holders of the means of legitimate, physical and symbolic violence, modern states possess a built-in, paradoxical tendency to undermine the very liberties and security they are constituted to protect. That even states that claim

to be liberal or democratic have a capacity when self-consciously pursuing a condition called security to act in a fashion injurious to it as do non-state security actors. Both inclined to proceed in ways that trample over the basic liberties of citizens; that forge security for some groups while imposing illegitimate burdens of insecurity upon others'. (Loader and Walker 2007: 7)

The allure of replicating the Western Weberian state, either consciously or sub-consciously, is no guarantee of a secure or stable post-conflict security and a localized approach to the restructuring and reforming of post-conflict security is more likely to succeed. In view of South Sudan's security complexes, this book also re-examines and explores the liberal peacebuilding approach to post-conflict security embodied by security sector reform (SSR) (Brzoska and Heinemann-Grüder 2004) and draws conclusions on its successes, challenges and shortcomings. It also examines Disarmament, Demobilisation and Reintegration (DDR), another key feature of the prevailing post-conflict approach to security and its role in South Sudan's attempts at reforming and reconstituting its security. By interrogating South Sudan's interactions with both SSR and DDR within the liberal peacebuilding frameworks, one can draw both theoretical and contextual lessons for not only South Sudan, but more broadly. In so doing, it sets the tone for the reorientation of post-conflict security reconstitution through a focus on demilitarization.

Security sector reforms (SSR) in South Sudan

In South Sudan's post-conflict reconstruction, security sector reform is a key component of the liberal peacebuilding vocabulary and lingua. Often viewed in line with parallel aspirations of post-conflict state-building, security sector reforms were pitched by both local and international agency interviewed for this book as an important part of the state-building process. In South Sudan, like in other post-conflict reconstruction programmes, views held in the international community about state-building proved to be competing, highly normative, not well-tested and often resulted in policies and measures whose success rate, when applied, was not very impressive (Brzoska and Heinemann-Grüder 2004: 122). Nevertheless, and despite the obvious shortcomings in the pursuit of SSR, not just in South Sudan but more broadly, its prominence in post-conflict international state-building and liberal peacebuilding has not waned. The prevailing approach to security in South Sudan is thus still presented and addressed as part of security sector reforms (SSR).

In view of the failures at redressing or reconstituting South Sudan's post-conflict security, it is timely to question the onset of SSR as the cornerstone of the liberal peacebuilding approach to post-conflict security. Current failures in securing a stable and secure post-conflict security in South Sudan can therefore be attributed to contemporary security debates and the primary focus on SSR and the liberal peacebuilding paradigm that underpins it. Arguably, while the literature on SSR makes a significant contribution to the study of post-conflict security, SSR like other approaches rooted in the liberal peacebuilding thesis can be a generic approach[3] with significant gaps between its theory and practice. Like the rest of the liberal peacebuilding thesis, the SSR approach in South Sudan was an externally formulated process, and that often put SSR aspirations on a different trajectory to the realities and needs of the country.

SSR and development

Security sector reform (SSR) has long been considered a critical component of establishing a secure environment conducive to long-term sustainable post-conflict development, especially in transitional societies. In South Sudan, like in other post-conflict countries, this has placed debates on post-conflict security alongside those of development.[4] SSR is a relatively new concept that was originally introduced by development donors in the late 1990s (Brzoska 2003, DFID 1999, 2000, 2002; OECD/DAC 2001; Welch and Forman 1998). However, although conceived by development donors, international organisations and consultants working for them (Brzoska and Heinemann-Grüder 2004: 123), SSR has moved on to become the de facto premise on which security in international interventions is based.

The onset of South Sudan's restructuring and reforming of security, however, exists within a broader international post-conflict intervention that generally perceives security as a prerequisite for development and democratization. It is therefore not surprising that SSR was a key feature of South Sudan's post-2005 reconstruction blueprint spearheaded by the United Nations Mission in Sudan (UNMIS) and subsequently the United Nations Mission in South Sudan (UNMISS). This presented South Sudan's attempts at post-conflict restructuring of security with the same challenges as those before it. In the presentation of SSR as the centre of the post-conflict security reconstruction narrative, South Sudan post-conflict security was intertwined with the parallel process of development and governance, further re-establishing the blurring of the lines between security and development (Duffield 2007). This presents an interesting starting point in addressing the successes, failures and restructuring of security in South Sudan since the signing of the CPA in 2005. Most importantly, it may play a major role in informing the next attempt with the signing of the August 2015 peace agreement and formation of the TGoNU in April 2016.

The importance placed on SSR in contemporary approaches of post-conflict security, however, does not reduce its critique, specifically that SSR is donor-driven. More so, as Brzoska and Heinemann-Grüder (2004) argue, that 'the development origins of SSR and the development agencies and donors that propel it generally have little experience, and often limited willingness, to deal with security institutions or traditional perceptions of security that do not fall within the development spectrum. This includes areas such as police reform and areas and institutions of civil–military interaction informed more by national cultures and interests than the liberal state' (Brzoska and Heinemann-Grüder 2004: 133). An internationally driven SSR is, however, not unique to South Sudan and has been used elsewhere (Brzoska 2000) including in Afghanistan, Azerbaijan, Bosnia and Herzegovina, East Timor, Georgia, Haiti, Iraq, Kosovo, Liberia, Macedonia, Mozambique and Tajikistan (Brzoska and Heinemann-Grüder 2004). A donor-driven attempt at restructuring and reforming security in South Sudan's post-conflict security did, nevertheless, present a number of challenges and a growing critique among the local structures. An army major general interviewed on the progress made by the Government of South Sudan in restructuring security in the country after the 2005 CPA argued:

> These things are framed and thought of by the Kawaja.[5] They then want us to implement. We are coming from the bush. Some of the things they ask are not possible. It will take time, but they say these things must be done and they give the funding for it. The money is used and reports are written but really we remain as we were. Deep down there is no change.[6]

These sentiments were echoed by local and international senior security personnel interviewed for this research in both South Sudan's military and police service, UNMISS and the private contractors working in the security reconstitution sector. They contribute to a growing debate on the extent and intent of SSR in South Sudan and reaffirm the arguments that 'he who holds the security development purse strings ultimately decides the direction, pace and scope of the restructuring and reform of security in the country'.[7] Although these sentiments were widely shared among local security personnel and practitioners, the main concerns the research found were in the fracturing of relationships beneath the surface between the donors and international practitioners on the one hand and the local elite on the other. Attending post-conflict security programmes and working groups all seemed well and good; however, there seemed to be disparities between what was alluded to in public and what the stakeholders said in private. In an interview with a zone commander and senior SPLA officer, extensively trained by the US Army as part of a bilateral training agreement between the two countries and a seemingly strong supporter of SSR, he said:

> The experts think we in the SPLA are stupid. I have been fighting since 1986. We have won many battles and we have good discipline. So we know a thing or two about military ethos. But when our colleagues come to help us they treat us like we don't know anything. I attend a lot of seminars but these are all useless; they are not telling me anything I don't know but I have to attend. Even now I've come from more workshops.[8]

Another officer asked about the current state of the security transformation process offered:

> The Republic of South Sudan is trapped. We are trapped between the ruthlessness of the international community who tell us the SPLA and security must look like this or like that and the dilemma of maintaining our national security.[9]

On the other side of the security reconstruction spectrum, a senior military official with the UN Department of Peacekeeping Operations at UNMISS also offered:

> Sometimes I don't know what we are doing here. We come, we raise the flag, we wear the blue hats and we go to sleep. We meet every day and talk about SSR and DDR but there is very little to show for the four years I have been in charge; the Sudanese don't really listen to us. Now there is another mission opening in Mali and many people are leaving Juba for the new mission. It's closer to Europe and the West African staff can go home often so it's better; also the danger pay may be higher in Mali than here in South Sudan, where it had been reducing, so there is no incentive to be here.[10]

While these sentiments may at one level be personal, they also raised all sorts of questions for this research. Specifically, they highlighted what fundamentally seemed like an exercise in futility alluding to a disunited front among the various actors and stakeholders in the processes central to the restructuring and reform of security in South Sudan. The sheer complexity of the security dichotomy in South Sudan, which will be addressed later in this chapter, is perhaps contributing to the existence of parallel post-conflict security processes often in competition with one another. Specifically, that many of those involved with the SSR processes did not believe in them was especially alarming. While this, to some degree, added to the critique of SSR, in no way did it diminish its relevance to the wider aspirations of post-conflict security reconstitution in the country conceived in this book as part of a wider effort in demilitarizing the country.

These add to the complexities of SSR in South Sudan which are more systematic than they are procedural and are dodged by structural challenges. These are indicative of a more fundamental problem that perhaps begins with the very definition of SSR in exact terms that can then yield a unified approach in its application. The lack of clarity in defining SSR has arguably translated in its application and in the case of South Sudan further entangled the already complex security dichotomy in the country. These might be responsible for the indifference expressed by SSR practitioners in South Sudan. As a case study, South Sudan also highlights the inconsistencies in SSR definitions and how that transcends to inconsistencies in its applications. It is from this premise that most of those who have reflected on the subject of SSR for any length of time agree with Fluri (2003) that SSR is indeed an ill-defined concept despite its popular use in post-conflict settings (Chuter 2006).

The lack of a clear definition for SSR is nevertheless odd, especially taking into account the large body of literature on the subject and that the subject has been extensively discussed since the late 1990s and most of its component parts go back much further than that (Chuter 2006). However, in reviewing SSR's application in South Sudan, it was clear that even in all its imperfections, SSR is not just a theoretical subject but the basis of security reorganizations around the world. It has, as such, been used to reallocate functions, terminate careers, reduce budgets and manpower and reconfigure the defence and security sectors in numerous countries (Chuter 2006: 1). Indeed, the first drafts of South Sudan's national security strategy were heavy on the promise of Security Sector Reform[11] although even then the challenge as presented by Chuter (2006) was in identifying what exactly this promise translated to for the country beyond the varying generic definitions and rhetoric of SSR.

In the August 2015 peace agreement, these definitions and rhetoric are nestled in what is referred to in the agreement as the Security Sector Transformation (SST) process which encompasses both SSR and DDR. Still, reform of the security sector with an even wider scope than the post-2005 process remains the centrepiece of transformation. The greatest challenge with reforms in the security sector thus remains the same and in South Sudan, like elsewhere, this is specifically in translating the broadness of their aspirations into a coherent articulation that could be translated into locally applicable concepts. This could begin by picking one working definition of SSR which can be confusing, given the many SSR definitions in existing literature and policy documents which according to Chuter (2006) can be narrowed down to:

> Helping 'developing countries improve the accountability and transparency of their security sectors' – United Kingdom's Department for International Development (DFID)
>
> 'Right-sizing, reorientation, reform and capacity building of national defence forces' – Paper for the Stability Pact Working Table III (on Security and Defence issues)
>
> Intended 'to create armed, uniformed forces which are functionally differentiated, professional forces under objective and subjective political control, at the lowest functional level of resource use' – Bonn International Centre for Conversion (BICC) (Brzoska 2000)
>
> '(r)educing the size, budget and scope of the security sector and reforming it to become more transparent and accountable to its citizens' – Women Waging Peace
>
> 'Prevent the proliferation of small arms in the country' – Peace Research Institute of Oslo project on Security Sector Reform in Malawi
>
> 'Includes weapons collection, munitions recovery and specialist EOD and Mine clearance (sic) training and advice' – UK consultancy offers its assistance in SSR
>
> 'Instead of focusing on the security of the state, SSR focuses on human security, i.e. it deals with threats to individual and community well-being, community-based policing and the introduction of measures to deal with the root causes of violence and conflict, including socio-economic deprivation (e.g. poverty and unemployment), are central strategies of SSR' – UN IDDRS

These varying definitions of SSR generally illustrate one of its greatest weaknesses, translating into its unfocused contemporary presentations and applications (Chuter 2006: 6). Still, none of these perceptions of SSR are wrong, but rather, according to Chuter (2006), reflect the genesis and parentage of SSR as a concept as 'the bastard child of Civil–Military Relations and Development Studies' (Chuter 2006: 3). As such and in view of this ambiguity, SSR is perhaps best explored from its intended outcomes, beginning with the work of Wulf (2004) which builds on Chalmers and Nicole Ball's earlier work presenting some of the SSR intended outcomes and goals as:

- Building the capacity of security sector organisations to perform their legitimate functions.
- Strengthening civilian management and control.
- Fostering respect for human rights and the rule of law within security sector organisations.
- Strengthening the capacity of civil society to perform monitoring functions.
- Fostering the transparency of security sector and budget management.
- Promoting regional confidence-building mechanisms.
- Technical assistance for the demobilization and reintegration of non-combatants.
- Tackling the proliferation of small arms.
- Incorporating security sector reform into political dialogue.

Although most of these offer a substantive presentation of what the reconstitution of post-conflict security entails, both in South Sudan and widely, the devil again remains in the detail. The divergence of views and intent presented by Wulf (2004) is in fact indicative of the divergence of SSR application already visible in its definitions. The trajectory of SSR in South Sudan after the 2005 CPA, characterized by parallel SSR programmes, was also reflective of this (Brzoska and Heinemann-Grüder 2004). The Security Sector Transformation (SST) road map set to drive the post-August 2015 reconstruction of security, however, does not detract from the post-2005 trajectory. In part, the road map was tasked with providing the details for the unification of the army and security forces, at the core of which are SSR and DDR processes.[12] Like the post-2005 process before it, the post-August 2015 process of security sector transformation will involve a multitude of processes. The post-2005 processes and their effect were summed up in an interview with a US Embassy official who stated that:

> Each donor country is engaged in a different track of the SSR process. We[13] are very interested in civil society and media development; the Europeans are more concerned with human rights, but even then individual countries seem to have a different interest. The Swiss are working on SSR, the Germans with GIZ have implemented DDR in Eastern Equatoria but they seem to have abandoned that. The international NGOs also seem to be working in different areas.[14]

Wider empirical enquiry revealed that this view was widely held. Indeed, not one single person interviewed for this research said they believed the SSR experience in South Sudan was working flawlessly, despite its importance in South Sudan's post-conflict security constructions. In fact, most of the interviews, informal and formal, started with the participant pointing at the work they were doing or knew of. However, when questioned further about the scope and extent of this book in view of South Sudan's country-specific challenges, interviewees asserted difficulties faced in the implementation of SSR and other related programmes in South Sudan. This prompted a number of questions for the research. Specifically, whether South Sudan after the 2005 CPA was an impossible case for SSR application or whether SSR and the related international peacebuilding effort were too rigid in their adoption of generic frameworks that made their successful implementation in the country almost impossible.

The premise of this research was that security sector reconstruction and reform needed to begin with an appropriate identification of the security-related problems to be solved in the short and medium term (Brzoska and Heinemann-Grüder 2004: 123). This nevertheless becomes increasingly difficult to attain, especially as SSR application in South Sudan in the post-2005 interventions becomes increasingly muddled and complex. This was particularly the case as security realities in the country evolved beyond the generic goals and outcomes of SSR and the underlying liberal peace thesis. Any attempt at the restructuring and reform of security in South Sudan must therefore move beyond prescriptions of SSR and the liberal peace thesis that underpins it, if it's to succeed in any meaningful way. This is not to discount contributions made by SSR in tackling some of the issues presented in Wulf's (2004) list, but rather to move it beyond its current limitations. This generally involves moving from the overly broad and generic goals and aspirations of SSR and paying more attention to a post-conflict restructuring and reforming of security that is case-specific.

This would specifically include involving local institutions responsible for both internal and external security in the planning of the country's post-conflict security strategy, rather than providing them with a blueprint in which to fit. In South Sudan, such institutions would include: the Ministry of Interior, the Ministry of Defence, the structures of national security, the commission on DDR and the Bureau of Community Security (Chuter 2006: 7). Although these institutions are all involved in the restructuring and reforming of security in the country, they had little input in the construction of South Sudan's post-conflict security strategy which arguably emanated from the UN manual – Integrated Disarmament, Demobilisation and Reintegration Standards (IDDRS).[15] However, even with the provisions of the IDDRS, the other guiding document in South Sudan's restructuring of security was the 2005 Comprehensive Peace Agreement. Like many of South Sudan's post-conflict engagements, the CPA included provisions setting out necessary frameworks for not only SSR but also DDR and other post-conflict security arrangements (Saferworld 2008: 14).

The August 2015 peace agreement in 'Chapter II: Permanent Ceasefire and Transitional Security Arrangements' does the same with specific mention to SSR and DDR.

As such, SSR and DDR form part of South Sudan's projected post-conflict architecture past and present. Nonetheless, post-2005, the UN IDDRS concluded that SSR establishes the basis for DDR within the various legal agreements that deal with the transitional period. As such, DDR could be perceived to be part of SSR. However, in the case of South Sudan, empirical observation shows that SSR and DDR are indeed different sides of the same coin; that the two were often used interchangeably in the fieldwork further reaffirms this. Subsequently, this prompts a number of questions, specifically: 'Which comes before the other, SSR or DDR?' 'What do these two processes set out to achieve?' and 'Are they both doing the same thing?' This chapter, in adopting a pragmatic approach to post-conflict security, argues that SSR and DDR are two separate but related endeavours and that they are often mutually dependent and, despite their shortcomings, they are both unavoidable in modern discussions of post-conflict security. As such, both SSR and DDR are central features in the reconstitution of post-conflict security.

Implementing DDR

From the onset, the DDR process in South Sudan post-2005 was beset by challenges and complexities which arguably stemmed from its contextualization. Although the IDDRS was hailed as the future of DDR, learning from past mistakes and offering a holistic approach, the DDR experience in South Sudan, like the liberal peacebuilding approach that underpins it, was a catalogue of failures.[16] On paper, the Interim Disarmament, Demobilisation and Reintegration Programme (IDDRP) launched in late 2005 from the IDDRS guidelines looked like a model of good practice. However, over eight years into the DDR implementation in South Sudan, the process did not achieve as much as was initially hoped.[17] This cast doubt over previous and current DDR engagements in the country. Specifically, it raised questions about the effectiveness of 'integrated' approaches to DDR and post-conflict security programming. The experience of DDR in South Sudan hence highlighted the significant challenges inherent in the 'integrated' approach and pointed at the need to better address the wide range of security challenges in countries emerging from conflict (Saferworld 2008: 8).

Initially targeting 180,000 participants from the north and south, the integrated approach became a victim of its own ambition. By projecting a unified multi-agency and multi-donor front under the flagship of the United Nations Mission in Sudan, the process was viewed with suspicion, primarily by the national government in Khartoum, but also by the regional post-CPA government in Juba.[18] As such, although DDR was an integral part of the CPA, and a requirement of the Permanent Ceasefire and Security Arrangements, signed on 31 December 2004, the actual DDR processes did not start until 2009, four years behind schedule. Yet despite this, the programme still succeeded in developing institutional structures needed for the institutional support deemed necessary for the wider DDR programme.

The pinnacle of this was the setting up of the National DDR Commission as well as the adoption of a National Strategic Plan in November 2007. This laid out a two-phase approach to DDR in South Sudan upon which DDR engagements, until the eruption of violence in December 2013, were still based. However, despite these strides, the DDR programme itself did not take off, with programmes existing more on paper at national and state levels with little action locally.[19] A senior UN official working on DDR in the South Sudan mission interviewed for this book indicated that there was little appetite from local partners and especially the DDR Commission to engage in any meaningful DDR exercise if there was no opportunity for the officials to access donor funding. More often than not, he said, these funds were then diverted from their intended DDR-related activities with little accountability.

This raises significant questions in the interrogation of DDR in South Sudan, especially if the challenges to DDR were indeed structural and procedural or if they were as a result of local agency. For those who'd argue that the challenges to DDR in South Sudan were indeed structural and procedural, its shortcomings are disappointing on many levels, primarily because DDR in South Sudan, like the rest of the post-conflict security architecture including SSR and the broader prospects represented in the liberal peace thesis, is supposed to have learned from previous experiences. However, the failure of DDR in South Sudan associated with local agency makes a significant case for those within the liberal peacebuilding spectrum who argue that the problem with liberal peacebuilding is not the approach but the way it's implemented and received. Whatever side of the argument one may take, the extent to which civilians rearmed and the fact that many joined the conflict post-December 2013, indicates that DDR in South Sudan may never have been effectively achieved in the post-2005 period, especially with regards to disarmament. As such, with post-2005 South Sudan as one of the most recent recipients of 'a better and improved' DDR, its failings are not just conspicuous but ultimately beg the question, 'Why?'

The challenges of DDR

Fieldwork observations indicate that the multitude of challenges that beset DDR in South Sudan emanated mainly from the structure and design of the process. These in turn resulted in the procedural and operational failures witnessed in post-conflict applications of not only DDR and the related SSR, but in the wider attempt at post-conflict security reconstitution. Indeed, taking into account the security and political complexity of South Sudan, the DDR process in the country had largely already departed from traditional notions of the practice.[20] Generally, DDR is traditionally the disarmament, demobilization and reintegration of former combatants, its primary purpose being the disbandment of armed groups and neutralizing military structures and capabilities outside state control (Brzoska and Heinemann-Grüder 2004: 134). However, the complexity of South Sudan's security outlook may have resulted in the inclusion of new parameters in South Sudan's DDR design. According to a UNDP consultant interviewed in the national capital Juba, DDR in South Sudan had to adapt because of operational limitations, like the reluctance of the SPLA, the former rebel army, in sharing information like the real numbers of soldiers/combatants in its ranks, present and past. That the success or failures of DDR was also measured by previous more standard and traditional applications did not help. Still, some DDR practitioners, like a senior UN DPKO military official in South Sudan who had also worked in the peace missions in Liberia, Sierra Leone and East Timor, maintained that sometimes DDR worked better when simply applied to address local conflict dynamics as opposed to when it's applied as an all-encompassing process. On this, he argues:

> When we first went into Sierra Leone as ECOWAS in 1999–2000, DDR was still new. The war in Sierra Leone had come with a lot of stigma and in South Sudan after war, many fighters just melted back into their communities, but in Sierra Leone this was not going to be easy. We knew that it was likely the communities would turn against the former fighters in Sierra Leone because these people had committed serious crimes. They had cut off people's limbs. The stigma of long sleeve or short sleeve was still there and for the people responsible to walk back into villages they had terrorised and be accepted was just not going to happen. We also feared that if these people went back to the villages and they were rejected they would turn against the villages again and that could very well restart the war.
>
> The peace in Freetown was holding by a shoestring. Any provocation from the countryside and it could come tumbling down. So the idea was to first

disarm the former fighters. Take away their guns by encouraging them to give them up. The war was over so they had no use for them anyway. We thought if we give them some things that are useful to their current realities, like seeds and tools and skills in carpentry etc., they could go back to the farming countryside where they had come from and resume their lives after we demobilise them from the Revolutionary United Front (RUF). Once this was done, we needed to find a way of getting them back into communities they had tortured. So the idea of reintegrating them involved rebuilding relationships between the former RUF fighters and the communities. This process was highly successful and I think it is what we have been trying to replicate for the last ten years or so.

But DDR is now a bureaucratic process. It has become too complicated with too many experts making it about everything and nothing at the same time. This is what I'm now dealing with in South Sudan. I'm coming to the end of my mission here but it has not been easy. We are talking about giving tools and seeds to pastoralists as part of DDR and giving people computer skills as part of ICT advancements. But these things look very good on paper but when it comes to implementing them they become difficult. In Sierra Leone, which is where I think the idea of giving people seeds and tools came from, the country is almost wholly agricultural and people come from farming communities. Here, people are cattle-keepers. It is unlikely that these same approaches will work. The idea of ICT I think is coming from East Timor and the Balkans. Again, applying it here is hard because the people coming for DDR are almost 90–100 per cent illiterate. This is the challenge of DDR. In Sierra Leone, we were there, we saw the problems, we came up with the solutions and they worked. Now we go to a meeting in New York. We draw up these plans and programmes. Then we come to implement. When we get here we spend all the time trying to get around the problems we find.[21]

Despite its 'humble' origins, DDR as it currently exists is indicative of the overwhelming change that the whole post-conflict thesis has undergone in the past twenty years. Nevertheless, it is also the case that Sierra Leone's DDR process is widely regarded as a success story, and elements of the Sierra Leone 'model' are often replicated (Solomon and Ginifer 2008) in modern DDR constructions. The departure from the normative approach to DDR in post-2005 CPA South Sudan arguably opened up the process to a wider section of society than would have otherwise been the case within more simplistic and traditional descriptions of DDR. The DDR process in South Sudan was opened up to include the elderly, disabled combatants, and women and children associated with armed forces and groups (WAAFG and CAAFG), all of whom being identified as Special Needs

Groups (SNG). Although this was presented as the beginning of a process that was broader and more integrated, behind closed doors, practitioners pointed at the lack of a consensus between the international community and the local authorities on the status of DDR in the country. On this, a senior government official in the Ministry of SPLA Affairs, renamed the Ministry of Defence after South Sudan's independence explained:

> The DDR process is complicated. We are still at war. We cannot afford to reduce the army because the SPLA is the reason we have the peace and the SPLA is the only thing that can keep Khartoum from spoiling things. So we must be ready. Khartoum will not reduce. They will just name their people police, but we know all of them are soldiers. So we are going to keep the army as it is. The people of DDR can go and take care of the Abubas and Yabahs (old women and old men) in the villages.[22]

Indeed, it has been the case that after the signing of the 2005 CPA, the SPLA grew in size, both from new recruitments and from militias being integrated into the SPLA. Arguably, therefore, the state of DDR in South Sudan further reinforces the argument that 'while DDR processes may seem straightforward and technical, their potential for success is often determined at the political level before the cantonment of a single soldier' (Bryden 2012: 206). The lack of an agreement on DDR among key stakeholders, according to a UNDP DDR consultant, is therefore responsible for South Sudan's 'wide and inclusive' approach to DDR:

> I have worked in DDR in many countries and the way it works is that when we come in we get to go to the barracks and fields of combat where the ex-combatants to be demobilised are. And we begin to process them by talking to them. We help disarm them, then we find out who wants to do what and we help them get skills, move them to areas they want to go to and those who want to stay in the army we work with them to reskill and even move their names to the Ministry of Defence. That is how we worked in Liberia, in Sierra Leone, in Kosovo, in East Timor [...] but in South Sudan things are different. We don't see the people we are supposed to do DDR with. The SPLA has provided us with a list and we are to work with these people to demobilise and reintegrate. The SPLA says it will do the disarmament, then we do demobilisation and reintegration.[23]

While the essence of the integrated DDR approach was to learn from previous mistakes, it is also the case that previous experiences can present a double-edged sword for post-conflict reconstruction endeavours. This is because, while providing the opportunity to learn from previous experiences, their service as a reference point may not always collate with present realities, as many of the interviews in this research indicate. Still, previous experiences contribute to the creation of the idea of a 'norm' from which generic approaches subsequently emerge, which can then be used as an intervention blueprint. Although these blueprints play an important role in informing and shaping the basic framework of interventions, their critique is that they rarely move beyond this function and remain as the sole basis upon which interventions are made, with little regard to country differences and changing empirical realities. The integrated DDR approach in South Sudan based on the IDDRS is one such example, widely informed by previous experiences and norms. It is from these perceived norms that the prevailing logic behind DDR emanates: that 'successfully reintegrating former combatants into civilian society reduces the likelihood that the "violence experts" will pick up arms again in order to secure their livelihood' (Brzoska and Heinemann-Grüder 2004: 134).

This remains the guiding principle, not only in DDR constructions but in the wider approach to redressing post-conflict security. Nevertheless, given the complexity of South Sudan's post-conflict security architecture, there are questions as to whether this presumably prevailing logic is indeed applicable to a country where the idea of the 'violence expert' has different manifestations. In South Sudan, 'violence experts' are undefinable, notably because nearly all South Sudanese men interviewed for this research knew how to use a gun, the only exception being those who went into refuge in other counties as infants.[24] Similarly, most homes in the research area, Eastern Equatoria State, continued to have guns. To a large extent, firearms ownership and use is arguably socialized and incorporated into everyday life, mainly owing to the country's long periods of protracted wars.[25]

The extensive accessibility of firearms in South Sudan also presents one of the challenges to, not only DDR, but the wider realization of post-conflict restructuring of security. More broadly, the high proliferation of arms, their accessibility and the casualisation of their use, not only highlights the challenges faced by DDR, but the depth of South Sudan's security conundrum. These also account for the seemingly two steps forwards, three steps backwards problem faced by security-related operations aimed at civilian disarmament in the country in the period before December 2013.

This is despite the emphasis placed on disarmament as a phased approach provided for in the 2005 CPA.

The CPA advocated for a locally led post-conflict approach with national institutions responsible for leading and implementing particularly DDR, while the UN and international partners fell into supporting roles. Specifically, the CPA dictated that 'the DDR process in Sudan shall be led by recognised state institutions and international partners shall only play a supportive role to these institutions' (Saferworld 2008: 8). The creation of these institutions was, nevertheless, part of phase one of the DDR process as discussed earlier in this chapter from which the National DDR Coordination Council and the National DDR Commission emanated. In accordance with the other provisions of the CPA, which included the establishment of the regional semi-autonomous Government of Southern Sudan, the Southern Sudan National DDR Commission was constituted, while in the north a similar outfit, the Northern Sudan National DDR Commission, was set up. Both of these commissions were each responsible for the design, implementation and management of the DDR process in their respective regions.

For its part, the South Sudan National DDR Commission[26] (SSNDDRC) presented its mandate to be the Disarmament, Demobilisation and Reintegration of military personnel into civilian life following the end of hostilities. However, it also suggested that its programmes should link with other national recovery and priority programmes aimed at returnees, internally displaced people and host communities. This included initiatives to reduce the number of small arms and light weapons in civilian hands. Nonetheless, another agency, the Bureau for Community Security and Small Arms Control (BCSSAC) under the Ministry of Internal Affairs, also presented a similar mandate. More specifically the BCSSAC mission statement stated:

The Bureau's mission is to address the threat posed by the proliferation of small arms and community insecurity to peace and development in South Sudan according to its mandate. The Bureau works to achieve this by:

1. Mobilizing, consolidating and building bridges between communities, government at all levels and law enforcement agencies that are tasked to carry out peaceful and voluntary civilian disarmament;
2. Advocating and leading the efforts on the formulation of small arms control policies and regulations;
3. Facilitating RSS solutions to address the root causes of community insecurity, through development, rule of law and peacebuilding measures.

While these two organisations within the Government of South Sudan seem to have similar aspirations in the issue of disarmament of civilians, they have also largely been criticized for being talking shops.[27] Indeed, neither made any significant inroads in disarmament, especially of civilian populations. In fact, at the height of inter-communal clashes in the eastern state of Jonglei in 2012–13, the army, the SPLA, was called in to disarm the civilian population.[28] According to the army spokesman: 'The Sudan People's Liberation Army had deployed about 10,000 soldiers to disarm the civilian population in Jonglei State in 2012. This was also the case in the research areas of Eastern Equatoria and across the country in the wake of increased local violence.'

Taking into consideration the levels of local conflicts in especially rural South Sudan and their impact on the overall security construction in the country, arms control is an integral part of South Sudan's disarmament and demobilization. This is underpinned in the importance placed on arms control or disarmament in the aspirations of DDR in South Sudan. In fact, in a 2008 report, Saferworld argued that 'the overall goal of DDR in Sudan is the promotion of community security and arms control' (Saferworld 2008: 8). With the amount of firearms in civilian hands outweighing those in the hands of the government,[29] civilian disarmament is essential for the country's post-conflict security. As such, attempts to address arms control can arguably be perceived as an exercise in DDR, although a direct link between the two, both in theory and practice, remains vague. South Sudan's wide accessibility of arms made this even more difficult with the problem likely to have worsened following the post-December 2013 conflict. Subsequently, despite the SPLA's efforts at civilian disarmament (Young 2007), successes were yet to be felt before the country plunged into a new civil war at the end of 2013.[30]

While this is just one example of the overlapping roles of different local engagements in disarmament, they do reflect the broader state of things. Away from official mandates and mission statements, disarmament efforts in the country, of civilians or otherwise, have not fared well. At the heart of all this is the issue of ownership and competing interests among South Sudan's many DDR players. This competition was not only visible within the national institutions like the SSNDDRC and BCSSAC, but among the UN agencies as well. Despite the adoption of the IDDRS as the guide to South Sudan's DDR, in practice, UN agencies were still learning to work together and more importantly to talk to each other. This was especially evident in the conspicuous and never-ending tugs of war between the Department of Peacekeeping Operations (DPKO), under which the mission in South Sudan falls, and UNDP.[31] The lack of synergy in the workings of UN agencies was especially visible to local institutions as one official at Kuron Peace Village explained:

> The UN people seem to be doing different things all the time and they quarrel all the time. Sometimes we are not sure whom we are supposed to listen to. The UN is supposed to work in coordination. To support with this mission of DDR. This is what UNMISS is doing but then you have the UN, like with UNDP, also working directly with projects and quarrelling with local organisations.[32]

These competing interests not only left the DDR programme in South Sudan in a shambles but they also left local and international actors often hinged against one another as opposed to working together. At the macro-level, this and other disagreements between the government and donors over the objectives and modalities of DDR in South Sudan left donors weary. This had a significant impact on phase two of the DDR programme characterized by a lack of donor funding and budget constraints for national efforts. However, with the challenges facing DDR, the buzz on South Sudan's post-conflict security seems to have shifted from an emphasis on DDR to SSR. Although this is an unquantifiable observation, it was the case that during the research period, emphasis shifted from DDR, even among people spoken to previously, who increasingly emphasized SSR. An SPLA training officer interviewed observed:

> DDR is proving difficult, but SSR is vague, hard to define and as such it is difficult to prove its implementation or lack of implementation. In DDR we talk of numbers of beneficiaries, so it's easy to tell it has not worked. In SSR, we talk about a principle, an idea and there is no way of quantifying that. So it's safer to talk of SSR when we cannot tell you for sure how much DDR was done when there is fighting in so many places in the country.

The decline of DDR's importance in South Sudan's security constructions could, however, also be attributed to time. DDR emphasis after conflict is acceptable but a continued focus on DDR almost eight years after conflict is harder to explain and raises uncomfortable questions. The shift of emphasis from DDR to SSR, however, seemed to have resulted in a frantic attempt to revive it by South Sudan's National DDR Commission which ultimately, according to the CPA, took responsibility for the country's DDR programmes. The commission in the fourth National DDR Council meeting held on 11 September 2013 unveiled the new DDR direction. At that meeting, the NDDRC chairperson released the following statement posted on the commission's website:[33]

Dear Friends, Partners, Supporters and Well-wishers

Warm greetings from the National DDR Commission!

It is with great pleasure that I wish to update you on the fourth National DDR Council meeting held on Wednesday 11 September 2013, chaired for the first time by His Excellency General Salva Kiir Mayardit, president of the Republic of South Sudan and commander-in-chief of the national armed forces. This fourth Council meeting, comprised of the newly appointed Cabinet Ministers, unanimously reaffirmed their unequivocal support for the National DDR Programme and committed to the fundamental principle that the programme must remain owned and led by the Government of the Republic of South Sudan.

They acknowledged that, whereas disarmament and demobilization were often accomplished readily within a short time, the reinsertion and reintegration components of the programme presented a longer-term challenge to the country with potential negative consequences if not well-addressed. In consideration of the aforementioned and the fact that ex-combatants are actually gallant liberators of this newborn nation, the Council owned up the challenge to make DDR attractive!

They pledged to ensure the successful reintegration of ex-combatants along with associated women and children, as well as veterans and wounded heroes. The Council also deliberated on alternative strategies that would help scale up and accelerate right-sizing the national armed forces faster than could be possible if only the National DDR Programme was in place.

Before adjourning, the fourth National Council meeting passed the following resolutions among others:

1. The inauguration of the National DDR Programme and graduation of ex-combatants should be postponed from 16 September to 18 September 2013.
2. The national line ministry proposals and budgets for the employment of ex-combatants' work brigades should be completed and consolidated into the National Reintegration Plan and Budget as soon as possible.
3. The National Reintegration Plan and Budget should be presented for the National DDR Council's approval and subsequently for Parliament's approval in time for December 2013 national supplementary budget allocation.
4. The Government of the Republic of South Sudan will commit its own national budgetary resources to make the National DDR Programme attractive. Notwithstanding, the Government will request security sector reform donors to contribute complementary financial support to the National DDR Programme.
5. The next National DDR Council meeting will be held after the inauguration of the National DDR Programme in Mapel.

I look forward to updating you on the next National DDR Council meeting deliberations and resolutions!

I thank you for your readership!

> Yours Sincerely,
> William Deng Deng
> Chairperson, National DDR Commission
> Secretary, National DDR Council

As the National DDR Commission propelled the DDR programme forward, despite donor reservations, the commission seemed to reflect the shifts within DDR and SSR in the country. Resolution four of the fourth National DDR Council meeting alluded to this shift stating:

> The Government of the Republic of South Sudan will commit its own national budgetary resources to make the National DDR Programme attractive. Notwithstanding, the Government will request security sector reform donors to contribute complementary financial support to the National DDR Programme.

This empirical development is unique to South Sudan's DDR experience but it also raises questions about exactly where the lines that distinguished DDR from SSR in the country at the time were drawn. More specifically, in a country with security construction as complex as South Sudan, was it possible to draw this line? Arguably, and consistent with the OECD/DAC handbook on Security System Reform, 'the two issues DDR and SSR are often best considered together as part of a comprehensive security programme' (Bryden 2012). This is in line with earlier arguments in this chapter that the two are indeed mutually dependent. However, there are still others who believe that SSR supports and assists DDR by providing ways to deal with immediate security concerns and strengthening state institutions which cannot also be ignored (Brzoska and Heinemann-Grüder 2004: 122). Whichever the case, South Sudan's experiences only reinforce the arguments that opportunities for coordinating DDR and wider security sector programming have until recently been largely missed, resulting in unforeseen and sometimes negative overlaps of different security processes (Saferworld 2008: 8).

On the whole, this can be summed up in the challenges that have beset the programme since its inception, specifically mistrust of the programme by recipients and hence a lack of political will to see it through. The lack of a clear direction is characterized by infighting between national and international actors on programme priorities and the adoption of an untested framework in the IDDRS which has been termed as too ambitious and unattainable by donors in view of its achievements (Saferworld 2008: 8). However, for the process to be viable, within a growing critique of the post-conflict liberal peace onslaught on which it is often based, DDR has to move beyond its current limitations as a generic framework with little regard to local context or flexibility (Muggah 2005). As a case study, South Sudan illustrates the challenge of reconciling the disparity between the aspiration of DDR and the reality of its application. Like any concept, the challenge lies in moving it from theory to practice. In South Sudan, DDR processes, by following a generic blueprint irrespective of the context, may have contributed to the current ambiguity of security instead of aiding its restructuring.

Informed by context, the processes, rather than following the IDDRS guidelines, would have started by asking the right questions. These, in view of South Sudan's complex security constructions, would have included questions on the suitability of DDR in South Sudan, its primary target especially for disarmament, given the armed civilian population, the fluid distinction between soldier and civilian and a legacy of protracted civil wars.[34] Similarly, who is demobilization for and demobilization from what, in view of the various armed groups in the south all excluded by the CPA but enjoined into the SPLA through the 2006 Juba Declaration? Finally, in view of an SPLA/M that commanded allegiances across most of the south, and the blurred lines between civilians and fighters with people dropping in and out of the war throughout the country's two civil wars, who would be reintegrated and into what?

As such, was reintegration ever a viable factor in South Sudan's version of DDR? While these questions were applicable to the post-2005 intervention, they remain relevant in South Sudan's post-August 2015 reconstruction and the perceived security sector transformation to which DDR remains a key feature. However, to even begin to answer these questions, the scope of enquiry must expand beyond the DDR target group often comprising of former fighters and armed civilians. In South Sudan, those still within various security institutions like the military and the police intelligence services are of equal importance in the realization of DDR in the country.

However, making the distinction between these two groups is not always straightforward in South Sudan. Notably, there were some overlaps between the theoretical aspirations of DDR, SSR and operational realities at the time of implementation. This was evident in the inclusion of personnel reforms within the SPLA in the department overseeing DDR. How this came about is an open question but most commentators suggest that it is linked to South Sudan's National DDR Commission's construction of DDR. SSDDRC particularly defined DDR as the 'Disarmament, Demobilisation and Reintegration of military personnel into civilian life following the end of hostilities'. This is broadly at odds with the more standard and traditional conceptualization of DDR as an exercise aimed at former combatants.

Still, South Sudan's National DDR Commission's official presentation of DDR was as a process conducted in three phases, notably: 'First, combatants and other individuals linked to the military are dispossessed of their weapons (Disarmament). Next, they are discharged from the military (Demobilisation). Reintegration, the third and final phase, is to help demobilized persons to be able to support themselves in the long term.'[35] However, in view of the empirical observations and evidence from the fieldwork, there were questions as to the suitability of this approach to DDR.

Conclusion

By mixing the exercise of disarming, demobilizing and reintegrating former rebel fighters with that of discharging active military personnel, South Sudan's National DDR Commission set the stage for the contextual confusion and implementation failings witnessed in South Sudan's DDR programme. As such, empirical observations indicate that parallel to the traditional constructions of DDR, South Sudan's National DDR Commission also took on the decommissioning of military personnel, ideally the premise of the military, its personnel department and part of a wider institutionalization, reform and restructuring of security. South Sudan's post-conflict restructuring of security in the post-2005 CPA period was far from a straightforward affair, despite the process evolving around two distinct and seemingly straightforward programmes of SSR and DDR. This in part can be attributed to the complexities associated with the country's post-conflict security infrastructure. Still, some of the challenges went beyond the complexities of South Sudan. There was, for example, no consensus on SSR between practitioners applying it on what exactly it entailed, which was illustrative of the wider critique of SSR as an ambiguous concept. The subsequent process of DDR did not fare much better with its application and was confined to a generic framework at odds with the country's realities.

Despite the entrenchment of DDR in the 2005 peace agreement, and its application forming a viable part of the post-conflict consolidation of security, DDR broadly failed to achieve many of its objectives owing to both structure and agency. South Sudan's interaction with DDR post-CPA proved that contemporary applications of DDR must never lose focus of individual post-conflict needs which are dependent on, among other things, the nature of the preceding conflict. The acknowledgement of local complexities may increase the likelihood of securing a stable post-conflict society than other approaches.

5

Realizing security restructuring and reforms

Restructuring security

The challenges associated with DDR in South Sudan are particularly important in understanding the development of the post-conflict security architecture in the country. Reforming security in South Sudan using prevailing approaches was turned on its head post-2005 and from the onset, post-conflict security reform could have benefited from an attempt to define the very idea of security in the country, and addressing local perceptions and understandings of security reform. As such, an understanding and consensus on what security reconstitution and reform meant in the context of South Sudan from the beginning may have resulted in a better intervention and outcomes.

After two civil wars spanning nearly four decades, both of which left a legacy of militarism as addressed in Chapter 3, what constitutes a stable and secure post-conflict security in South Sudan may significantly differ from the 'norm'. Arguably, the ambiguity of security in the country, both in definition and operationalization, contributed to the failings of conventional approaches to post-conflict security reform and reorganization including DDR. The answer to addressing the restructuring of South Sudan's security, therefore, perhaps exists primarily in the assessment of the state of its post-2005 security which was indicative of a security sector caught somewhere between its past and the aspiration of its future. Specifically, it was a security system that directly descended from the systems that preceded it, notably the highly paranoid security system of the old Sudan and a system based on 'tactics of the bush' in the SPLA.[1] Understanding this preceding legacy to South Sudan's constructions of security not only helps explain the country's contemporary security complexities, it also provides a valid starting point for any attempts at restructuring and reforming it. This remains true in the post-August 2015 period where the security sector transformation plan must take a good look at the conflict and constructions of security and insecurity from which it must attempt a transformation.

After the 2005 peace agreement, the institutional and structural changes in South Sudan's security were heavily based on the governing cultures of Sudan and the SPLA. The internationally led SSR and DDR processes, therefore, only served to institutionalize and strengthen already heavily securitized systems and in the south extend the dominance of the SPLA in the country's security infrastructure (Lokuji, Abatneh and Wani 2009). As a result, South Sudan's other security structures, like the police, remain relatively weak in comparison to the SPLA.[2] For the most part, even after South Sudan's independence, the SPLA was consistently called in to take on day-to-day law and order matters like crowd control during national events. This was certainly the case during the country's independence celebrations in July 2011, the first anniversary of independence in 2012 and the second anniversary in 2013 where the army took over roles including the direction of traffic. The arrival of important foreign dignitaries visiting the country also sees the army taking over policing roles.

This encroachment by the SPLA into the functions of the police service is nevertheless perhaps more capacity-driven. Empirical evidence from interviews and extended participant observations specifically point to a weak and non-factional police service.[3] The army, on the other hand, gives the impression of being more organized.[4] Indeed, interviews with both local and international security actors presented that in view of the wider security infrastructure in South Sudan, only the army had the capacity to intervene in matters of security, both internally and externally. As such, despite the different roles and jurisdictions of the various security actors as envisioned in the many institutional and legal frameworks on which security in the country is based, the army, the SPLA, not only leads the way but dominates the field. This domination extended to everyday life, reaffirming the monopoly and hold of the SPLA over security in the country. Arguably, however, this is a position that the SPLA finds itself into not by design, but by default, illustrating some of the army's greatest challenges.

> The security forces of the Government of South Sudan (GOSS) are engaged in reform and development processes to improve their ability to respond to current and emerging threats, while facing a lack of resources and growing pressures to be more professional, affordable and accountable. (Snowden 2012: 6)

The issue of affordability is especially potent to South Sudan's restructuring and reform of security, particularly as the country's military is not only overtly large but also virtually unaffordable in view of the country's economy (Warner 2012).

While this was true post-2005 CPA and before the December 2013 crisis when the country had about $2 billion in reserves,[5] the situation is likely to be extensively worse in any post-August 2015 intervention. In the post-2005 intervention, the South Sudan's military and other security services in the ministries of defence and internal security received over 45 per cent of the national budget.[6] Then, force reduction was a big component of the country's restructuring and reform of security, although any such efforts remained mainly cosmetic (Mwanika 2012: 2).

The imperative to reduce the size of the SPLA was not only a condition demanded by donors but was also driven by internal realities. This was a major goal of the SPLA transformation strategy of attaining a conventional force by 2017, also referred to as 'objective force 2017' with a total force count of 120,000. The size of the SPLA pre-2013 remained largely unclear with numbers ranging from 190,000 to 210,000 and thus requiring an almost 90,000 reduction to attain the objective force 2017. While a 90,000 force reduction is an ambitious task, it was further complicated by institutional challenges like the lack of comprehensive records on current personnel (Baas 2012: 164). The records of the SPLA payrolls have also been subject to ghost soldiers and are not a reliable source of SPLA numbers.[7]

Similarly, the growing of the SPLA by militia integration, especially in the 2006 Juba Declaration, did not help the process. Arguably, it was with the Juba Declaration that the blotted post-2005 CPA army that could not decommission a large part of its personnel emanated. The fear that mandatory decommissioning could have led to new militia insurrections remained real within the SPLA top brass.[8] A broad range of interviews with both government and military officials further revealed a fear of turning the wider population against the army command as a result of mandatory decommission.

> The people have always stood with us. We have asked them to go to the bush and fight and they responded without complaint. Now, at the end of the war when there is peace, if we remove these people from the army there will be trouble. The people will not be happy with us. This will be a betrayal of the heroes of this country. So we know we need to make the SPLA smaller, it is too big, and even many of the people we have are drunkards, not really soldiers, but we can't do anything.[9]

It is from this premise that the research began to comprehend the overlaps between the exercise of DDR usually aimed at former combatants and the recent warming-up to the process by the SPLA. With the required downsizing of the SPLA not only grossly overdue but also hinged on a number of political and security minefields, approaching the issue of SPLA decommissioning from the premise of DDR offered an opportunity; specifically, a less explosive solution to an SPLA that had, since the end of the war in 2005, continued to grow in numbers rather than reduce. This was the reality post-December 2013; however, with a new civil war, there are questions as to new force numbers. In particular, how many remained in the SPLA ranks, how many joined the former vice president Riek Machar in the new rebel outfit dubbed the SPLM/A In Opposition and how many civilians joined either side? This will, of course, have serious implications for the next attempt at the restructuring of the forces, although the challenges are expected to remain the same as those pre-December 2013.

In view of the strategy adopted in the restructuring and reform of security post-CPA, this research reiterates that the idea of including active solders by virtue of being on the staff payroll for extended periods (up to eight years) to a process that's traditionally aimed at former combatants might ultimately not yield much, particularly taking into account the precedence of DDR in the country. Although the SPLA's involvement and commitment in the process might actually have helped it succeed, there are still concerns that DDR in the SPLA was based on a false premise that sought to negate the increasingly complex issue of personnel realignment and force resizing to the perceived easier option of DDR.

Force reduction

In the 2005 period, the challenges facing attempts at SPLA force reduction, which was a key element in the wider SPLA transformation and security reform, were primarily based on history. Throughout the 21-year civil war, the SPLA functioned mostly as an unpaid army of volunteers and conscripts. After the end of the war, and with the signing of the 2005 CPA, the SPLA embarked on a process of 'professionalizing the army'. The idea of professionalization, however, meant different things to different people and, in the early days of the CPA, professionalization was interpreted by many officials interviewed then[10] to mean the beginning of the payment of soldiers' salaries. However, although many responded to the call for the first official convergence of SPLA soldiers after the CPA 'reporting', many more did not and just melted back into their villages and local towns. This raises one of the biggest questions for South Sudan's restructuring and reform of security and especially the DDR process that soon followed the CPA and the call for 'reporting'. A fundamental question to this was whether the former fighters who did not 'report' to start collecting salaries became former combatants and what was their status in the debates on post-conflict security that followed and more specifically DDR?

Empirical evidence in interviews and participant observations, as well as focus group discussions, indicates that this group of former SPLA fighters who did not join the SPLA or the militias largely fell through the cracks in the post-2005 discussions of post-conflict security. However, although these soldiers melted back into their communities and were no longer in what could be vaguely called active service, they retained their SPLA identity and their weapons. Indeed, 'I am SPLA' was a phrase heard often in the course of the fieldwork while talking to particularly young men who did not 'report' and who stayed in their villages, either because they had been in SPLA units near their homes and so just went home after 'peace came'[11] or they were too far from the site where soldiers were asked to report; in Eastern Equatoria the fieldwork site was in Kiyala. While this illustrates the different dynamics in contemporary debates on South Sudan's restructuring of security, it also illustrates the complexity of drawing clear lines between former combatants and present SPLA.

While these were the considerations before the post-December 2013 conflict, it did highlight the reality of the complexity of SPLA force reduction and the army's late inclination towards DDR. Still, those who 'reported' and ended up on the payroll could no longer be defined as an ex-combatant but active service soldiers whose departure from the army should be addressed under personnel retirement or redundancy. The issue of retirement, however, proved to be the Achilles heel in South Sudan's attempts at SPLA force reduction in the post-2005 period, the point of contention being who exactly was eligible for retirement? In view of almost 40 years of military engagements in the southern civil wars, based primarily on voluntary service, there were disagreements, both within the government and the military top brass as to what service should be deemed admissible for retirement benefits.[12]

This especially stemmed from the SPLA's tradition as a movement and the overall feeling that everyone contributed to the war and, as such, giving pensions only to those leaving the SPLA post-2005 would have been unfair.[13] The issue of inclusivity also re-emphasised the fact that South Sudan had been through two civil wars, the post-December 2013 one notwithstanding. As such, a compensation programme for only SPLA veterans would also be unfair because it would exclude the veterans from the First Civil War, the Anyanya 1. Nevertheless, including everyone was not evident and even if the line was to be drawn at the SPLA, a pension programme would still be unrealizable, not only from a logistical standpoint but also from the point of funding.[14] Privately, senior government and military officials conceded there was no money to pay pensions because 98 per cent of South Sudan Government revenues came from oil with the revenue used mainly to service government expenditure, largely paying government and army salaries.[15]

It is arguably from this reality that the alternative but imperfect solution of addressing the issue of force resizing found its way into the remit of DDR. However, even then there were still questions to be asked about not only the viability of DDR as an approach, but also about the merits of the process beyond procedural competencies. Effectiveness of the DDR process was also questioned in part owing to numerous mistakes associated with the process. One of the first SPLA soldiers to be inducted into the DDR process in 2009 for example carried a discharge certificate from the DDR process that stated he had been disarmed 12 years earlier.

Despite such endemic errors, the DDR process involving SPLA decommissioning was, until the December 2013 fallouts, widely accepted as part of phase two of the DDR process in South Sudan. Subsequently, there was a lot riding on its success, not least of all being the whole SPLA transformation strategy of which objective force 2017 was a key component. Force reduction was especially a pressing matter, because up to the December 2013 crisis, 40 per cent of the SPLA budget was spent on personnel salaries (Warner 2012: 2). The rest of the SPLA transformation was to be achieved in line with other complementary legal, constitutional and policy frameworks at the time namely:

The Comprehensive Peace Agreement
Interim National Constitution
Interim Constitution of Southern Sudan
SPLA Act
2008 SPLA White Paper on Defence
SPLA Rules and Regulations
SPLA Retirement Policy

Although these formed part of a larger picture that was aimed at the reorganization of the SPLA into a peacetime force, most of the SPLA reforms framework was already written into the CPA. However, the ideal remained to transform the SPLA into an organized, professional and effective peacetime force.[16] Yet taking into consideration the complexity of the country's security, it was the case that the idea of a peacetime force was in effect a falsification of a reality characterized by permanent suspicions, risk of war with its northern neighbour and continued internal conflicts. The idea of a peacetime force was thus ultimately an ideal that offered a starting point in the restructuring and reforming of the post-CPA SPLA, and by extension the country's post-conflict security.

SPLA restructuring

In order for the reconstruction of security in South Sudan to even begin, the process must start with the 'elephant' in the room, the SPLA. Here, 'the term "reconstruction" of the security sector pertains to the necessity of rebuilding domestic public security institutions to particularly re-establish a legitimate monopoly of violence' (Brzoska and Heinemann-Grüder 2004: 121). However, as the main security player in the country, any success in the reconstitution of security in South Sudan was heavily reliant on how much space the SPLA yielded in the security sector. In the post-August 2015 reconstitution of security, this remains true with reference to not only the government's SPLA but the armed opposition's SPLA-IO as well.

In the post-2005 period, the SPLA restructuring seemed on course with the army seemingly moving to the background in South Sudan's security and the top brass asserting the military's subordination to the civilian structures. Despite these declarations, in practice the SPLA's dominance did not reduce, leading to conclusions that the rhetoric of reform was aimed more at the international community that drove the security reform process as part of the liberal peacebuilding intervention in the country. Similarly, there was a challenge of circumstances. In most instances, post-conflict security reconstruction is necessitated by the inability of the war army to provide order and protect citizens, either because they were de facto dissolved after the conflict, are too small, or suffered from a loss of credibility in the war' (Brzoska and Heinemann-Grüder 2004: 121). In South Sudan, the reconstruction of security was driven more by the opposite and specifically the dominance of the former rebel army.

> The SPLA, either by design or by default, continue to dominate the security landscape in South Sudan. The restructuring and reform of security in the country that you talk about is mainly about 'taming' this dominance. Telling the generals that this country is not just theirs is not going to be easy because they feel they made a lot of sacrifices during the war. The generals and the SPLA were in charge of security in the south and in areas under its control for more than two decades. Taking control from them is not going to be easy. We are starting to see some changes with the building of institutions but even then, the SPLA still

asserts itself. For a long time, the Ministry of Defence had little influence over the SPLA. It is only a general from the SPLA who can be an effective minister there.[17]

In post-CPA South Sudan, attempts at mitigating the SPLA dominance were illustrated in the interview above based on the institutionalization of security. As such, although the processes of building institutions were part of the more long-term reconstitution and reconstruction of security, some of the processes akin to the SPLA were entrenched in the 2005 CPA. This included the reorganization of the SPLA and the SAF. Specifically, the SPLA after the signing of the CPA was organized into six divisions and four independent brigades in mid-2005. Following the death of John Garang on 30 July 2005, the SPLA reorganization that existed on paper was not implemented until after the Juba Declaration with the main phase starting in late 2007. The SPLA reorganization was primarily necessitated by the absorption of nearly 50,000 additional men into the SPLA following the Juba Declaration in 2006 (Richard Rands 2010). At the time, the new SPLA structure constituted (Table 5.1).

Although this reorganization was hailed as an important step in the restructuring of security in the country, it is also from this reorganization that conflicts in the country, primarily with the neighbouring Republic of Sudan, can be traced. After South Sudan's Independence, Divisions 9 Nuba Mountains and 10 Blue Nile were left on the Sudan side of the border with over 20,000

Table 5.1 SPLA divisions and locations

1st Division	Upper Nile State
2nd Division	Equatorias
3rd Division	Northern Bahr el Ghazal and Warrap states
4th Division	Unity State
Old 5th Division	Lakes State HQ support when the Capital was Rumbek
New 5th Division	Lakes State including the independent brigade that was in Raja
6th Division	SPLA elements of the JIUs
	Over 50,000 men reintegrated into the SPLA at independence
7th Division	Upper Nile State (Also referred to as a mobile division)
8th Division	Jonglei
Old 9th Division	Nuba Mountains (South Kordofan)
New 9th Division	Around Jau
Old 10th Division	Blue Nile
Independent units	Special Force (Commando) – Brigade of four battalions

Source: SPLA Officers Interviews.

men and women.¹⁸ They subsequently rebelled against Khartoum and in 2012 joined three Darfur rebel groups, Justice and Equality Movement (JEM), the Sudan Liberation Army factions of Minni Minawi (SLA-MM) and Abdul Wahid (SLA-AW) to form the Sudan Revolutionary Front (SRF). The issue of Divisions 9 and 10 remained at the heart of conflicts between the two Sudans with Sudan often accusing South Sudan of continued support to the former SPLA Divisions 9 and 10, now renamed SPLA-North, an accusation that South Sudan denies.

Nevertheless, the SPLA to a large extent established some form of structural reforms through the reorganization, with not only new divisions but also four professional categories: Infantry, Air Force, Navy (Riverine) and Intelligence. The disintegration of the SPLA after the December 2013 conflict, however, casts doubt on the success of the SPLA transformation, and especially its institutionalization. This begs the question what went wrong, with the most suitable answer being perhaps everything. The institutionalization of the SPLA as the overall goal was set within an international framework and standards for a professional army. However, the almost 'warlord' nature of South Sudan's military constructions presented several challenges to the attainment of this goal. The greatest hindrance was the fact that the SPLM, and its national army, the SPLA, were fragile coalitions of various militia and political entities that often fought against one another during previous civil wars.¹⁹ This factionalism forms the basis of South Sudan's warlordism, further institutionalized by the Juba Declaration which opened the door for militia integration into the SPLA in a programme a senior diplomat in Juba called 'the coalition of the bribed'. This set the wrong cause for security reform and restructure in the country.

The vast number of militias and armed groups in South Sudan has resulted in the creation of various commanders who often answer to no one. In the post-2005 period, attracting these commanders into the SPLA through the Juba Declaration and the various amnesty offers from GOSS with huge cash awards was arguably an elaborate exercise in creative persuasion. This persuasion was embodied by the ultimate status symbol in post-CPA South Sudan, the Land Cruiser V8 costing about US$100,000 and infamously nicknamed 'Miithapuol' (the children are all right) thus warranting the vehicle. The December 2013 conflict, however, strained and tested alliances and the fluid agreements they were based upon, reigniting old rivalries. This once again illustrated the difficulty of reforming and restructuring security in South Sudan in the post-2005 period. In the security sector transformation envisioned in the August 2015 peace agreement, the challenges of reforming both parts of the SPLA – the government forces and the armed opposition forces – and reconstituting them into the National Defence Forces of South Sudan (NDFSS) will be even greater. Therefore for the transformation to succeed, it must learn from the previous 2005 experiences. More importantly, it must be holistic and include other security players who have grown in dominance like the National Intelligence and Security Service.

National Intelligence and Security Service in South Sudan's post-conflict security

Taking into account the space and time dedicated to the SPLA in South Sudan's post-conflict restructuring of security in the 2005 period, it was clear that the SPLA had dominance over other security apparatus in the country.[20] This dominance was especially reflected in the country's post-conflict intervention where the bulk of the intervention was directed at the former rebel army with numerous consultants attached to the Ministry of Defence and, before July 2011, SPLA affairs. Liberal peacebuilding-based security sector reforms were also primarily aimed at the SPLA. As such, despite conceptual development of other national security organs, the SPLA maintained a lead over the pack, often overshadowing others including the police and the intelligence services. One branch, National Intelligence was especially left out of discussions and engagements about security sector reform. The outfit known as 'National Security', however, developed to occupy a role as key as the SPLA in South Sudan's security infrastructure, despite remaining outside the SSR scope. On this matter, Blair (2012) suggested that:

> There is still no formally constituted national security architecture. South Sudan has not yet debated what national security model it wishes to implement. The main reference point for this issue is the Constitution, which currently conflates national security with national intelligence functions. (Blair 2012)

Blair's views were widely shared by many people interviewed for this study. There were especially diverse views with regards to the functions of the National Intelligence Service and these were summed up by a South Sudanese scholar:

> The national intelligence in this country is increasingly looking and behaving like the National Intelligence and Security Service (NISS) in Khartoum. Constitutionally they sit in a vacuum, yet they seem to have more power than the police. The national security people are always stepping on each other's toes with

the SPLA, fighting for supremacy with one another. That they fight each other is strange because these two should exist in two very different legal frameworks. But, national intelligence and military intelligence of the SPLA can't seem to see eye to eye and most of the time they want to shoot each other.[21]

This analogy was echoed by Haken and Taft (2013) that 'the National Security Service in South Sudan is a security apparatus whose functions and mandate have never been defined by law' (Haken and Taft 2013: 2).[22] Still, NISS legacies remain a major factor in the country's security. The extrajudicial modus operandi of the entity known as 'national security' often contradicted the emphasis placed on national security strategy and policy first echoed in the post-CPA interim constitution and in the SPLA defence white paper (2008). The exclusion of the National Intelligence and Security Service in the wider post-conflict security reforms framework in the post-2005 period illustrated the contextual gaps that existed in the attempt to overhaul the country's security sector.

Arguably, 'national security' were deliberately excluded from discussions on restructuring of security, primarily owing to their seemingly extrajudicial workings. With South Sudan's security priorities remaining focused on the SPLA, empirical observations, especially in the field site at Torit and in the national capital Juba, illustrated that the public was, at the time, generally less aware of national security than the SPLA. Despite the lack of a legally constituted framework for its existence, the populace awareness of national security was fearful despite its lack of a visible formal role, unlike the SPLA. As such, it is the case that national security and intelligence services in South Sudan, like the SPLA, are also key players in the country's security infrastructure. Their role in the attainment of a stable post-conflict security is thus a subject for further inquiry.

Reform by institutionalization

The gaps, both legally and structurally, found in the existence and operation of some of South Sudan's security actors like the national security, especially highlight the importance of developing institutions in the country. Despite the challenges to the restructuring and reform of security in the country, the building of security institutions was a key component of the various processes. This pursuit of institutionalization succeeded to some degree, especially by providing the country with viable security management structures. In the post-2005 period, the South Sudan Security Committee and the Southern Sudan Defence Council, according to Mwanika (2012), were the most prominent ones:

The South Sudan Security Committee, also referred to as the RSS Security Council, meets weekly to review the internal national security situation in South Sudan and is chaired by the vice president, and often includes the Inspector General of Police (IGP) or the Deputy Inspector General of Police (DIGP), the Governor of Central Equatoria State as the seat of Government, the SPLA Chief of General Staff (COGS) and representatives from the ministries of defence, military intelligence personnel and national security. The committee decides on how internal national security matters are handled, either by national security institutions in Juba and then passed on to the State security committees, or directly by the SPLA.

To a large extent, the South Sudan Security Committee and the Southern Sudan Defence Council illustrated the endeavour for pluralism capable of realizing a stable and secure post-conflict security in the country in the long term. That said, the greatest challenge remained in harmonizing the empirical reality – the aspirations of an internationally led liberal peacebuilding intervention and the complexities and theory of national security. Blair (2012) referred to this as 'Switching Gears from Concepts to Implementation'.[23]

Despite the optimism presented by the policy outlook for national security, the reality of South Sudan's security infrastructure could not be glossed over. This was reflected in the continued SPLA dominance, especially in internal security matters despite efforts at institution building. There was, nevertheless, significant progress made in evolving and shaping South Sudan's post-conflict security system beyond the legacies of its liberation struggle origins, one of the major institutional hallmarks being the creation of more operationally relevant institutions like the South Sudan Police Service (SSPS). Institutionalization as an approach thus contributed profoundly to the reconstitution of security in post-2005 South Sudan and especially in addressing the liberation movement hangovers.

The South Sudan Police Service

The establishment of the South Sudan Police Service (SSPS) and its subsequent institutionalization and reform was unavoidably entangled with the reform and restructuring of the SPLA. However, like in other post-conflict countries like Uganda, Rwanda and Sierra Leone, the police in South Sudan have been shaped by their experience of war (Baker 2007). This raises issues in addressing the police occupational culture which, in the case of South Sudan, culminated in a history and continuum of militarism. The influence of South Sudan's protracted conflicts within the police service has been far reaching with the police culture in the country hinged on war traditions and practices (Baker 2007). With this in mind, several questions come to the fore, specifically, 'What is the role of the SSPS in the wider security construction in the country and what influence does this have on the demilitarization narrative?'

The parameters for South Sudan's post-conflict policing are particularly wide and can be drawn from any list of policy areas pertaining to policing in a fragile or post-conflict state. These include 'police-military relations, political economy of policing, police development in militarized societies, and AK-47 cultures and security delivered by the state through social processes of patronage and policing provided by non-state actors'.[24] As such, although the subservience of the police service in favour of the army is endemic in South Sudan, the institution is a key part of the post-conflict security infrastructure written into the CPA and equally important in the August 2015 peace agreement.

Even so, the SSPS has received considerably less attention in South Sudan's post-CPA restructuring and reform of security in comparison to the SPLA. Indeed, although the creation of the SSPS was a requirement of the CPA, little attention was paid to its frameworks in comparison to that paid to the defence sector and the SPLA in particular. Specifically, the security provisions in the 2005 CPA informed the constructions and formulations of policing in the Interim National Constitution and the Interim Constitution of Southern Sudan and gave precedence to military reform and DDR over issues related to the rule of law and public security. Arguably, the same is likely to be the case in the August 2015 peace agreement with its focus on security sector transformation. In the 2005 agreement, Chapter VI of the CPA illustrated this imbalance, with 30 pages devoted to the military and DDR and only two pages to issues of public security (Sedra 2009: 4). On the whole, the SSPS was set up on the basis of three specific provisions in the CPA and the subsequent interim constitution, specifically entailing that:

> Structures and arrangements affecting all law enforcement organs, especially the police and national security shall be dealt with as part of the power-sharing arrangements and tied where necessary to the appropriate level of the executive. (CPA Chapter VI – Security Arrangements, Article 8)
>
> Powers of the Government of Southern Sudan stipulated that the exclusive legislative and executive powers of the Government of Southern Sudan included 'police, prisons and wildlife services'. (Schedule B – CPA p. 40)

The law enforcement agencies and security service in Southern Sudan sets out the broad parameters for the organisation of the SSPS and the requirement of ensuring appropriate legislation for the police and its functions and the democratic requirements for the police as an institution. (Chapter III in the Interim Constitution Act 162, 10–14)

These three provisions provide the broad frameworks upon which South Sudan's police services are based. Established in 2005 under the interim constitution, the SSPS marked the beginning of the realignment of security in post-CPA South Sudan. In the 2015 Agreement on the Resolution of the Conflict in the Republic of South Sudan, the composition of the police beyond the immediate transitional security arrangements is likely to remain within the existing post-2005 frameworks. The police service thus remains an important component in the restructuring of security in post-conflict South Sudan despite its weaknesses. For the most part, the SSPS could assume greater responsibility for internal security with the SPLA focusing on external defence. The success or failure of the SSPS and its development efforts therefore have widespread implications for the entire security system. This would give both the SPLA and the SSPS a greater chance of successfully implementing individual reform and development programmes (Snowden 2012: 8), essential for the success of the wider restructuring of security in the country and more broadly its demilitarization.

However, beyond reform, the challenges that beset the South Sudan Police Service are mainly to do with institutional and capacity weakness. While this can be attributed to the newness of policing, both theoretically and practically in the south, it can also be associated with the legal evolution of policing after the CPA. This is often at odds with societal and cultural complexes which in South Sudan evolve around a policing culture fashioned from the cloth of the SPLA. While policing in general implies the collation of a set of activities aimed at preserving the security of a particular social order (Reiner 2010: 4), in South Sudan up until the signing of the CPA in 2005, this role was primarily fulfilled by the SPLA.

From the shadows of the SPLA

The South Sudan Police Service, therefore, from its inception in 2005, struggled to move from beyond the shadows of the SPLA, despite it being a key component of South Sudan's post-conflict security reconstruction. In looking at the set-up of policing in the country, the research revealed:

There is a general lack of respect and appreciation of the very idea of policing which is often an afterthought. Even in the CPA, policing was an afterthought in the broader formulation of the post-CPA security infrastructure.[25]

This sentiment is shared by many in the security services interviewed for this research, and especially in the SPLA and SSPS, as well as within GOSS. It also points at deeper-rooted contextual challenges associated with policing in South Sudan and, more specifically, the morphing of a police service from the shadows of a rebel movement. This results in a knock-on effect on the institutional cultures of not only policing, but also other internal security aspects in the country.

While policing may be done by a variety of agents and professionals employed by the state in an organization with an omnibus policing mandate (Reiner 2010: 4), in the case of South Sudan and the SSPS, the constitution of the agents is equally important. This is particularly true of the SSPS which, at the end of the civil war in 2005, took on the personnel previously in the SPLA. In fact, the initial police service comprized mainly of former SPLA fighters and the armed forces.[26] Specifically, it drew from two distinct constituents: former police of the government of Sudan that were in garrison towns and personnel from the SPLA/M. The former garrison town's police were treated with suspicion by the local communities and seen as part of the Khartoum/NCP establishment. The SPLA-drawn police, however, comprized of two elements: those who played the role of civilian police in SPLA/M-administered areas and soldiers passed on to the SSPS after the CPA.[27]

This notwithstanding, it is the case that those who played the role of civilian police in SPLA/M-controlled areas were in effect still drawn from the security units of the SPLA (Metelits 2010: 69). The soldiers passed on to the police service from the SPLA were also those largely perceived as unfit for military service. This contributed to the subservience of the police to the SPLA as the less fitting of the two institutions, further increasing and justifying the bravado of the SPLA.[28] Although most of the challenges that beset South Sudan's police service and policing in the country could be traced back to its formation and its institutional culture of subservience to the SPLA, the challenges to policing in South Sudan go beyond the contextual security challenges in the country.

Beyond the empirical challenges: contextualizing the challenges to policing

Policing and police reform are fairly new in comparison to other security disciplines (Reiner 2010). In Africa, the study of the police and policing is newer and the study of policing as part of post-conflict reconstruction of security newer still. Primarily, the study of policing tends to revolve around immediate policy issues often taking for granted and assuming the notion of the police and their proper function (Cain 1979; Reiner 2010). Whereas most people living in a modern society have an intuitive notion of what the police are, mainly identified as a body of people patrolling public places, with a broad mandate on crime control, order maintenance and some negotiable social services functions (Reiner 2010: 3), these roles are not very clear in South Sudan. As such, the articulation of the role of the South Sudan Police Service in post-CPA and post-independence South Sudan is not only a matter of urgency but one of significant importance in the overall post-conflict security.

However, although the blurring of military and police lines has created confusion in the articulation of police roles, the legislation does provide guidance. It sets out police roles to include 'the prevention, combat and investigation of crime, maintaining law and public order, protecting the people in Southern Sudan and their properties, and upholding and enforcing the constitution and the law'. Drawn from the 2011 constitution, these roles not only set out the remits of police authority in the country, but the constitution also details the command structure which gives significant authority to State Police Commissioners in a decentralized police system. In decentralizing policing, the post-2005 CPA construction of policing spread the SSPS jurisdiction to ten southern states.[29] Post-CPA, though, the onset of policing was primarily based on building the police service as an institution and especially its command and structures including personnel. Notable among these was the police training school that was set up in Rajaf from where the first 6,000 police trainees were dispatched to the ten states in December 2010. At its inception, South Sudan's police service had started out with an aim of 3,000 police per state. The reality as of December 2013, however, was a service in crisis and bewildered by the lack of capacity, training, essential infrastructure, resources and equipment. This adversely affected its ability to extend security to the community.[30]

These limitations of SSPS were especially linked to its perceived failings seen in the deteriorating security in the country (Jok 2013). With the exception of border conflicts with the Republic of Sudan and prior to the post-December 2013 rebellion, South Sudan's conflicts remained internal, which essentially exposed the weaknesses of the police service. It is these weaknesses and failures that informed the National Police Service Inspector General's strategic action plan for reforming South Sudan's police. As such, the 2011 police reform plan specifically set out to increase SSPS capacities, both operationally and legislatively.[31]

However, although the police reform plan did not receive as much attention as the SPLA transformation, it was still an important piece of the country's security jigsaw. As a result of the strategic plan, the number of police in the SSPS increased in the years before the 2013 conflict. Still, the Achilles heel remained that many recruits continued to come to the police from the SPLA. Similarly, despite the overall increase in the number of 'trained' police, there was little to no change on police personnel numbers at local levels. At an operational level, senior police officers complained that despite the increase in numbers, police capacity remained negligible as the SSPS officers were largely functionally illiterate, with over 65 per cent not being able to read or write.[32] Yet the same officers maintained that the service remained committed to improving its overall capacity:

> We have been trying to improve ourselves. We are trying to get people who have some education to join the police but the money is not there. The austerity has put some of our plans on hold. Also we have been trying to get a headcount in the police so we are sure how many officers we have, but this is not easy. Many of the police we have are no good. They drink too much, they are too old or not effective and they were sent to us from the SPLA. For us to fully adopt the police reform strategy we need money and this is not there.[33]

While the role of policing in post-conflict restructuring of security is not as well-defined as perhaps those of DDR or SSR, its validity to the overall post-conflict security complex is unquestionable. However, discussions about policing and the SSPS circumnavigate back to the same debates – the extraction from the SPLA of policing roles and that not much thought seemed to have been paid to policing in comparison to the military. This seems true for most post-conflict countries, especially that issues of policing are hardly ever properly addressed in peace agreements. However, there are exceptions to this, the most notable ones in recent history being the Good Friday Agreement in Northern Ireland and in post-apartheid South Africa. While there are distinct differences between South Africa, South Sudan and other examples of post-conflict policing, South Africa and Northern Ireland after the Good Friday Agreement are a few of the instances where extended dialogue on the role of policing was integrated into the peace process as a key component.

South Sudan falls within the post-conflict countries where the military, embodied by the former rebels, becomes the focus of the post-conflict security reconstruction.[34] Within the context of South Sudan, policing and police reforms were never the centrepiece of the post-conflict security constructions, so it always lingers in the background. Unlike the various post-conflict approaches applied to the army and ex-combatants that have been associated with the recurrence of violence and a return to hostilities, approaches to the police have been almost dismissive.[35] Police in post-conflict countries are thus addressed more in terms of the overall structural and institutional building, than a threat to peace.

However, in countries like South Sudan with a long history of militarization, a blurring of police-military relations and militarized societies with an AK-47[36] culture (Carr 2008; McCaskie 2008), the police, like the military and ex-combatants, must command equal attention in relation to their role in the country's security. Still, even with this in mind, the reality of the SSPS has been one of a service delegated to cosmetic and generic discussion on the building of post-war structures and institutions. In South Sudan, this has been highlighted by the division of labour and specialization of the police into other civil policing roles like the fire brigade, wildlife, prisons, etc.

Need not dogma

Arguably, this is part of the wider aspiration of liberal peacebuilding at the heart of which are governance and rule of law. The police are thus vital to this process and, as discussed earlier, approaches to post-conflict policing are often driven by the attainment of law and order and rule of law. Arguably, this is a pursuit that is broadly informed by the onslaught of liberalism from which liberal peace is derived. The specialization of South Sudan's police service, be it more structurally than in practice, is an example of this. Specialized policing is often linked to economic specialization and differential access to resources that occur in the transitions. This is often applicable in stable countries and the extent and breadth of police specialization is often reflected in the country's embodiment of liberal, political and economic principles (Robinson and Scaglion 1987: 109; Reiner 2010: 6). In South Sudan, where both of these factors are missing, police specialization runs into some empirical challenges articulated by a police commandant:

> Most of the fire brigade services in the country don't have fire engines. Even for those that do, we don't have running water in the country. Even in Juba, the engine, if it works, has to go to the river Nile to get water together with all the commercial trucks that provide water in the town. The wildlife has many officers but we have no roads and our so-called national parks are bushes like

they always have been. We should have used these people better if they were in the police, so we can train them to stop all these robberies and insecurity. The tukuls (round huts with grass thatched roofs) will be completely burnt by the time the fire brigade comes; better they be chasing the thieves.[37]

The empirical challenges facing policing like these are thus perhaps an indication of the need for a post-conflict approach that is more needs-driven than dogma-based. The lesson drawn from this experience is that although some of the SSPS internationally led pursuits are good on paper, the case study and the curveballs it presents also has to be taken into account. This is especially the case because pursuits based on a theoretical approach to policing, underpinned by internationally led liberal peace-based programmes, also bring with them a certain degree of comparisons.

Notably, in South Sudan, the police service developed hand in hand with social inequalities and hierarchy (Reiner 2010), common in policing. These hierarchical inequalities were especially visible in the country's capital Juba. In the research area of Eastern Equatoria, the police, for example, in the state capital Torit were less visible in comparison to police in the capital Juba. Similarly, the police in Torit are more visible than police at the county level. From the county level going down, police visibility goes down from little to none. This dwindling of police and policing at the basic community level outside the national and state capitals was not only the epitome of hierarchical inequalities in South Sudan's policing, it also contributed to rises in insecurity in the country.[38] However, although the lack of personnel and poor training are some of the challenges facing the police service, a more important problem persists: that of a police service that refuses to behave like a police service. Arguably living in awe of the more seemingly 'superior' SPLA, the police behave like a mini-SPLA.

> South Sudan is the only country where the police behave like they are the army. Our police drive around town with 2.5 inch mounted machine guns. This is a police that behaves like the military. Most of the boys were ours (SPLA) and now they are in the police, but they behave as if they are still on the front line. This makes policing a bit shaky.[39]

This once again gravitates back to discussions on SPLA dominance and societal militarization where the practice of delegating police roles to the SPLA has provided for a militarization of policing, both past and present. The SSPS officers thus work in a continuum that prioritizes the SPLA, which often takes over policing every time the SSPS falters owing to its institutional and capacity challenges. This systematic and continual domination of the SSPS by the SPLA has, in effect, turned into a vicious cycle that almost always guarantees SSPS failure in its policing.

This not only made it difficult for the population to make a clear distinction between the roles of the police to those carried out by the military, it is also difficult to distinguish between the police and SPLA personnel. Roadblocks are a good example: sometimes set up by the police, sometimes by the SPLA and sometimes by locals with police or SPLA uniforms. Incidents of people in SPLA uniforms robbing civilians are not uncommon.[40] The question that this raises, both for South Sudan and more widely, is how does South Sudan begin to distinguish between the police and the military and, more importantly, between policing and military operations? Still, distinguishing between the SPLA and SSPS and their functions is part of the reform and restructuring puzzle that South Sudan must address. Also important is the need for what Reiner (2010) calls the distinguishing between police and policing which he urges is equally important; specifically, presenting police as referring to a particular kind of social institution, while policing he argues implies a set of processes with specific social functions (Reiner 2010: 4).

Whereas it is problematic to define contemporary police mainly in terms of their supposed function (Klockars 1985), in South Sudan the problems with policing and the wider constructions of security are perhaps less institutional and structural and more functionally basic. Although Reiner's (2010) presentations of police and policing are simple, in South Sudan their realization is not as dependent on societal perceptions. More specifically, how the security institutions, including the police, truly see themselves and more generally how they perceive societal expectations, especially of policing. On this a former child soldier explains:

> During the war, the SPLA civil police were in charge, so everybody in the villages knew the police and the SPLA to be the same. With the peace and now independence, very little has changed in the countryside. The SSPS is made up of people who were in the SPLA. Also, during the war, most young men had an association with the movement. Most of these are now police. It is very difficult to delink the SPLA from the police and other security organs because most of the people in these institutions – fire, prisons, wildlife, as well as the police – were all with the SPLA at one point or another. There is a history here. Even most of the young people who can fight and handle their weapons were mainly trained in the SPLA. I was one of them. We were called the Jesh Ahmr – the Red Army or child soldiers.[41]

With this in mind, it seems that delinking the SSPS from the SPLA is a herculean task. But given the dynamics of South Sudan's post-conflict security, it is not surprising that constructing a police and policing in a country emerging from two protracted civil wars is bound to be challenging. Still, as part of the post-conflict realization of security in the country, the need to contextualize policing cannot be overstated. This is especially in line with broader questions that arise from the aspiration of policing in South Sudan, especially if the expectations placed on the SSPS are comparable to those of contemporary policing in Africa. More specifically, if the expectations placed on the SSPS are at all realistic, taking into account the country's contextual and empirical challenges (Reiner 2010: 4), it is especially impossible to ignore the fact that South Sudan's police service is evolving at a critical time in the development of policing, a time when contemporary Africa is embracing technological advances, especially in security discourses including policing with technology, such as CCTV cameras (Goold 2004, 2009; Norris and Armstrong 1999; Sheprycki 2000). As such, with evolving functions of the police and scopes of policing, there are questions to be asked on the effects and impact of such advances on South Sudan's aspirations of policing and its police service.

Nevertheless, although the questions asked of the SSPS and policing in South Sudan in general are more basic, changes to policing elsewhere, like the inclusion of technology, does affect the SSPS, both in its development and its aspirations. More generally, how do regional police organizations like the Eastern Africa Police Chiefs Cooperation Organisation (EAPCCO) impact on the SSPS and its struggles for professionalism and efficiency in a security architecture dominated by the army? Key to this is South Sudan's reflection of self, beginning with a national approach to reconciling the existing gaps between the rhetoric of rule of law and law and order with the reality an egalitarian approach to justice. Subsequently what is acceptable, not only constitutionally and in the statute, but in the parallel traditional systems which, although unlegislated in the hierarchical system of governance, dominate social interactions in South Sudan? These reconciliations will address some of the main challenges to policing; more notably in identifying the scope of policing that looks beyond the statute.

By so doing, the SSPS would be setting its own parameters for policing, independent of external influence and dependent on its own policing needs. This is especially important in the post-August 2015 period and would offer an insight into why South Sudan interacts with security and its security organs like the police in the way that it does. More importantly, why the post-2005 approaches to security, including policing, did not produce the liberal peace envisioned in the country's post-conflict interventions. This reaffirms the theoretical and conceptual arguments presented in Chapter 1, re-emphasizing the importance of taking a society's cultures and traditions into consideration in addressing its demilitarization.

The legacy of war: societal constructions of security and the paradox of armed youth

The legacy of war in South Sudan has arguably had a major effect on the country's construction of post-conflict security, many already discussed in this book. These include the impact on social attitudes to violence, societal perceptions of security and the paradox of armed youth left by the legacy of war. A major factor in this legacy is in the story of the Jesh Ahmr or Red Army.

The Jesh Ahmr or the Red Army are a key feature in the legacy of the 1983–2005 Civil War in South Sudan, as these were the child soldiers in that war and today's young adult population, whose lives are a direct result of events during the war. As such, they arguably are the custodians of the legacy of the civil war in the country; a legacy that is embodied in the narrative of their lives, which perhaps offers some insight into South Sudan's armed youth and their role in the country's renegotiations of post-conflict security. The post-2013 conflict created a new generation of children recruited into the conflict by both sides, re-establishing the complexity of militarization embodied by the Jesh Ahmr in the pre-2005 conflict. Although Jesh Ahmr rarely feature in discussions about militarization in the south, they are an important part of that narrative.

The best known of these southern units of young men and boys that made up the Jesh Ahmr were the boys known as the Lost Boys, whose stories cultivated the world in the early 1990s (Pur 2012). These were thousands of unaccompanied children who walked for months from Ethiopia to Kenya after the toppling of the Mengistu government in Ethiopia that forced the SPLA/M to leave western Ethiopia. These boys primarily ended up in the refugee camps in Kenya and many were resettled, mainly in North America but also in Australia. However, despite similarities in the story of the 'Lost Boy', empirical enquiry and protracted fieldwork periods indicate that after the departure from Ethiopia, the lives of the Jesh Ahmr took different forms. More specifically, that most of the children that formed the Jesh Ahmr may have remained in Southern Sudan.

> It is difficult to tell the exact number of the Jesh Ahmr. At first we were between 30,000 and 40,000 in Ethiopia but thousands went to the front line. We were left with about 25,000 in Ethiopia but, of these, only about 16,000 ended up in Kakuma in Kenya.[42]

Most notable is that although the biggest number of the Jesh Ahmr stayed in Sudan, their story is the least known, raising the question: 'What happened to these boys?' The answer to this question is especially important to grasping the country's security complexes. In the memoirs of one 'Lost Boy' he says:

> The Red Army were brainwashed into war in order to become future destructive and hostile strong soldiers in the rebel movement. I never feared taking away the lives of those who were weak and innocent. We used to live as a group, Squad Company, and a battalion of Red Army with no families or relatives. We were liberators for the land that our grandfathers died for, fighting for the same causes. I was planted the military seed of a conflict and was motivated to fight for an unknown grievance. As the tougher black army (elderly soldiers) became extinct at front line war zones, Red Army troops served as interior reinforcement to refuel the war that divided the largest African country, Sudan. (Pur 2012)

Although Pur's (2012) account of the Red Army is by no means conclusive or representative of the almost 40,000 boys that made up the Jesh Ahmr, it cannot altogether be discounted. The account, though, does offer a snapshot of the underlying narrative to southern militarization and, as such, the Jesh Ahmr might also have a role to play in its demilitarization. This begins by addressing the legacy of the Jesh Ahmr on a generation of children, now adults, who arguably hold the key to the stability of post-independence South Sudan. To understand the legacy is to understand the stories and shed some light on the different trajectories of the lives of the Jesh Ahmr boys:

The Lost Boy

I come from Bor and I'm Jec El Amer. I was about 12 years old when I joined. I was in our area and, like many other boys my age, we would go to the cattle camp and come back to the village when there was pasture in our area. One day when we had just returned from the cattle camp, there was news that the commander in our area had asked for a meeting. In that meeting, Kuol Manyang, who has been the governor of Jonglei and has just been appointed Minister of Defence, was the SPLA commander. In the meeting, it was said that every family should give a son to go to Ethiopia to be taken to school and to be trained. My father took me and there were many other boys there also. Before we left, my father told me to take care and to work hard and that I should not expect to be given things. This principle has guided me in my life – that the world owes you nothing. This was the last time I ever saw my father. I think it was around 1987. From then, we walked for almost two months to reach Ethiopia.

When we got there, there were a lot of boys but I was also a bit older than most, so it was not so bad for me but life in Ethiopia was not easy. We went to school and we got training and some of the women in the camp took care of us; the big boys like myself also took care of the young boys. When Mengistu fell from power, we left Ethiopia and came back to Sudan; we walked for a long time until we reached Mogos. We stayed there for a long time before we went to the camp in Kakuma, Kenya. I went to school in the camp for nine years before I was relocated to the United States.

The SPLA soldier

I went to Ethiopia with other boys from my village. We stayed there from 1986 but then we were told we could not stay because of the war in Ethiopia. We came back to Sudan and we walked to Mogos. When we got there, I and some others went on to New Kush. I have been fighting for liberation since then. I was injured in Kapoeta on the front line and was taken to Narus. Since peace came, I have just been around Torit.

These two encounters from two men roughly the same age are, however, not isolated. These are just two representations of two different trajectories in the lives of the southern child soldiers. However, even for those children at the same age who did not end up in the Jesh Ahmr, the war had a profound effect on their lives and more so on their present. Below, another two men, again roughly the same age:

From Uganda with love – the NGO worker

When the war became worse around 1986 we had to run. We had stayed in our area, Loa, for as long as possible. Then we had run to Yei but then things also got difficult in Yei and we decided to run to Uganda. I was young but I remember it was me and my late older brother. We walked for many days and I got too tired sometimes and I could not walk so he carried me. We were hungry and I cannot forget. I had these shorts that had holes everywhere and especially two big holes at the buttocks. This thing has stayed with me. We got to Uganda and we went to Adjumani refugee settlement in northern Uganda. We had heard from relatives that my mother was there. When we got there we found her, and she was with my sister. We stayed in Adjumani and went to school there. My brother died but my mother is still there. My wife and children are in Kampala but I don't want them to come to South Sudan because I remember that journey with my brother and I'm afraid that if things ever got bad they would go through the same. So I leave them in Kampala. I don't want them to come here.

Although this young man did not fight in the civil war, his life was turned upside down, with a life lived in refuge and afraid of the memories of the war. The other man, also the same age, has a different story that illustrates the militarization at the micro-level.

The cattle raider

More specifically, the cattle raider, like the NGO worker, did not go to Ethiopia and neither was he Jesh Ahmr. He is, however, from Mogos, a village that was a stopover for the Jesh Ahmr on their way to Kakuma refugee camp in Kenya and from them he and those in his village learned to use the AK-47. These guns became an important part of his life, which has many similarities to the lives of many armed youth that litter the new country's hinterlands. His life is the illustration of the micro-militarization and its social and cultural integration in South Sudan. He represents the mwenyemuji in Eastern Equatoria, the White Army in Jonglei and Upper Nile and all the other bands of armed youth across the country who can instantly be commanded into an organized fighting force as was the case in the conflicts after 15 December 2013.

The narratives of these four men, different as they are, all bear particular significance to the state of contemporary South Sudan. They are especially representative of the many narratives encountered during this research. The stories of these men, now in their late to mid-thirties perhaps, better illuminate the diverse legacies left by the Second Civil War and how these experiences continue to affect the conception and realization of security in the country. Those actively involved in the civil war, like the Jesh Ahmr, bring the military training they acquired along the way to the independent South Sudan. For those who ended up in refugee camps in neighbouring countries or in north Sudan, especially in Khartoum, access to education sets them apart in the new country. This has placed them in government jobs or within South Sudan's emerging private sector and in the third sector.

However, for most of those who stayed within the south during the war, access to education was limited. This has a number of effects on their interaction with both the structure and agency of independent South Sudan. Especially among the Jesh Ahmr who melted into the countryside, joined the SPLA or local youth who make up village defence groups and forces, illiteracy is especially high and has a direct impact on the processes of post-conflict security.[43] A senior consultant with the Ministry of Defence put this in context:

> ## Box 5.1 The cattle raider – photo journal
>
> I am not sure how old I am, but believe I am about 35 years old. I was born in a village near Mogos town in Southern Sudan. My mother died the day she gave birth to me and my elder brother and sister and I were brought up by my father's other two wives, who took it in turns to care for us. From a small child I was taught how to use a gun by other boys and at around nine years old my elder brother gave me an AK-47. We are pastoralists and livestock, especially cows, is our way of life.
>
> The women take care of the homes, the small boys herd the goats and the big boys look after the cattle. When I learned how to use the gun I also started looking after the cattle, which is a big responsibility because sometimes other tribes come and steal our cows. We in return will go and raid someone else and take their cows. I went for my first raid with other young men from my village when I was around 12 years old.
>
>
>
> **Figure 5.1** Akwilino Lokwar Lopir herding cattle.
>
> It is a day I will never forget. I was scared but you must show bravery at all times. My brother was also with us but the enemy fought back hard and he was killed. After every raid you are grateful if you are not killed. I have spent the better part of my life as a cattle raider, but two years ago, things changed. I tried to marry a girl but she was taken by someone else. I got so angry that I decided to leave Mogos and come to this town, Narus. I got a job as a watchman for a kawaja or foreigner, who gave me somewhere to stay and food to eat. I like it and since I am away from home I do not go raiding.
>
> My employers are good to me and their two small children were trying to teach me how to read and write. Then I started going to class with them, but they were learning too fast for me. So when the school for older people started, I asked if I could join it. They agreed so now every afternoon I go to school.
>
> The lessons have been good and I have been going there for about a year. I say it is good because now I also know how to count my money

Figure 5.2 Lokwar working as a guard.

Figure 5.3 Attending school.

Figure 5.4 Learning basic maths.

and I have even started a small shop outside the house. I sell small grocery goods like soap, cigarettes, sweets, sugar and salt and people come to buy from me.

After school, I go back to my work and fetch water from the borehole. In class they have taught us not to drink from the pools so I get my water from the borehole when I go to get water for the kawaja. Here, most people don't send their children to school, but I will send mine because then they can make money and help me. I know that this will be a good thing because I want them to know how to read and write and my children to understand better.

I have a very full life with my new friends and I am very happy. I guard the house at night with my gun and in the morning after I've finished my chores in my employer's compound, I open up the shop. I now even go to Lokichogio in northern Kenya to get things for my business. Our tribe, the Toposa, was neutral during the long civil war which made it easy to get guns, but now it is over it is easier to go about normal business.

Figure 5.5 Fetching clean water.

I haven't stopped raiding altogether. In July I raided the Koroma people of Dima in Ethiopia when I went back to my village. But I was almost killed, so I don't want to raid any more. I got 37 cows for participating in the raid. There were 25 of us men, two got killed, and we took 300 cows from them.

I have now found another girlfriend and I want to marry her. Her name is Madalena. I will use the cows that I already have at home to pay for her dowry. Then I will take care of her by just doing my business, not raiding.

Figure 5.6 Using skills from basic maths to run small business.

Source: Nyambura Wambugu.

The SPLA wants to transform, the police want to transform, and there seems to be political will to move the security actors, especially the SPLA, from a rebel force to a professional one. The SPLA has the right priorities. If its transformation strategy works, it will not only make it more operationally effective but also cheaper. This will fundamentally change the outlook of security in the country. If this strategy fails, it might not be for the lack of trying but rather just the circumstances and the hand that is dealt, because most of these challenges are to do with capacity. So far only 15–20 of the SPLA officers' corps can read and write. In the rank and file it's worse; there are few who can be middle managers to effect the change that we are consulting on. We opened a training school in Lanya along Yei road and this is hailed as a success and a big step towards restructuring security in the country by offering training. The small print is that the training is offered in English and less than 10 per cent of the recruits can speak or understand English, even at the very basic level. So in effect the training school, although it exists on paper, achieved little in the restructuring of security.[44]

Conclusions

The arguments above affirm that the prospect of restructuring and reforming security in South Sudan is a big undertaking, not least with the complexities of the post-December 2013 civil war. Specifically, they point at the underlying challenges facing South Sudan's restructuring and reform of security and the wider demilitarization endeavour.

Contextually, the greatest challenge to South Sudan's post-conflict restructuring of security is to be found in reconciling contradictions on how security is perceived locally and how it's perceived in the liberal peace thesis. As the empirical enquiry and the fieldwork reveal, societal views on the state of security and the roles of the different security players in the country differ significantly from the liberal peace aspirations in the country.

The Second Civil War has also had a major impact on the militarization of South Sudan's youth and on contemporary negotiations regarding security in the country and South Sudan's demilitarization. Still, these chapters focus more on the period after the signing of the 2005 peace agreement. In fact, demilitarization of the youth is paramount for the success of demilitarization of the country. Empirical enquiry already suggests that these youths are indeed two sides of the security coin, a deterrent and a threat at the same time. A deterrent because the militarized youth serve as a standing army in South Sudan's many conflicts and may deter external aggression. However, following the post-December 2013 conflict, the threat caused by a heavily militarized youth to the country arguably outweighs any benefits. A militarized youth is, in South Sudan, undoubtedly a destabilizing factor, especially in their engagement in inter-communal conflicts and primarily because more often than not they have no central government allegiance. This was the case post-2005 CPA and more so since independence.

To reconcile the idea of war legacies and the everyday realities, the research attempts to demonstrate the impact and divergence of the war legacy through the narratives of four men. Interviewed in the research site, they are all roughly the same age. The stories of these men illustrate the paradoxes facing post-conflict South Sudan. The young man who learned military skills and firearms handling from the army as a child soldier in the Jesh Ahmr, but who left Southern Sudan for Kenyan refugee camps and later North America. The young man, also a child soldier, who stayed in Southern Sudan and joined the army until the CPA after which he just went back to the village; not decommissioned, still in possession of his weapon and effectively still a soldier but not part of the official DDR programmes. The young man who, after escaping the civil war, is still haunted by memories of that war making him reluctant to fully commit to an independent South Sudan and finally a young man who epitomizes life in the countryside as a cattle raider, his life revolving around the AK-47 he possesses and uses to great precision, despite the fact that he never joined the SPLA but learned his firearms skills from friends, peers and family.

The story of the cattle raider especially draws parallels to the research focus group question: 'Do you know how to use a gun and where did you learn?' The majority of the respondents said they learned to use firearms aged between eight and 14 years old from family or peers who had been in the SPLA or who had learned from someone in the SPLA. Also resounding of the legacy of the war was the expression by young men in five focus group discussions that as young men there was an expectation that one must know how to use a firearm for 'protection'. While this illustrates the legacy of the war in South Sudan, it also illustrates the extent of militarization in the country. At a micro-level, this militarization is directly linked to the normalization of the acquisition and handling of firearms and their integration into everyday life, especially within the cattle-keeping communities.

The limited access to education is also another legacy of the war which continues to haunt South Sudan and which, together with the normalized militarization of rural youth, provides for a lethal mix. Illiteracy in South Sudan compounds poverty in a changing country and creates vulnerability easily manipulated by the political elite. It also makes it difficult for communities to understand changes to their way of life where, in most instances, it has not changed for generations. These changes include the establishment of some of the structures envisioned in the 2005 peace agreement, that is, a parliament at national and state levels, administrative structures and a government, judiciary and economic structures like a bank and currency. In the research process, over 80 per cent of the focus group discussion participants could not answer questions about what a government is or what an election is, despite having voted in an election in April 2010 and a referendum in January 2011. It was also clear from the field research that participants were highly dependent on 'our person', used to mean someone from the area in a position of power or who could read, write or speak some English or Arabic and thus was the community's contact with any visitors as the representation of 'government'.

This was not at odds with the patriarchal nature of South Sudan's communities. However, illiteracy and the inability of communities to interpret for themselves things like the peace agreement, the constitution, or to engage with training offered to them in any meaningful way had a profound impact on post-CPA interventions in the country, especially those relating to the reform and restructure of the security sector. Arguably this especially explains why it is so 'easy' to start rebellions in South Sudan, even with the backing of a handful of local men it appears. In the post-December 2013 conflicts, the militarized youth of South Sudan's countryside got drafted into yet another civil war, again serving their purpose as a standing army for anyone's taking. In the post-2013 conflict, the former vice president called on the White Army and the government, through Vice President Wani Igga,[45] was also drafting in youth to join the SPLA, both sides presiding over the militarization of the next generation of South Sudanese youth.

6

Restructuring governance

Introduction

This chapter explores the restructuring of governance in South Sudan as part of the country's demilitarization. It engages with key events relevant to the restructuring of governance in post-CPA South Sudan and focuses on the post-2005 period as the most significant for the restructuring of governance in the country's recent history.[1] It examines the promises made against the contemporary reality of South Sudan and pays close attention to the overlapping relationship between the SPLA and the SPLM, its transition from a rebel movement into a government (de Zeeuw 2008) and questions the extent to which this transition has occurred and its influence therefore on the wider restructuring of governance in the country.

It is necessary to deconstruct the various arguments surrounding post-conflict political consolidation and systematically apply them to South Sudan while examining their relevance, links and manifestation in the country's demilitarization. Although the links between democratic elections, democratic institutions and democratic governance and their role in consolidating peace (Bastian and Luckham 2003: 2) were central to the international liberal peacebuilding engagement in the country, the relationship between governance and democracy in South Sudan was not mutually exclusive. Subsequently, the growth and expansion of democratic practices did not result in the desired restructuring of governance or peace consolidation (Chadda 2000).

Examining the premise of elections in the country vis-à-vis the trajectory of demilitarization, it is important to question the significance placed on elections at the onset of democracy and peace consolidation (Carothers 2011; Grimm 2008; Jarstad and Sisk 2008; Lyons 2009). With South Sudan returning to war in December 2013, the presentations of elections as a safeguard against a return to conflict (Snyder 2010: 3) raises further questions. To a large extent, despite the importance placed on elective politics in post-conflict settings, if held too soon elections can serve as a revolving door back into conflict rather than as a stabilizer (Brinkerhoff 2005; de Zeeuw 2008; Grimm and Merkel 2008) as was the case in Angola with Jonas Savimbi in the 1990s (Snyder 2010).

Measures required include restructuring politics in the country by taking the military out of politics, growing political space illustrated by building political parties and, most importantly, removing the SPLA from the SPLM and growing democratic institutions and procedures like elections and referendum on independence. However, although the referendum on independence resulted in the ultimate restructuring of governance in South Sudan – its secession – this restructuring remains incomplete and primarily top-down (Rolandsen 2007: 15). There has in fact been little to no change in governance outside the national and state capitals (Rolandsen 2007: 13), although there have been some successes in the restructuring of governance with the building of some institutions and structures.

Restructuring governance

The charge of restructuring governance in a post-conflict country is a particularly complex one, but what exactly constitutes the restructuring of governance? Although on the one hand 'governance' is a word that has been used routinely over the course of many centuries to refer to the exercise of authority within a given sphere (de Alcántara 2002: 1), it is also a concept that is applied to many situations in which no formal political system can be found and so it can imply the existence of a political process. This is the case with the 'governance' of SPLA-held areas.

That 'governance' also involves building consensus or obtaining the consent or acquiescence necessary to exercise authority in an arena where many different interests are at play, not only added to the challenge but also brought forth the many approaches to governance (de Alcántara 2002: 1). These all have in common an understanding of governance that refers to the setting, application and enforcement of rules (Kjaer 2004; Pillora 2011). Anne Mette Kjaer suggests that these rules have to be legitimized, either through democracy or some form of efficiency (de Alcántara 2002; Kjaer 2004), and she draws a link between governance and democracy.

This is particularly important because democracy has not only become a prominent feature in the post-conflict reconstruction agenda, but it is also one of the strategies adopted by the international community (Diamond 2006;

Englebert and Tull 2008; Lyons 2004; Ottaway 2003)[2] as part of the post-conflict reconstruction effort. Indeed, Carrie Manning in an article on post-conflict elections in Bosnia and Herzegovina argues that elections have been at the centre of virtually every negotiated settlement to end a civil war since the end of the Cold War. They form an integral part of the de facto formula for internationally supported post-conflict state-building (Manning 2004: 2). As a more recent post-conflict country, South Sudan has been no exception and, as such, democracy has arguably been one of the strategies adopted in South Sudan's restructuring of governance. However, despite the weight placed on democracy by today's quest of the perfect post-conflict political system (Kjaer 2004), there is also a growing concern among governance theorists who argue that representative democracy on its own is increasingly inadequate in meeting the broad requirements of governance (Baral 2006: 13; Boudreau 2013: 3; Kjaer 2004; Norris 2012; Pillora 2011; Powers 2001: 184). Some of these inadequacies are present in the case of South Sudan and will be addressed later in this chapter.

Nonetheless, with all the different presentations of governance, this research presents governance normatively, and for the purpose of this research defines it as: the exercise of power to manage a nation's affairs (Mkandawire 2007: 679). The chapter thus sets out to explore the importance of the restructuring of the exercise of power in South Sudan and argues that it plays a fundamental role in the country's demilitarization.

Building or rebuilding governance?

After more than four decades of war in the south of Sudan, the destruction of war and a history of underdevelopment left the region with limited state infrastructure. In post-conflict South Sudan, this raised a number of questions on the restructuring of governance. These questions have evoked numerous debates on the state of governance in the country. At a training of election observers held in Torit in November 2009, a representative of the Southern Sudan civil society asked of the exercise on reforming and restructuring governance:

> Shouldn't this be building governance rather than restructuring governance? There is nothing here to restructure, we are building everything from the beginning.[3]

This assertion came up often in the course of the fieldwork and played a significant part in the shaping of this book. That South Sudan was starting the building of government infrastructure from zero post-2005 CPA was a fact that could not be ignored, especially in view of the fact that the restructuring of governance must be preceded by some sort of governance.[4] History of the Sudanese state as illustrated in Chapter 2 shows the persistent absence of a central government in Southern Sudan during the war years and the discontent that existed between the region and the government in Khartoum. However, the lack of central government control in the south saw the rebel movement, the SPLA/M, create parallel government structures in southern regions under their control.[5] An unlikely proposition, the SPLA/M indeed governed towns and villages in the southern hinterlands beyond the Government of Sudan's control while Khartoum kept control over the few garrison towns under its control. As such, despite the absence of a central government in the south, the presence of SPLA/M structures made up for the vacuum left by the absence of central government structures.[6] This exercise of governance by the SPLA/M during the Sudan civil war makes a significant contribution to addressing some of the research questions raised in this book.

The SPLA/M institutions and structures set up during the war also offer an insight into the governance of contemporary South Sudan. The SPLA governing structures and institutions, as the only available form of governing authority, were the blueprint for institutional behaviour, style and governing traditions that emerged in the south after the signing of the CPA. During the war, the SPLA not only built governing institutions, it also created an administrative structure in the areas under its control (Kevlihan 2013). Although the rebel structures and systems remained military, adhering to a top-down military command structure, they also exhibited a degree of sophistication.[7] They included local administrators known as commissioners, a humanitarian relief structure in the SPLA's relief wing – the Sudan Relief and Rehabilitation Association (SRRA)[8] – and customs and border control like in Nadapal, a border crossing town on the border between Kenya and South Sudan (Metelits 2010: 69; Rone 1996). The SPLA 'government' was especially visible for anyone dealing with the rebel movement or working in the rebel-controlled areas as Kevlihan (2013) observed:

> At first glance, the institutional configuration of the SPLA and the government of Sudan mirrored each other. Where the government had the Humanitarian Aid Commission (HAC) as their primary interlocutor with NGOs, the SPLA had its aid arm – the Sudan Relief and Rehabilitation Association (SRRA). Where HAC controlled the issuance of travel permits, the SPLA also issued visas to enter Southern Sudan. (Kevlihan 2013: 24)

The issuance of visas or travel permits in the south of Sudan by the SPLA/M and the disregard of visas issued by the Government of Sudan in SPLA-controlled areas was one indication of the rebel movement's authority in the territories it controlled. This continued even after the signing of the CPA with both parties continuing to issue different permissions for travel despite being part of one government of national unity. After the signing of the CPA, the creation of the Government of South Sudan (GOSS) as the authority over the south, being part of a national government of Sudan in which the president of Southern Sudan was also the national first vice president, entrenched and constitutionalized these dual systems of government.

As such, after the signing of the CPA, the government of Southern Sudan took over the issuance of visas from the SRRA. Empirical enquiry reveals that this played out outside the country as well. In the Kenyan capital Nairobi and Uganda's Kampala, for example, the government of Southern Sudan set up offices that worked parallel to the already existing Sudanese embassies. These offices, referred to as liaison offices for the southern Ministry of Regional Cooperation, took over the issuance of visas in post-CPA Southern Sudan. However, the visas remained, as officials called them, travel permits as they had been during the war with little differences between the two as illustrated in Figures 6.1 and 6.2. Although these were issued independently and not placed on the passport, their issuance was one of the elements of the administrative set-up of the SPLA/M passed on to the Government of Southern Sudan. More broadly, the SPLA/M was widely recognized by the people in areas under its control as the government, which is still reflected today in discussions with South Sudanese about administration during the war. In focus group discussion six, when the idea of the rebel movement as a government was queried by quoting the SuNDE elections observer, who felt that there had been no governance during the war and that the country was just starting to build governance, the participants disagreed. This focus group consisted of senior South Sudanese working for a USAID-funded democracy and governance NGO and on the matter they said:

> During the war, the SPLA ran a government which had structures and all these structures were all structures of governance, which means we are right to talk about the restructuring of governance today because we are improving what was there.[9]

This raises questions about how a rebel movement like the SPLA/M became the 'government' during the war. The answer to this is perhaps simply that the SPLA/M made itself the government. The rebel movement in 2002

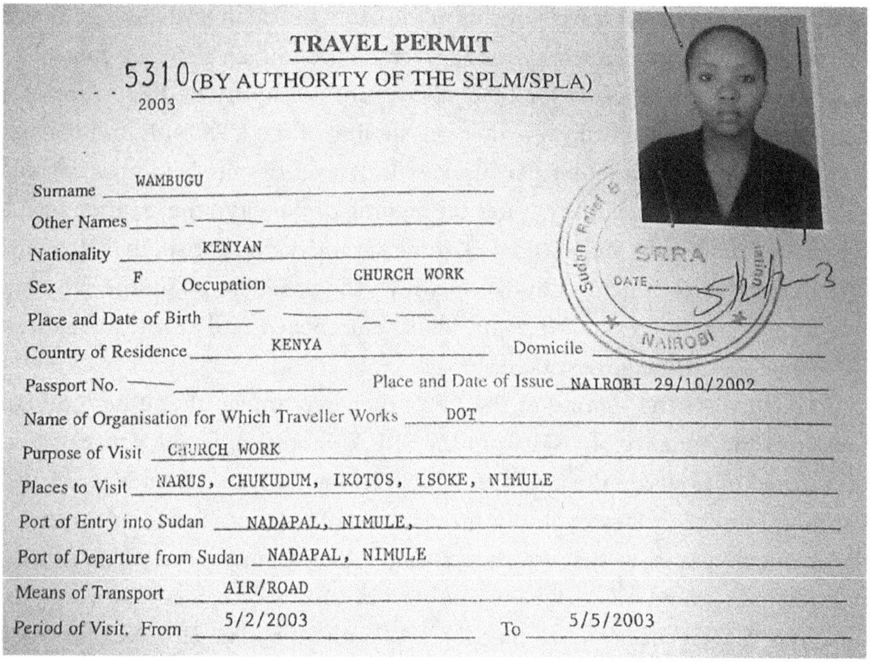

TRAVEL PERMIT

5310 (BY AUTHORITY OF THE SPLM/SPLA)
2003

Surname WAMBUGU

Other Names

Nationality KENYAN

Sex F Occupation CHURCH WORK

Place and Date of Birth

Country of Residence KENYA Domicile

Passport No. Place and Date of Issue NAIROBI 29/10/2002

Name of Organisation for Which Traveller Works DOT

Purpose of Visit CHURCH WORK

Places to Visit NARUS, CHUKUDUM, IKOTOS, ISOKE, NIMULE

Port of Entry into Sudan NADAPAL, NIMULE,

Port of Departure from Sudan NADAPAL, NIMULE

Means of Transport AIR/ROAD

Period of Visit. From 5/2/2003 To 5/5/2003

Sudan Relief ... SRRA DATE NAIROBI

Figure 6.1 Pre-2005 CPA travel permit.
Source: Nyambura Wambugu.

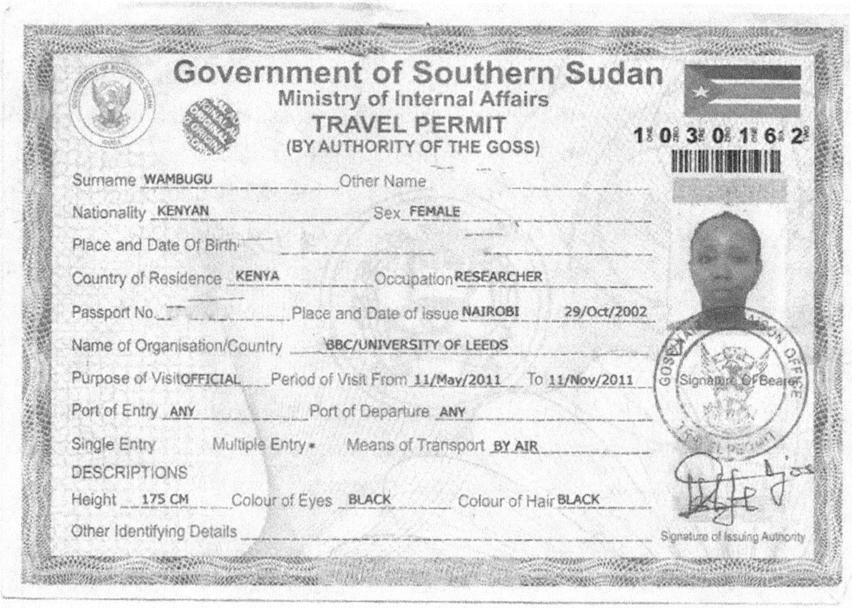

Government of Southern Sudan
Ministry of Internal Affairs
TRAVEL PERMIT
(BY AUTHORITY OF THE GOSS)

1 0 3 0 1 6 2

Surname WAMBUGU Other Name

Nationality KENYAN Sex FEMALE

Place and Date Of Birth

Country of Residence KENYA Occupation RESEARCHER

Passport No. Place and Date of issue NAIROBI 29/Oct/2002

Name of Organisation/Country BBC/UNIVERSITY OF LEEDS

Purpose of Visit OFFICIAL Period of Visit From 11/May/2011 To 11/Nov/2011

Port of Entry ANY Port of Departure ANY

Single Entry Multiple Entry Means of Transport BY AIR

DESCRIPTIONS

Height 175 CM Colour of Eyes BLACK Colour of Hair BLACK

Other Identifying Details

Signature Of Bearer

Signature of Issuing Authority

Figure 6.2 Post-CPA travel permit.
Source: Nyambura Wambugu.

declared that it alone possessed 'governmental' authority in areas it controlled (Metelits 2010: 69). This assertion made the SPLA/M the de facto government in Southern Sudan and point to the problems at the centre of this book: the legacies of the SPLA/M and a history of militarization that continues to beset contemporary South Sudan. Although this reaffirms the validity of the inclusion of the restructuring of governance as a major factor in the demilitarization of South Sudan, it also points to its greater challenge of removing the SPLA from government and governance in South Sudan which it founded. While the form of governance exercised by the SPLA/M in its territories may have been flawed, it was the only system many in the south knew and, as such, it was the norm. The challenge in contemporary South Sudan thus begins with attempts at completely re-engineering governance away from the military governance purported by the SPLA.[10]

However, in the constantly evolving politics of South Sudan, the role and influences of the military in southern politics are not always straightforward. Even less clear are the more recent overlaps of political and military conflicts in the country. They do, nevertheless, raise questions on the militarization of politics, government and governance in the country. This can be attributed to the dominance of military ethos in South Sudanese society which presents the greatest challenge to the restructuring of governance and more widely the aspirations for demilitarization. The militarization of South Sudan, be it conscious or sub-conscious, makes the country, its people and its politics especially versatile. This demands a rethink of the pursuit of governance in the country; a rethink that must work with the empirical reality that the country's military ethos may make political expediency more challenging in the country than would otherwise be the case.

Rethinking the restructuring of governance in South Sudan

The restructuring of governance in South Sudan is exemplified by the international liberal peacebuilding intervention in the country. The whole exercise, in many ways, is geared towards the institutionalization of the state and the planting and growing of liberal values in post-conflict South Sudan. However, all this starts by pulling back the sweeping influence of the military in a country which is profound as Rolandsen (2007) explains:

> In areas (mainly rural) held by SPLM/A for a longer period, wartime CANS[11] structures remain present to various degrees. Within these structures, there was no distinction between the SPLA/M and the administrative structures [...] therefore when establishing SPLM party and government structures at the local levels, the SPLM leaders will be attempting to redefine already existing channels of popular participation. (Rolandsen 2007: 11)

That the current civil administration in South Sudan evolved from a tradition of governance by the SPLA/M during the war years is perhaps an indication of the magnitude of the challenge ahead (LeRiche 2007). However, whereas the challenge starts with redressing the dominance of the military ethos in the political sphere, this must begin with addressing the balance of power from the army, the SPLA, to the SPLM, the ruling party.[12] According to a Catholic missionary who has worked in South Sudan for more than 30 years, this redress began with the end of the civil war.

However, the fieldwork questions the extent and success of this redress. In particular, the Catholic missionary who has lived through the different forms of government and governance in the south observed that although most of the people who took up Government of Southern Sudan positions were the same people who had held the positions in the SPLA administrations, there was a change in the way power was exercised, in that it was more legitimate and more absolute. After more than 30 years of interacting with the different power and governance structures in Southern Sudan, the missionary contends that the war was widely used as the justification and affirmation for the contemporary exercise of power.[13] This sentiment was shared by many people interviewed for this research. The feeling that the ruling class had attained absolute power with the end of the 1983–2005 Civil War, and with independence, was common. There was a feeling that the former rebel movement simply moved its power base from the barracks to government offices.[14] The SPLA officers therefore became SPLM officials, although to many it was more a game of musical chairs among the same SPLA/M officials.[15] This sentiment was echoed by senior South Sudanese employees of an international governance organization who participated in Focus Group 6 (FG 6). One participant felt that:[16]

> The restructuring of governance in South Sudan after the war has not been done with regard to what is best for the country or who is best placed to do the job for the benefit of the country or how to best serve the country, but rather it has been driven mainly by the need for appeasement. Government positions and institutions have been built as a reward for having fought the war. The

restructuring of governance has therefore been driven by giving dividends for the war effort and not by nation-building.[17]

The post-December 2013 intra-conflict in South Sudan was therefore arguably an extension of the struggle for power and the redistribution of the spoils of independence rather than about the pursuit of democracy. This reaffirms the assertions of military dominance to carve out political gains and while this can be viewed as a side effect of the country's history of militarization, it also generally illustrates South Sudanese everyday interactions with power in their individual communities. This has a direct impact on their perceptions and understanding of the exercise of power. Although the CPA structurally provided for some restructuring of governance by underwriting key events like the national census, voter registration, national elections and ultimately the referendum on independence into the peace agreement,[18] the process of restructuring governance in South Sudan went beyond these CPA hallmarks. These processes, however, collectively illustrate the difficulty facing the former rebel movement now the government is shifting from an exercise of power informed by the barrel of the gun to one that involves cross-societal consensus.[19]

The overarching influence of some of the CPA milestones like the census, national elections and referendum drove and dominated efforts aimed at the restructuring of governance in post-conflict South Sudan.[20] Still, the successful establishment of institutions, structures and procedures associated with the restructuring of governance like the legislature, judiciary and executive, both at the national level and in all the ten states, cannot be ignored. However, despite this, participants of FG 6 felt that in reality the restructuring of governance in the country was largely cosmetic. This sentiment was affirmed by interviews with senior government officials at the Ministry of Justice (Figure 6.3).

Public forums on democracy and governance held in the capital Juba restated the same. However, there was also a feeling that the building of government structures and institutions was one of the successes of restructuring and reform of governance attempts in post-conflict South Sudan.[21] In a joint public seminar held by the South Sudanese think tank the Sudd Institute, in conjunction with the German organization Friedrich-Ebert-Stiftung in the capital Juba, participants – mainly young men and women in formal education[22] – pointed at the establishment of institutions as the most tangible change in the country post-2005 CPA. Although participants of FG 6 held similar views, they also felt that despite these achievements in building institutions, there was still much to be done.

Figure 6.3 Flyer – democracy public forum in Juba, South Sudan.
Source: Nyambura Wambugu.

More specifically, that a total restructuring of governance in South Sudan was still necessary but was unlikely to happen because there was a lack of political will to see it through.[23] The conclusion of this FG 6 discussion was therefore that although a genuine restructuring of governance in South Sudan was necessary for the country to move forward, it would require a total change in the way South Sudan did its politics.[24] However, the group maintained that in view of the country's current political dispensation, this was unlikely to happen as the favour was in maintaining the status quo, where power remained with the SPLA through the SPLM and the small ruling class in Juba.[25] As such, this chapter argues that to reform and restrict governance in South Sudan, the effort must begin with understanding and addressing the relationship between the SPLA and the SPLM and, more importantly, delinking the two.

Building a party from the ashes of a rebel movement: from SPLA to SPLM

The complex relationship between the SPLA and the SPLM personifies not only politics in South Sudan but the very existence of the South Sudanese state. The political fallouts that turned into military fallouts at the end of 2013 are a clear indication of this. At the height of the post-December 2013 conflict, President Yoweri Museveni of Uganda, whose army was sent in to support the South Sudanese Army, attempted to explain this complex relationship at the fifth International Conference on the Great Lakes Region (ICGLR) in Luanda, Angola:

Recently, we had an outbreak of serious fighting in our young brother country of South Sudan. There are two versions of how that fighting started. The government says that there was an attempted coup which was defeated in Juba but spread to the provinces of Bentiu, Jonglei and Malakal. The opposition says that it is the government that provoked the fighting by trying to disarm some of the soldiers on a sectarian basis. The truth will come out with time. What is clear is that the problem started within the SPLM, the ruling party, as a power struggle. You detect ideological, organisational and disciplinary issues in this situation. Why should there be sectarian undertones or overtones in a political debate? Why should intraparty matters go public before they are resolved within the party?

The SPLM party should resolve their disagreements within those structures. If some people are not satisfied with the SPLM, they should go out and form another party and the government should neither stop them nor impede them. However, to turn a political problem into a military one, having mismanaged the political problem itself in the first place, is not acceptable. In my opinion, if Riek Machar had not planned a coup and it had all been mistakes on the government side, he could have done two things: withdraw to a remote area of the country to avoid attack and to start talks unconditionally so as to resolve the problem quickly and not to protract it.[26]

President Museveni's speech touched on some of the key issues in South Sudan's restructuring of governance, not only in the SPLA/SPLM relationship but the absorption of party politics into southern politics. Broadly, political parties and political party formation after conflict is one of the hallmarks of post-conflict political consolidation and a gem in the liberal crown. It not only provides for the rearrangement of political participation through political parties, but it also provides the political class with a vehicle to seek the legitimization of their rule by going through elections. This, however, can be a challenge, especially for countries coming out of prolonged conflicts like South Sudan. Here the challenge is not only one of political organization, but mainly of transforming stakeholders to the conflict into political entities. In South Sudan, this involved shifting the country's political focus from the SPLA to the SPLM. It also perhaps explains the power wrangling in the party and the unwillingness of parties to these conflicts to leave the SPLM to form another political party.

Looking at the history of the war in Sudan and the formation of political processes in the south in Chapters 2 and 3, it was clear that although often referred to as the SPLA/M with the A for army and M for movement, in reality the army and the movement were synonymous with each other.[27] Nonetheless, in the later years of the war, especially after the first SPLA/M convention in Chukudum in 1994, there was a shift in the movement with increasing reference to the SPLM as the political wing of the liberation movement. Despite this, the SPLM remained in the shadows, with the SPLA as the dominant partner (Nyaba 1997; Young 2007: 5). After the signing of the Comprehensive Peace Agreement, it was only after 2006 that the first steps towards establishing the SPLM as a proper political party were taken with the introduction of interim party structures.[28] In January 2007, the president of Southern Sudan, Salva Kiir, announced the year of the SPLM when launching the process of organizing the first party congresses at the grass roots. This was also the first time the party – the SPLM – had formally gone out to recruit members (Rolandsen 2007: 6). Still, it was not until May 2008 that the party held its second national party convention, 14 years after the first one in Chukudum in 1994. While this marked the beginning of the shift in focus from the SPLA to the SPLM in post-war South Sudan, it is also the case that like most former rebel groups turned governments, the sudden change in the SPLA/M was not entirely voluntary, but rather a result of global political and normative pressures to democratize (Metelits 2004).

The legitimacy of the former rebels' commitment to democracy is often questionable and South Sudan is no exception. This is evident in how the SPLA/M leadership interprets 'democracy' largely in Schumpeterian terms: more concerned with the procedures that the international community deems 'democratic' than with the outcomes (Metelits 2004). This is in tune with FG 6's assertions that the strides and gains in the restructuring and reform of governance in post-conflict South Sudan have been cosmetic and thinly spread. As such, although there seems to be a clear distinction between the SPLA and the SPLM in South Sudan's post-independence politics, perhaps brought on by international pressure and the liberal peacebuilding efforts in the country, in reality, the line between the two remains blurred. This came across in many of the interviews conducted during the fieldwork as illustrated by a Swiss diplomat working with the SPLA in training and restructuring. He explained:

> The SPLA and the SPLM are changing because we are telling them to. We want to deal with the government and party officials and not the generals. The only problem is that all directors I work with are all Brigadier Generals or Lieutenant Generals, but they are in government offices running states and commissions. (Interview with Swiss army officer, Swiss Embassy, Juba in July 2012)

The assertions in this interview are repeated many times over in interviews in Juba's diplomatic circles and are affirmed by my own observations. In my interactions with the SPLA and the SPLM, there was an attempt to draw a distinction between the two. The communications department of the SPLA in particular was keen to assert its role as an army under a civilian government,[29] while the SPLM-led government appeared to use the institutions of government to pass through legislations, especially those that pertain to war.[30] However, these progresses were then overshadowed by practice. The old military habits in South Sudan are arguably a default setting such that 'when important decisions have to be made, they are made by the security clusters in the party hierarchy and the government led by military men'[31] before they are handed down to the legislature to pass. Generally, as one SPLM Member of Parliament put it:

> Our party officials at the top organs were all commanders; even if some might not have been in the front line, they were commanders. We were all involved in the army. When we were in the bush, the only law was that of the army – even at the village level, chiefs were given military rank so that they were not harassed by the soldiers. There are some party officials today that might not have been in the front line, but still they were representing the movement abroad and were also installed as commanders and ranked accordingly.[32]

This interview perhaps summed up what this book observed to be a contradiction in the theory, rhetoric and practice of governance in post-CPA South Sudan, especially as pertains to the SPLA/M. Empirical observations have been that while the Government of South Sudan and the ruling party the SPLM have worked to create a party structure and the impression of a separation of powers through institutions of parliament, executive and judiciary, the reality tells a different story. The reality tells the story of an SPLM/SPLA that is still intricately linked. This reality was particularly reflected in the interviews with people working closely with the different structures of governance in the country. Although the assertions in these interviews were largely opinions, they were opinions of people working on issues of governance in South Sudan and, as such, perhaps offer some insight into the exercise of governance. They present that:

> The shift in emphasis from the SPLA to the SPLM has been one of the biggest changes in post-conflict South Sudan, but I'm not sure in reality it has happened. I believe the president and some generals in the SPLM Political Bureau are still running this country. (Interview with IRI Programme Officer in February 2013)

> The SPLA still works as the SPLM's private army and the SPLM takes its orders from the SPLA. The party does not do anything without directions from the army; that's just the reality. (Interview with a manager in a private security company in November 2012)

> There is no difference between the SPLA and the SPLM; all top government officials are all military men. They wouldn't get those jobs if they were not. (Interview with a South Sudanese CEO of a private media company in September 2011)

Interviewed up to eight years since the signing of the peace agreement in 2005, these interviews, although a drop in the ocean, suggest that the SPLM had not moved from the shadow of the SPLA.[33] The extended fieldwork and the empirical observations in this book further affirm this, especially in the divergence between public rhetoric and practice. Whereas military officials interviewed in public were keen to show a distinct separation between the army and the movement,[34] in private they concede that this was not the case. One army officer offered:

> We liberated this country by our guns. We must also make sure we protect it, especially from those returning and taking our peace for granted.[35]

The literature on the post-2005 period also illustrates a lack of distinction between the SPLA and the SPLM. Rolandsen (2007), for example, in assessing the progress made by the SPLM in transforming from a guerrilla movement to a political party and its domination in the run-up to the April 2010 elections writes:

> It is difficult to imagine that parties other than the SPLM/A would be able to gain any significant influence in the countryside. (Rolandsen 2007: 11)

Most writers on South Sudan still referred to the SPLM/A when writing about the party, the SPLM, notably, not differentiating the A – army from the M – movement (political party). Although a subtle assertion, it is one that illustrates the inherent link that still exists between the two. As such, there are questions as to whether it is possible to delink the SPLA and the SPLM. This addresses some of the research questions, especially why the application of prevailing post-conflict paradigms like liberal peacebuilding has been challenging in South Sudan. Similarly, how the evolution of South Sudan's post-conflict politics has influenced its demilitarization. Attempting to answer both questions raised by this book requires a bottom-up approach rather than a top-down one. On the question of how demilitarization affects present-day peacebuilding, and the extent to which demilitarization can deliver societal post-conflict civil–military relations and the possibility to achieve this post-conflict societal transformation with an illiterate and non-urban population, this research asserts that interventions must go beyond perceptions. That if the measure of success on the different components of demilitarization is based on perceived success rather than real changes, then South Sudan's demilitarization would exist only on paper but unrealized in the country.

The danger of perceived success rather than real changes continues to be shared among party officials and ordinary citizens, again raising the fear that the SPLA/SPLM transition has been cosmetic. This perhaps stems from an even greater concern in the pursuit of international liberal peacebuilding and its aspiration for the SPLM to be the dominant entity in the SPLA/SPLM matrix (de Zeeuw 2008: 156). Nevertheless, the success of the restructuring of governance in the country is still dependent on the successful transformation of the SPLA/SPLM balance of power. Although the shift from the SPLA to the SPLM was immediate after the signing of the 2005 CPA, in reality the shift never occurred. The lines between the SPLA and the SPLM remained blurred as South Sudanese society arguably still treats them as different sides of the same coin. In a cycle of overlapping roles, soldiers say they are SPLM, the SPLM is the government and the government is both.[36] Consequently, the blurred lines between the SPLM and the SPLA undermine the whole exercise of restructuring governance in the country. Nonetheless, it is also the case that managing such a transition and the transformation of an armed rebel movement into a political party is arguably one of the hardest peacebuilding challenges there is, especially when the transition is done alongside a multitude of other transitions into democracy and multiparty politics (de Zeeuw 2008: 156).

Despite this challenge, the extent of the SPLA dominance in the SPLA/M dual act in South Sudan is unparalleled. Still, even from under the shadow of the army, the SPLM dominated South Sudan's multiparty political system, holding over 90 per cent of parliamentary seats in the country.[37] It is, however, not surprising for political parties affiliated to former rebels in post-conflict elections to exert this kind of dominance. The success of similar parties can be found elsewhere like the ANC in post-apartheid South Africa and in El Salvador, among others. However, their success is never a foregone conclusion as the Revolutionary United Front Party (RUFP) in Sierra Leone lost the post-conflict elections in 2002 as did Angola's UNITA in 1998.

SPLM dominance: undemocratic democracy?

As the dominant political party in post-conflict South Sudan, the SPLM is also the governing party. As such, the development of the SPLM party structures was seen by many international peacebuilders as the first step in reorganizing the politics of the country.[38] The international intervention effort in the country especially paid considerable attention to the party and to helping it create 'proper' party structures with the belief:

> If the SPLM changes, then it will change the government and the country. But if the SPLM does not change, then nothing else will change. What the SPLM does for the party, it does the same for the country.[39]

There is credence to this assertion, that despite more than a dozen political parties in post-independence South Sudan, almost all were arguably briefcase parties that existed only on paper, with few members and questionable structures and institutions. However, American organizations International Republican Institute (IRI) and National Democratic Institute (NDI) invested heavily in developing political parties, party systems and electoral democracy in South Sudan with the SPLM being the main recipient of this investment. As the ruling party, in control of 90 per cent of the national legislature and the country's oil revenues, the SPLM's dominance in South Sudanese political society was entrenched despite its incomplete divorce from the SPLA. Still, there are assertions that the SPLM's dominance is, in part, made possible by its links to the SPLA.

The SPLM and its journey from the shadows of the SPLA thus mark a significant juncture in South Sudan's restructuring of governance. These links are especially important in assessing the state of governance in post-conflict South Sudan. More importantly, though, are the legacies that precede them, that arguably account for the incomplete divorce between the two. Similarly, it seems that the SPLM, as the dominant political party, is still dominated by soldiers and an administration-based military ethos and traditions (de Zeeuw 2008: 159).[40] These notwithstanding, some of the challenges facing the SPLM, like the lack of a clear political ideology, are resonant with its past where the movement shifted ideology and doctrines to ensure external backing (Cordesman 1993; ICG 2002).

In its early days, for example, the SPLA/M adopted a Marxist-Leninist socialist agenda (Johnson 2003: 62–63; Sidahmen and Sidahmen 2005: 42–43; Soderlund 2008: 74) influenced by its then backers, the Derg.[41] However, when Mengistu was overthrown in 1992 at the end of the Cold War, the SPLM/A shifted its ideology and aligned itself to Christian groups mainly in the United States (de Zeeuw 2008: 156; Young 2006: 19). Soderlund (2008) perceives these shifts in ideology to be tactical and strategic by an SPLA/M leadership which he argues to have been more pragmatic than ideological (Soderlund 2008: 74). The effects are thus the lack of formative political ideologies in South Sudan's modern political history. Subsequently, the semi-autonomous government formed in Southern Sudan after the signing of the peace agreement in 2005 came to power with not only little experience, but also with the lack of a clear political ideology to root it. This has continued to be one of the greatest critiques of the SPLM-led government often accused of lacking in ideological direction.[42]

However, despite having established administrative structures in SPLA-controlled areas during the war, the SPLA/M, which formed the regional Government of Southern Sudan at the signing of the CPA, was largely inexperienced in governance. This inexperience plagued the SPLM throughout the six-year transitional period. Despite this, the SPLM at the same time became the recipient of the southern share of oil revenues from the national government in Khartoum. This mix of inexperience and extensive access to funds with little institutional oversight arguably set the stage for the misrule, corruption and conflicts that have beset South Sudan since independence. Being in the SPLM and close to the centre of power automatically translated into access to South Sudan's new found oil revenues and the multitude of donor funding aimed at supporting the country's post-conflict reconstruction efforts.

This redefined the SPLA/M dominance in South Sudan and further institutionalized it by devolving state power to predominantly SPLM-appointed legislatures and administrative structures, effectively installing a one-party state. Attempts at pulling back some of the SPLM's dominance witnessed in the push for multi-partism in the country were therefore futile. At the national level, the SPLA/M was the co-signatory of the peace agreement and, as such, to all intents and purposes, the only legally recognized entity in the political process in the south. The exclusion of other southern entities outside the SPLM is thus, arguably, not only one of the critiques of the CPA but also the act that institutionalized SPLA/M domination. For the most part, this domination left the SPLA/M to write the initial nation state narratives of South Sudan's birth unchallenged. These narratives formed the trajectory the country took after independence in 2011 and arguably borrowed heavily from the Republic of Sudan, especially the democratic deficits and securitization approach to governance.[43]

As part of the national government in Khartoum, there are those who argue that in the six years' interim period that the SPLM were partners with President Omar al-Bashir's NCP, it not only learned the NCP style of governance, but embraced and adopted it in the south. The NCP dominance in northern politics and the securitization of politics that is characteristic of Khartoum was replicated in the south by the SPLM. However, there are still those who feel that filled with mistrust, the SPLM indeed learned nothing from its northern partners. On this, a consultant working with the Government of South Sudan presents:

> The time that the SPLA/M officials spent working in Khartoum and national government should have been sufficient to gain some experience of running a country and then lack of experience would not be used so often as an excuse for bad governance.[44]

Still, another argument persists, that of an SPLM that learned what it needed to dominate, control and guide the south into independence. Overwhelmingly, most people interviewed, with regards to the role of the SPLM in the post-independence period in this study, said that the SPLM's biggest task at that time was not primarily to govern Southern Sudan but to see it to its independence. This meant remaining the majority and dominant party in the south which, according to a senior SPLM party official, was important in order to 'counter NCP manipulations in the south'. This required the SPLM winning the elections in April 2010 and ensuring a successful referendum on independence in January 2011.[45] These were fundamental requirements of the CPA, central not only to the restructuring of power in the country, but also to the legitimatization of the power already held by the government of Southern Sudan through its nominated officials and guaranteed through the SPLA.

This was particularly important as, at the signing of the peace agreement, government posts and parliamentary seats were shared according to fixed quotas between the two signatories, the National Congress Party (NCP) and the SPLM (Dargatz 2011: 2). However, at the time of the April 2010 elections, there was growing resentment[46] against officials appointed through these quotas. In the south, many of them at the time of the elections in April 2010 had been in office for over five years. The absolute power exercised by many of these SPLM-appointed leaders bordered on undemocratic and illustrated a continuum of the SPLA/M war years' style of governance.[47] The April 2010 elections were therefore seen as the first real chance for the restructuring of post-conflict governance in Southern Sudan, and thus the stakes were high.

The elections

> Sudan's political culture is a zero-sum game in which any gains by one side are necessarily seen as a loss by the other. Today, the two principal parties are on the

defensive, mutually sizing each other up, testing one another and assuming the worst of one another. (de Waal 2010: 13)

This was the background that preceded Sudan's first national election which took place on 11–15 April 2010. However, the holding of elections as part of the post-conflict reconstruction effort is not unique to South Sudan as post-conflict elections are considered a turning point in the recovery and reconstruction of countries emerging from civil war (Snyder 2010; Thomas 2009: 10). In countries like Mozambique, Namibia, Sierra Leone, Liberia, El Salvador, Nicaragua and Cambodia, elections were an integral part of the post-conflict narrative (Kuhne 2010: 2) and the Sudan followed on the same trajectory. The elections in South Sudan, like many in post-conflict countries, were central to the realigning and restructuring of governance in the country (Willis and El-Battahani, 2010: 192). In the case of the Sudan and, in particular, in Southern Sudan, the elections were particularly important as they provided the first real sense of the people engaging with the peace process through political participation.[48] As the post-CPA government was wholly appointed as part of the negotiated settlement in the CPA, the 2010 elections, especially in the south, were seen as an essential part of the legitimatization of the new political dispensation.

The post-CPA appointments in both the north and the south had provided for the creation of not only a national government, but also the creation of the semi-autonomous Government of South Sudan. While the signatory to the CPA nominated members to the national government and the national assembly in Khartoum, in the south, the SPLA/M nominated members of the Government of Southern Sudan both at the national and state level. More generally, the April 2010 elections allowed the citizens in the south to elect their leaders for the first time.[49] Although before the 2010 elections there had been 17 other national elections held in the Sudan after 1967, none had ever fully included the south, although they purported to (Dargatz 2011: 3). This was evident in the fieldwork when few in the focus group discussions outside the urban areas understood what elections really were and what their intention was.[50] Answers to the question, 'Why did you vote?' were varied and the further away from the urban centres, the more inconsistent the answers were. The following extracts of two FGs illustrate this. Participants of FG 1 were secondary school students in Isoke, a town centre, while participants of FG 5 were men in a village in Mogos, EES.

While these findings are just a reflection of two focus groups out of six, they are representative of answers to the same question (see Appendix 2 for all focus group data). Although participants of FG 1 illustrated a better understanding and

Table 6.1 Focus Group 1 data extract

Focus Group 1 – 13/06/11
Isoke St Augustine Secondary School
Participants: 3 female, 10 males
Q. Did you vote?
• Everyone except one had voted in both the election in April 2010 and the referendum in January 2011
Q. Why did you vote?

Participant	Answers
Male 1, Female 2, Male 6	To have freedom
Male 2, Male 9	I voted to get the right leaders
Male 3, Male 4	I voted because it's my right to get the right leaders
Male 5, Male 10	I voted to be like other countries
Female 3, Male 11, Male 7	I voted to have democracy
Male 8, Female 1	So that we could be like other countries

Table 6.2 Focus Group 5 data extract

Focus Group 5 – 19/07/11
Mogos, Lokochot Village, Kapoeta South County
Participants: 6 males
Q. Did you vote?
• All said they voted in the referendum on independence
Q. Why did you vote?

Participants	Answer
Male 1	Because of the Sudan
Male 2	So that Toposa land can be free from the enemy
Male 3	We want to settle peacefully without a problem
Male 4	Because someone was trying to cheat us and this is our land
Male 5	Because we want the land to be ours
Male 6	So that we separate from the Arabs and our land becomes ours

participation in the April 2010 elections, the same cannot be said of participants of FG 5 held in a village away from an urban centre. In FG 5, participants showed a localization of issues that participants perceived to be the reason for their participation, both in the April 2010 elections and January 2011 referendum. In fact, there was a lack of understanding of even the basic procedures associated with the elections (Dargatz 2011: 6). This especially interacts with the research questions on whether it is possible to achieve post-conflict societal transformation with an illiterate and non-urban population. More specifically, are there any tangible gains to the liberal peace-informed pursuit of elections in communities and societies where there is little comprehension of the liberal principles it seeks to entrench and reaffirm? Still, procedurally, the significance of the elections could not be overlooked because for all the people interviewed, these were the first elections they had ever taken part in. This was the case not only in former SPLA-held areas, but also in former garrison towns like Kapoeta and Torit, which had been under the government of Sudan administration and would have been eligible to participate in previous elections in the Sudan.

The importance placed on the April 2010 elections was therefore colossal, not least because they were the first truly national elections, but also because they were written into the peace agreement.[51] The entrenchment of elections in the CPA was one of the strategies adopted to move the country forward.[52] In the peace agreement, the holding of elections was set as a precondition for the holding of the referendum on independence. This perhaps helps shed some light on the emphasis that was placed on the elections by both parties to the CPA. For the south, the SPLA/M insisted that elections had to be held because not holding them was an impediment to the referendum.[53] For the Government of Sudan and the ruling party, the NCP, the elections were a half-hearted affair that they found themselves pushed into; hence, the postponement of the elections twice and the constant accusation by the south of a lack of political will on the part of the NCP to hold them.[54] Writing on the paradoxes of elections in Sudan, the Enough Project summed this up:

> The NCP, under heightened pressure, views elections as both a threat and an opportunity. The party is broadly unpopular and has much to fear from any ballot that genuinely opens Sudan's constricted political space. However, the NCP agreed to elections during CPA negotiations, hoping that they could head a political partnership with the SPLM that would draw democratic support and gain international legitimacy while simultaneously subordinating the SPLM's national ambitions and reducing SPLM presence in power-sharing institutions. (O'Brien 2009: 6)

The elections in April 2010 were therefore not just another piece in the post-conflict narrative jigsaw in the Sudan; they were a vital component in the successful implementation of the peace agreement.[55] They were a litmus test for the Sudan as to whether they would usher the country across a threshold that would consolidate peace and democracy or serve as a revolving door that could spin the country back into war. The immense mistrust between the two major parties – the SPLM and the ruling party NCP (Snyder 2010) – made the threat of returning back to war very real. This made the overwhelming importance placed on these elections a zero-sum game that bore great influence in the second restructuring of governance in the south.[56] The first restructuring of the post-CPA-appointed government of Southern Sudan is often argued to have been illegitimate but necessary.[57] Nevertheless, the post-CPA government, legitimate or not, ushered in a new era of governance and set the stage for the second restructuring of governance embodied by the elections.

This went beyond local politics as 'credible elections in the Sudan were a central component in the multilateral strategy to help the Sudanese people fundamentally alter how their country is governed' (O'Brien 2009: 2). In particular, the elections played a monumental role in setting up the referendum on independence in which perimeters in the excise of power in the Sudan were permanently determined. Despite the importance placed on these elections, they were postponed twice, which ultimately resulted in a hurried election marred by serious irregularities that were largely ignored and swept under the carpet.[58] It is here that the impact of elections in South Sudan's demilitarization became clear. Those who felt aggrieved by the elections process and the failure to resolve election irregularities had a significant impact on South Sudan's demilitarization or lack of demilitarization in the post-CPA era. Election irregularities and flaws, especially in the Greater Upper Nile regions, resulted in former political aspirants abandoning the political processes and returning to armed rebellion. Therefore while the April 2010 elections provided much needed legitimacy for the political engagements in the country, the elections also fulfilled the revolving door back into conflict critique associated with post-conflict elections. This seriously affected the trajectory of demilitarization and peace consolidation in South Sudan and arguably provided the basis for contemporary security complexes post-CPA. However, although the April 2010 elections created significant obstacles to demilitarization, they were still, arguably, a significant part of the restructuring of governance aspiration which is an important component of demilitarization.

A flawed election and resurgence of armed rebellions in South Sudan

The importance placed on the April 2010 elections played a significant role in how the elections were handled. Empirical inquiry[59] points to a lack of confidence in the Sudan's and especially the south's preparedness and readiness to hold the election in 2010 (O'Brien 2009). The Southern Sudan High Elections Committee chairperson in Torit, in the run-up to the elections in a telephone interview, conceded that 'the elections will be done because they have to be done. But we are facing a lot of challenges. Some of the material is late. The rainy season in some places has started early and our officials are having difficulty reaching them. But we shall manage.'[60] The importance placed on the elections within the context of the CPA was nonetheless well-understood, as was the lack of preparedness attributed to it. A common charge was that the ruling party – the NCP – made little preparation for the elections through the National Elections Commission (NEC) as an attempt to derail the election and, by extension, the wider peace process (Curless 2011; Jooma 2011). Although the elections were finally held after being postponed twice, they were largely flawed and marred by irregularities, which Anja Dargatz, writing on elections and conflict in Sudan, observed as:

> ranging from logistical deficiencies – such as the late arrival of ballot papers, late opening of polling stations and incorrect ballot forms and lists – to more politically motivated practices such as intimidation, not allowing party agents to observe, instructions given to voters to vote for the NCP by staff at the polling stations (the same for SPLM in the south), allowing children to vote, pitching of NCP tents close to polling stations and even the systematic completion of ballot papers by polling staff (a video spread worldwide on YouTube made this famous). (Dargatz 2011: 4)

While Dargatz (2011) contends that most of the illegal practices were observed in the north, done by (or in favour of) the NCP, she also points at serious fraud observed in the south among competing SPLM candidates (Dargatz 2011: 4). This was particularly the case in the Greater Upper Nile and western Equatoria regions,[61] but it was also widespread across the wider south (Carter Centre Report 2010: 166). Though there were numerous reports of irregularities, including an acknowledgement that the elections were neither free nor fair, they were still viewed as a success. A newspaper article in the *Sudan Tribune* on 19 April 2010 stated:

> The United States said today that the elections held in Sudan over the last week were 'neither free nor fair' and suggested that it has now shifted its focus to the 2011 referendum for the south in accordance with the Comprehensive Peace Agreement (CPA) signed between the north and the south. (*Sudan Tribune* 19 April 2010 – Washington)

The same article went on to quote the then US State Department spokesman P. J. Crowley as saying:

This was not a free and fair election. It did not, broadly speaking, meet international standards. That said, I think we recognise that the election is a very important step towards carrying out the 2005 peace deal that gave the south autonomy, a share of oil revenues and a route to independence via a referendum by January 2011. (*Sudan Tribune* 19 April 2010 – Washington)

After the elections, observers' reports from the Carter Centre, the European Union (EU), the African Union, IGAD, the Sudanese Group for Democracy and Elections (SuGDE) and the Sudanese Network for Democratic Elections (SuNDE) all indicated that the Sudan elections fell short of international standards; that they were marred by poor preparation and irregularities, but, like Crowley, they subsequently called on Sudanese officials to fully implement the 2005 peace accord[62] (The Carter Centre – Final Report 2010; O'Brien 2009; SuNDE 2010).

Arguably, the importance placed on reaching the referendum resulted in the international community and regional players ignoring irregularities in the April 2010 elections. In the Sudan, the argument carried the day that even when the electoral process is manipulated, elections still offer an alternative to violence and serve as a strategy to institutionalize authority without war and gradually regularize electoral politics (Snyder 2010: 2). Unfortunately, the decision to overlook the electoral malpractices and manipulations by the NCP in the north and the SPLM in the south only entrenched their dominance. In Southern Sudan, the dominance of the SPLM continues to have a serious impact on the restructuring of governance in the south.[63] Whereas the CPA had, to some extent, mitigated the SPLM dominance by providing some quotas to represent all the marginal political groupings in the country, the April 2010 elections changed all this. On this, an IRI programme officer working with political parties in South Sudan in an interview said:

> There were more political parties and other groups in parliament and government institutions in the CPA-appointed government because it provided quotas, but with the elections the SPLM became dominant and completely wiped all the other parties from parliament, both nationally and at state level. There are fewer non-SPLM members in parliament and even fewer in government institutions like government commissions which should be all inclusive.

Was this intentional on the part of the SPLM?
> No. The SPLM in the elections of 2010 was elected overwhelmingly. They just trampled over all the smaller parties that had been in parliament because the CPA had accommodated them.

How did the SPLM do this?

The people were grateful that the war was over and, for many, the SPLM is the only party they know. Other parties that might have been in parliament because of the CPA had little visibility outside Juba and so, when people came to elections, they elected the SPLM. Even with all the economic problems, if an election was held today, the SPLM would still win about 80 per cent of the votes.

Although the intended purpose of post-conflict elections is to offer the country an alternative way of doing politics and opening up democratic space,[64] in some countries like in South Sudan, elections can have the different effect of legitimizing dominance. This is one of the challenges of competitive elections; on the one hand, they offer the country an alternative way of doing politics and in the case of the Sudan, it was a departure from the norm of armed rebellions and counter-rebellions that had dogged the country since its independence.[65] On the other hand, electoral competition can lead back to conflict, especially when the election loser chooses to escalate election disputes rather than accept the results (Lyons 2004: 147–9, 152–7; Mansfield and Snyder 2008; Snyder 2010: 2; Stedman and Lindberg 2006: 15). In the case of the Sudan, the April 2010 elections, especially in the south, resulted in what is now commonly referred to as post-election insurrections.[66] Political competitors, who were all former military men, unhappy with the elections, launched rebellions against the government. These insurrections, at a time when the south was preparing for the referendum on independence, compounded a fear that the south would slide back into war and would become yet another case where post-conflict elections provided the 'revolving' door back into conflict.

Elections and the re-emergence of war

The revolving door argument thus illustrates the limitations of elections and the wider liberal peace thesis on which they are based. However, the contribution of elections to the wider post-conflict restructuring of governance also cannot be ignored. In countries like Namibia, Mozambique, Sierra Leone and Liberia, elections have been used as successful tools in peace consolidation. As in these countries, 'post-conflict elections can jump-start the democratization process by offering all citizens the opportunity to be involved' (Goldsmith 2005: 12). In the Sudan, despite the flaws and irregularities, the election was also largely seen[67] as a critical step in consolidating the peace (O'Brien 2009) at least at the macro-level between the two signatories to the CPA, the NCP and SPLM/A. Still, in the case of Southern Sudan, the election also resulted in new armed rebellions (see Appendix 4), which was indicative of a failure in peace consolidation at the micro-level.[68]

The use of elections as a platform for restarting armed rebellions is not unique to South Sudan. In 1990, following elections after the protracted civil war in Angola, rebel leader Jonas Savimbi of UNITA restarted the civil war when he lost the elections (Boas and Dunn 2007). This illustrates the thin line between the success or failure of using elections as a tool of restructuring governance in post-conflict countries and the challenge of using elections as a guarantee for lasting peace. Nonetheless, there is also a realization that competitive elections held in the early stages of democratization can lead directly to major civil wars (Snyder 2010: 3). Still, the proponents of competitive politics as a hallmark of post-conflict reconstruction argue that elections offer the only real hope of realigning power and politics in a post-conflict country. Essentially, despite the acknowledgement that elections at the initial phase of a democratic transition bring with them a heightened risk of civil war (Goldstone et al. 2005; Hegre et al. 2001), the prevailing liberal peace approach to post-conflict reconstruction seems to perceive them as a risk worth taking. In South Sudan, in spite of the armed insurrections that followed the elections, they were essentially a meaningful first step in the country's restructuring of governance.[69] One interviewee suggested:

> The restructuring of governance in South Sudan meant restructuring the movement which was a rebel army. This certainly meant dividing it into three separate functions and entities: the military, the government including the executive and legislative branches and the political party. Transforming the SPLA/M into all three of these was a very difficult challenge – the elections was the first time there was an indication that the three were indeed separate.[70]

The elections, therefore, while they resulted in legitimizing SPLM governance and more generally its dominance, they were also the first real attempt at a restructuring of governance in South Sudan (O'Brien 2009). This was also the first time that the country looked beyond its military traditions.[71] The elections, therefore, made a significant contribution to South Sudan's demilitarization processes which broadly engage with the dominance of military traditions in the country. Although the SPLM still scored a major victory in the elections, the 2010 elections also forced the party to think about its dominant position and not take it for granted.[72] From this premise, the April 2010 elections, despite providing the revolving door back into conflict in post-CPA Southern Sudan, also provided the first steps towards South Sudan's engagement with democratic practices and the building of democratic institutions and procedures which are an essential part of the complex web that weaves together elections and democracy.

Democratizing governance

Democracy and elections, especially in post-conflict countries, often exist alongside each other. Democracy has particularly gained prominence in the post-conflict reconstruction nexus and in South Sudan has not been an exception. After the signing of the peace agreement, many donors, and especially the United States Agency for International Development (USAID), concentrated mainly on building democracy.[73] American organizations the International Republican Institute (IRI) and the National Democratic Institute (NDI) mentioned earlier in this chapter led the way. However, apart from these politically inclined American organizations, other INGOs arriving in South Sudan as part of the international peacebuilding efforts also directly or indirectly contributed to the 'democratic' pursuit.[74] The idea that democracy should empower citizens and help them overcome exclusion (Bastian and Luckham 2003: 1) is broadly one of the viable outcomes of the liberal peace onslaught. It is especially a persuasion that is widely acceptable in the post-conflict pursuit of 'democracy'. For example, the pursuit of democracy in South Sudan accounted for more than 80 per cent of the USAID budget spend in the country.[75] Still, the irony of the vigorous pursuit of democracy in a country with no social economic structures is not lost on Bastian and Luckham (2003), for example, arguing that:

> Democracy can contribute to the prevention and resolution of violent conflict, both through democratic institutions and through democratic political institutions that can provide procedures under which conflicts can be managed through negotiation and debate rather than violence. Democratic politics can pose democracy. And democracy can encourage good governance alongside social justice, more inclusive government, the rule of law and other values as substantive political demands to counter the narrower agendas of the conflicting parties. (Bastian and Luckham 2003: 5)

Although the prominence given to democracy in post-conflict liberal peacebuilding has propelled it beyond its historical struggles against despotic rule and social injustice (Luckham, Goetz and Kaldor 2003: 15), its new use also comes with new critiques. The emphasis on building a Western-style democracy to which elections are central is particularly central to this critique (de Waal 2010; Ottaway 2007). More broadly, this is also the critique to liberal peacebuilding and one of the anomalies that this book examines. Even with its current status promising peace and stability, the pursuit of liberal principles in the construction of post-conflict states is still widely perceived as an imposition of Western ideals on fragile post-conflict countries usually disregarding local conditions. Some of these critiques have already been tackled in Chapter 1 and elsewhere in this book. However, the pursuit of liberal principles in post-conflict countries and their successes and failings are not entirely a new subject for discussion. On this matter, a number of scholars offer different views, including Marina Ottaway who argues:

> Coercive democratisation as practised since the early 1990s has not been a successful method to seal agreements and consolidate shaky peace in countries emerging from conflict. (Ottaway 2007: 614)

On the same thing, Alex de Waal in a 2010 essay proposed that:

> International state builders begin with a blueprint of what a modern country ought to look like, and how it ought to be run: Afghanistan needs to become more like Austria and Sudan more like Sweden. […] The economists and political scientists who advise international institutions argue that no country should follow its own unique rules, and human rights advocates insist there should be no second-hand solutions for countries just because they are poor and war-torn. Too often, the same coterie of international civil servants decamps from contracts in Kosovo to East Timor to Liberia, bringing with them the same working culture and the same formula for state-building. (de Waal 2010: 28)

Although de Waal is writing more recently, the same critique was levelled in Eastern Europe after the Balkans War:

> In Bosnia and Herzegovina, outsiders do more than participate in shaping the political agenda – something that has become the norm throughout Eastern Europe, as governments aspire to join the European Union. In Bosnia and Herzegovina, outsiders actually set that agenda, impose it and punish with sanctions those who refuse to implement it. (Knaus and Martin 2003: 61)

These types of critiques point at some of the empirical challenges that generic democratization programmes are likely to encounter in South Sudan. The most prominent of these challenges, this research presents, is the realization of liberal principles in a country where the political space is shaped and dominated by military norms and attitudes. The other big challenge is the promotion of liberal principles to remote and isolated populations who may not understand them due to illiteracy.

Changing military structures and attitudes

The lack of understanding of liberal terms and pursuits may also explain the dominance of the military culture, norms and attitudes which present the most daunting challenge to South Sudan's restructuring governance. The challenge, nonetheless, lies not only in attempting to change the structures of governance from military to democratic ones but more in changing attitudes from the absolute, top-down command of the military to a civil and consultative system.[76] After more than four decades of war, South Sudan was structured in military terms (Rolandsen 2007). As such, even after the CPA, military credentials still carried a lot of weight and favour in the new government.[77] The favour carried by military credentials was particularly discussed in Focus Group 6[78] in which participants noted that having military credentials was one of the main criteria used unofficially in allocating positions of power and influence in post-2005 South Sudan.[79] The focus group particularly pointed to the distribution of power in South Sudan's ten states pre-December 2013, where from ten state governors only two did not have military titles (Table 6.3).

In the Government until the sacking of Riek Machar in 2013, both the president and the vice president had military titles. The president was a general

Table 6.3 South Sudan's Governors

State Governors	
Eastern Equatoria Brig Gen Aloisio Emor	**Central Equatoria** Maj Gen Clement Wani Konga
Jonglei Lt Gen Kuol Manyang Juluk	**Lakes** Lt Gen Daniel Awet Akot
Northern Bahr el Ghazal Maj Gen Paul Malong Awan	**Upper Nile** Maj Gen Galuak Deng Garang
Unity Brig Gen Taban Deng Gai	**Warrap** Mr Toor Deng Mawien
Western Bahr el Ghazal Gen (Police). Mark Nyipuoch	**Western Equatoria** Mrs Jemma Nunu Kumba

Source: UN OCHA (correct as of June 2013).

while Vice President Machar was a lieutenant general, again illustrating the prominence of the military in the country. Although the ministers have shed their military titles, they were all active in the liberation movement,[80] either directly on the front line or in the diaspora dispensing other duties.[81] Still, even with the replacement of military uniforms with suits, it was the case that on 16 May every year, when celebrating SPLA Day now dubbed 'Heroes Day', the politicians and government officials would reclaim their military titles and uniforms in public, if only for one day. On this, a programme officer working with the American INGO IRI noted:

> The military in South Sudan has transcended to the political space and you see it in the political culture of the country. In South Sudan when a decision is made from above, it's not questioned or disagreed with. There is just no culture of questioning authority.[82]

As such, notwithstanding the elections and investments in democracy and governance, the greatest measure of success in the restructuring of governance in South Sudan would be the replacing of military norms by political ones.[83] This would ultimately reflect a key argument in this book in that, broadly, 'demilitarization is a restructuring of civil–military relations in post-conflict countries and part of the wider redressing of the balance of power from the military to the civil'. The question of changing military norms and attitudes in South Sudan was therefore one that was often discussed in interviews and one that would completely change the balance of power in the country.[84]

This is especially an issue that comes up often in conversations with INGOs and senior government officials, perhaps indicating an acknowledgement of the problem. But the casualness with which it also crops up in conversations in South Sudan also indicates acceptance of military norms and attitudes as the rule rather than the exception. Addressing this, however, presents the country with its greatest challenge to not only the restructuring in the country but to the whole demilitarization exercise as well. In South Sudan, the shift from military norms and attitudes to a political system not dominated by a top-down military ethos will be one of the biggest successes of demilitarization.

Illiteracy and democracy

However, apart from the challenge of addressing military norms in South Sudan, the other challenge to the restructuring of governance, democratization and the wider liberal peace thesis has been the levels of competencies and basic comprehension of the processes, procedures and principles involved. This directly addresses the question, 'Is it possible to achieve post-conflict societal transformation with an illiterate and non-urban population?' By any statistics, the education levels in South Sudan are dire[85] and illiteracy is placed somewhere around 80 per cent of the population not being able to read or write.[86] This raises a number of questions, not only for this book but for the wider post-conflict intervention in the country. Specifically, how do such low rates in literacy affect the prevailing pursuit of liberal peacebuilding in South Sudan and this book's aspiration of demilitarization? More essentially, how do you promote and harness democracy in a largely non-urban and non-literate society? These issues, this book argues, significantly influence the outcomes of the liberal peacebuilding pursuits adopted in post-conflict South Sudan; specifically, the success of democracy and liberal peace, as measured in the emergence of things like a strong and vibrant civil society that works consistently, not only to democratize politics but also to hold the state accountable (Beetham 1992; Gruglel 2001: 1; Held 1996; Schumpeter 1976: 268–70). These challenges in the absence of a literate and, to some extent, urban society, transcend aspirations of demilitarization and re-emphasize the importance of adopting a post-conflict reconstruction framework like demilitarization that takes contextual complexities into account.

Although issues of literacy are not prominent in the discussions about democracy in South Sudan, they cannot be ignored as they present the biggest critique to the liberal peace thesis in the country and the generic liberal peacebuilding programmes that come with it. The population's lack of literacy significantly affects the whole exercise in the restructuring of governance and, by extension, the country's post-conflict reconstruction. It not only brings into question the issue of election credibility, but it also draws questions on issues of legitimacy and local ownership of political transitions, especially in complex post-conflict settings like South Sudan. During the fieldwork period, empirical observations revealed that the issue of illiteracy was key to the success or failure of most post-conflict interventions. Here, this book takes into account some of the answers provided by respondents and interviewees to the question, 'What is government?' by assessing answers from five focus group discussions (Tables 6.4–6.8).

The answers to the question, 'What is government?' clearly illustrate the challenge to post-conflict intervention in South Sudan. More specifically, these answers raise questions on whether South Sudanese populations at the

Table 6.4 Focus Group 1 – Ikotos County

Participant	Answer to the question: What is government?
Male 5	It's a system where government is formed
Male 10	It's the authority of the state
Female 3	It's the state general
Male 2	It's the state general
Male 4	It's the authority at the state
Male 7	It's the authority of the state

Date 13/06/11, Participants: Male 10, Female 3

Table 6.5 Focus Group 2 – Magwi County

Participant	Answer to the question: What is government?
Male 1	We are the government
Male 2	The people are the government
Male 3	Government is in town
Male 4	It is with the president
Male 5	Government includes everybody
Male 6	People who know how to read and write so that if there are visitors they can talk to them; it is everybody who has gone to school
Female 3	The government is the chief, sub-chief, headman, the soldiers, fire brigade, police
Female 2	Everybody is in the government

Date 14/06/11, Participants: Male 6, Female 12

Table 6.6 Focus Group 3 – Budi County

Participant	Answer to the question: What is government?
Female 1	Government is the government
Female 2	They are responsible for the people; if there is hunger they bring something for the people
Female 3	They bring the orders of the people we voted for
Female 4	It is an element that makes people not fight, that people listen to
Female 5	Government is the eyes of the people

Date 15/06/11, Participants: Female 11

Table 6.7 Focus Group 4 – Lafon County

Participants	Answer to the question: What is government?
Male 1	The government is the person who keeps us in peace with no aggression
Male 2	Government means the person who leads us
Male 3	It's someone who can lead us together
Male 4	Someone who can keep peace
Male 5	Someone who can keep the enemy away
Male 6	Government means the person who leads us
Male 7	Government means the person who leads us

Date 19/06/11, Participants: Male 7

Table 6.8 Focus Group 5 – Kapoeta South County

Participants	Answer to the question: What is government?
Male 1	It is the school
Male 2	The school
Male 3	The school
Male 4	The school
Male 5	Someone who has been nominated and gone to school and comes to help the community, that is government
Male 6	Someone nominated from family and comes to help the community

Date 19/07/11, Participants: Male 6

micro-level broadly understand the basic constructions of the contemporary liberal state on which the restructuring of governance in the country is based. More essentially, this raises significant questions about what this means for the legitimacy of the exercise of restructuring governance, the related processes of elections and democratization and, more broadly, the liberal peace thesis that underpins them. Similarly, they revisit the research question of whether it is possible to achieve post-conflict societal transformation, and indeed demilitarization, with an illiterate and non-urban population. Although not the focus of this study, issues of illiteracy do have serious consequences for South Sudan's post-conflict reconstruction and the challenges of low literacy in the restructuring of governance have certainly not evoked the attention that they seemingly deserve in South Sudan's post-conflict reconstruction.[87]

Still, there were considerations made during both the elections and the referendum to include the majority of the population that could not read or write

Figure 6.4 Voting cards.
Source: Nyambura Wambugu.

in the democratic process associated with the restructuring of governance in the country. During the voter registration for the referendum on independence in November 2010, an official with the Southern Sudan Referendum Commission (SSRC) in Torit noted, 'Because our people can't read we had to make things like the voting cards very simple.' (Figure 6.4).[88]

Even with this, the attention paid to the impact that the lack of literacy has on South Sudan's post-conflict reconstruction remains negligible. This is reflected in everyday interactions with the country since the signing of the 2005 CPA. This was broadly expressed in FG 6 where participants' discussions pointed to the impact of illiteracy on the post-conflict restructuring and reform of governance yet none of the participants directly identified illiteracy as a problem. Asked about what they perceived to be the key difficulties in the post-CPA interventions, the participants said:

> Since the CPA, the focus has been on building institutions; we had nothing so this has been the area that has been given most attention (NDI 1).

> In South Sudan we were starting from nothing, so the priority has been in building institutions and structures. Like creating the parliaments, the courts, the counties […] whether they work was not the problem (NDI 2).

> We have built institutions, but the people running them are not there. You find we have a court system that includes cultural/traditional courts and the people running those courts have never heard of the law. So you find them even giving people life sentences for things like stealing (NDI 3).

> It is not only our courts that have this problem. The police are even worse. You find they arrest someone as a guarantor, that if your brother does something and he disappears they arrest you as a proxy for your brother and keep you in prison until the day they find your brother. There are people who have been in prison like this for even one year. You go and tell the police that this is illegal; they tell you they are the police. But how do you start explaining the law to someone who thinks they know the law but they can't read and the one they are depending on is the law of the bush during the war? (NDI 4).

> At least here in Juba, it is better; in the villages it's worse. Even the commissioners can't read, yet they are the chief executives of counties. Most of them are just former commanders who sit under the trees all day (NDI 5).

Although these represented real examples of the impact of illiteracy on the effort to restructure governance, they predominantly highlighted the issue of building post-conflict institutions. On the importance of post-conflict institutions, Kjaer (2004) argues that building institutions is indeed a major feature of governance which focuses on both input – concerned with democratic procedures – and output – concerned with efficient and effective institutions (Kjaer 2004: 4). As such, while effective institutions are a significant part of the post-conflict narrative, their role in the wider democratic consolidation process is not always straightforward. The links between building institutions and the restructuring of post-conflict governance can, however, be found in literature on democratic consolidation and particularly in Adam Przeworski's work. He perceives democratic consolidation to be 'when under given political and economic conditions, systems of institutions become the only game in town; when no one can imagine acting outside the democratic institutions, when all losers want to do is to try again within the same institutions under which they have just lost' (Przeworski 1991: 23).

To a large extent, the need for the restructuring of governance, democratic consolidation and building institutions is made by Gunther, Diamandouros and Puhle (1995). Specifically, that democratic consolidation can only be attested to 'when there has been a genuine adoption of democratic institutions, processes and values by the political class and the masses' (Gunther, Diamandouros and Puhle 1995). However, despite the significance attached to building democratic institutions, especially in post-conflict countries, it is also the case that democratic institutions alone cannot account for the holistic approach to restructuring and reforming of governance needed in post-conflict South Sudan. This holistic approach is especially important if the restructuring of governance is to significantly contribute to the wider demilitarization of the country. However, the institutionalization of democracy is no guarantee of democratic processes or politics (Luckham, Goetz and Kaldor in Bastian and Luckham 2003: 14). In South Sudan, this reality is even more poignant as illustrated by the political fallouts post-December 2013 and the ensuing conflicts.

Institutions and restructuring governance in South Sudan

The challenges, therefore, to not only the establishment of institutions but also to making them work for the restructuring of governance and demilitarization more broadly are many. Some are a reflection of the contradictions between the empirical reality of the country and entrenched traditions and history. As Chapter 2 has already illustrated, the influence of Sudan's history on the state, its institutions and processes is vast. More essentially though:

> The long civil war in Sudan destroyed whatever few institutions existed before the war. Similarly over the past half century since its independence, the Sudan was ruled by a hybrid of institutions and patronage systems with the patronage system taking dominance owing, in part, to the neglect of institutions and social norms in its modern history'. (de Waal 2010: 16)

In the case of Southern Sudan, where the neglect of institutions in the south of Sudan was systemic, dominance of the patronage system emerged as one of the biggest obstacles to the restructuring of governance in post-conflict South Sudan.[89] Indeed, Bayart's observations of the 'factionalized struggle for patronage' points to this challenge. In particular, the reproduction of the big man politics in South Sudan is evident across the national and state governments that emerged post-CPA. An extension of a century-old authoritarian local structure established by the Sudan Condominium government, the patronage system in contemporary South Sudan festers in tradition. Its legacy in South Sudan is especially compounded by the SPLM/A militaristic style of leadership (Rolandsen 2007), primarily addressed in this chapter. As such, factionalism in the Sudan remains a structural condition at the heart of the country's politics (de Waal 2009). On this, and in light of Sudan's politics, Bayart contests that:

the precariousness of national political equilibrium is not a manifestation of the organic inadequacy of the state, nor even a supplementary proof of its extraneity. On the contrary, it reveals its narrow symbiosis with the grassroots that sustain it. (Bayart 2009: 221)

This arguably forms the basis on which the patronage that threatens to overwhelm South Sudan is based. The big man / small man syndrome that comes with patronage is especially widespread in South Sudan. At the local level, this is perpetuated by the fact that the drive for institutionalization of power witnessed in Juba and state capitals is largely lacking. The rise and entrenchment of patriarchal politics in South Sudan therefore extensively undermine the restructuring of governance in the country. Post-CPA, local patronage exercising local powers of the executive is more pronounced and in most places has not changed from its pre-CPA existence (Rolandsen 2007: 13). Subsequently, there are those who still feel that the answer to South Sudan's patronage systems is to be found in the institutionalization of the country's structures of governance. As such, institutionalization in South Sudan offers the same remedy to the politics of patronage as in the rest of Africa (Mansfield and Snyder 2005, 2008).

In looking at the role of institutionalization in post-conflict reconstruction, Snyder (2010) argues that when institutions that cut across traditional cultural groupings are poorly developed, ethnic or religious groups are easier to mobilize, especially in comparison to class or secular constituencies (Snyder 2010: 2). This is particularly relevant to South Sudan where politics is dominated by ethnic patronage (Berman 1998). The dominance of ethnic patronage in South Sudan (Deng 1995: 539; Kevlihan 2013: 99) is cited as one of the grievances by the post-December 2013 armed opposition and rebellion. Arguably, therefore, patronage has a profound effect on South Sudan's post-conflict reconstruction and is an obstacle to the reform and restructuring of security, governance and livelihoods in the country. Similarly, patronage in the country continues to be the major cause of resentment, discontent and conflict.[90] This arguably makes the need to build institutions that can safeguard peace in the country (Snyder 2010: 3) more urgent.

Following the political fallout that led to the post-December 2005 conflict, the emphasis on building institutions was further highlighted by Snyder (2010). He especially argues that in post-conflict countries, transition is easier in countries with working institutions as they act as one of the facilitating conditions for democratic politics (Mansfield and Snyder 2005: 61–2, 2008; Snyder 2010: 3).

In South Sudan, despite the challenges and some of the shortcomings that have beset attempts at institutionalization of governance, there have been some successes. Although most of these successes have largely been wiped out by the country's return to war in December 2013, they cannot altogether be dismissed. In particular, and for the most part, successes in institutionalization are vital in the overall reforming and restructuring of politics and governance in the early stages of a democratic transition (Mansfield and Snyder 2005: 61–2, 2008).

Conclusion

The restructuring of governance is essential to the reconstitution narrative in South Sudan and, as illustrated, forms part of the strategies for its demilitarization. This chapter therefore attempts to answer some of the questions raised in this book and especially, 'How does the evolution of South Sudan's post-conflict politics influence its demilitarization, but also whether it is possible to achieve post-conflict societal transformation with an illiterate and non-urban population?'

Shifting the balance of power from the SPLA to the SPLM and, more specifically, to the political entities in South Sudan is essential to the attainment of demilitarization and the redressing of South Sudan's post-conflict civil-military relations. On the whole though, the restructuring of governance is a key part of the redressing of the balance of power. However, it has also suggested that this is, to a large extent, dependent on a number of outcomes, specifically on the growing of procedural and structural democracy including political parties, holding of elections and building institutions. Still, the restructuring of governance in post-conflict South Sudan continues to face a multitude of challenges, including the adoption of liberal peacebuilding as the overarching post-conflict approach and its lack of empirical sensitivities and flexibilities. These challenges are nevertheless addressed in relation to this book with broader arguments that take into consideration South Sudan's cultural and traditional peculiarities in relation to its restructuring of governance and, ultimately, its demilitarization.

That success, however, is dependent on the concordance between the SPLA, the former rebel movement, the country's political elite and the broader South Sudanese populace. Similarly, such a concordance would offer a break from a liberal peacebuilding approach that prioritized the pursuit of liberal principles as the centrepiece for any reconstruction. Without these, the restructuring of governance in this country, whose people remain sympathetic and indebted to the movement, is likely to fail. This also perhaps vaguely explains why South Sudan snowballed back into a civil war at the end of 2013.

In exploring some of the challenges facing the pursuit of liberal peacebuilding in South Sudan's reconstruction, it is necessary to draw particular attention to the country's low literacy rates, and especially to the complexities of pursuing liberal politics and liberal economics in an illiterate and non-urban society. Although the challenges caused by illiteracy are not sufficiently addressed in South Sudan's reconstruction narratives, they do present a formidable challenge to the broader aspirations of liberal peacebuilding in the country.

The challenges faced, however, also present a unique opportunity for the conception of an intervention in keeping with the empirical reality in South Sudan. This reality is subjugated by a dominance of military norms and their normalization in everyday political and social interactions. In this regard, it is only in rolling back the influence of the military culture and attitudes from the political, in theory and practice, that a successful restructuring of governance in South Sudan can be achieved. Apart from redressing the balance of power from the military to the civil in South Sudan, the restructuring of governance further opens up the space for social economic growth in the country, which is another key component of the demilitarization jigsaw.

7

Arms and livelihoods

Introduction

African conflicts and wars often invoke a socio-economic crisis involving the youth in which a generation defined by its political and economic marginalization forms a discontented constituency ripe for political manipulation, recruitment for rebellion and violence (Richards 1995). This is particularly true for South Sudan, considering that much of the country's unstable and insecure post-conflict security is linked and associated to armed rural youth. This chapter explores the role of securing socio-economic development in a post-conflict country where arms and livelihoods are intrinsically linked. It argues that the onset of social economic development is an important component of demilitarization and addresses the reliance on the gun, not only as a source of livelihood but also as a protector of livelihoods. To some extent, it engages with the current literature and arguments on the security development nexus, especially the importance of social economic development and livelihoods in post-conflict reconstruction, arguing that an alternative source of livelihoods not based on firearms is the final piece in the demilitarization puzzle in South Sudan.

Through extensive fieldwork with the Catholic Diocese of Torit development programmes, which comprised attachment with the veterinary, food security and health programmes, this chapter explores the role of developing sustainable livelihoods in the demilitarization process. The fieldwork carried out in four of the most militarized counties in Eastern Equatoria State – Lafon, Kapoeta, Ikotos and Budi – revealed that militarized livelihoods are a real challenge in South Sudan and must be addressed as part of the demilitarization efforts. Conflicts in South Sudan, including the post-December 2013 conflict, not only heavily militarized large parts of the countryside but completely disseminated livelihoods. The post-December 2013 civil war, for example, created a situation worse than that in the post-2005 period, including a man-made famine.[1] In this regard, existing links between arms, livelihoods, the broader pursuit of social economic development and demilitarization in the country are explored. It specifically engages with two arguments. On the one hand, those that perceive demilitarization as a necessary precondition for any meaningful attempts at securing social economic development through the reduction of military spending and the redirection of such funds to social economic pursuits. On the other, those who see demilitarization and the post-conflict security it seeks as a precondition for the redress of the links between arms and everyday livelihoods in South Sudan.

Arguably, these two are indeed mutually dependent and a society devoid of both social and economic development is unlikely to successfully demilitarize. A rethink of the construction of social economic development, especially by breaking the links between arms and livelihoods in post-conflict South Sudan, is therefore necessary. Here, like in the other chapters in this book, the research presents that the best approach to post-conflict social economic development should be primarily informed by the reality that the country presents. The militarization of livelihoods encountered in the research that informs this book is at the centre of that reality. This chapter draws attention to the gaps between the aspiration of a locally perceived idea of social economic development which evolves around livelihoods and the prevailing perceptions of development offered by international development practitioners and donors. Drawing on a vast pool of empirical data collected over different fieldwork periods, the chapter presents that after the restructuring and reforming of security and the restructuring of governance, a country must then address its population's social economic challenges in order to complete its demilitarization. This is a priority not only for demilitarization, but also as an important part in post-conflict peace consolidation.

It was clear from the fieldwork that social economic development played a significant part in addressing the question of what to do with populations after the end of conflict. Presentations in the second global conference on agriculture research for development held in Kigali, Rwanda in November 2012, which concluded that in post-conflict spaces, sustenance of peace depends on robust economic growth, are of specific influence to this book; that, for the vast number of households, agriculture constitutes the prevalent livelihood base and is a key driver for recovery and overall economic growth (Annor-Frempong and Ojijo 2012: 1).

On many levels, the extent to which development can be pursued as a viable strategy for tackling demilitarization at the micro-level in South Sudan is explored and presents that the extent to which development can succeed in its contribution to the wider demilitarization process can only take place over extended periods of time. South Sudan's return to conflict re-emphasizes the issues associated with the resurgence of violence and draws significant parallels to arguments by Christopher Cramer in his 2006 work *Civil War is Not a Stupid Thing*. Cramer (2006) brings to the fore the complex interactions between development and security. As a case study, South Sudan embodies some of these complexities.

The arguments in this book are an interaction with some of these complexities, especially in reconciling the theoretical perceptions and constructions of development with the empirical reality of their realization. It attempts this by focusing on a localized idea of development and on social economic development pertaining to post-conflict livelihoods in South Sudan; more importantly, on their links to the high proliferation of firearms in the country and the challenges this then causes to the aspirations of demilitarization. This brings to the fore the social economic complexes that devolve from South Sudan's history of militarization and not just at a grand, theoretical level, but at a micro-level, both practical and personal. On the whole, it looks at the reality and the challenge of demilitarization as a way of reversing the militarization of livelihoods in the post-war country.

Social economic development and demilitarization

> If we want to prevent violent conflict, we need a comprehensive, equitable and inclusive approach to development. Development is moving to the centre stage of the global political agenda, largely on account of the realisation of current leaders of global governance agencies that development and security are intimately linked – World Bank President James Wolfensohn's address to the UN Security Council. (January 2000)

This statement sums up the shift that accelerated the merging of development and security in the new millennium. Although this focus might be slightly different from that presented by Wolfensohn, the role of livelihoods in South Sudan's demilitarization is largely informed by the broader links between development and security. These are arguably intimately related, that one cannot be achieved without the other (UK Parliament 2006). However, in spite of this rhetoric, in theoretical terms, the causal links between security and development that inform the arguments on livelihoods, social economic development and demilitarization in South Sudan are yet to be adequately explained (Klingebiel 2007; Youngs 2008). This presents a particular challenge to this study and, more broadly, to understanding the synergy between post-conflict social economic development and security. Despite this, issues of development remain high on the priority list of liberal peacebuilding, interweaving social economic development into the post-conflict intervention fabric. Recent literature especially argues that 'robust economic growth has proven to be more crucial than political reform in preventing a return to conflict' (Collier, Hoeffler and Söderbom 2008), and, as such, the emphasis on the merging of social economic development and security has grown beyond the rhetoric, both in theory and practice.

Still, it is the prevailing wisdom that social economic development is impossible without stability but also that security is not sustainable without social economic development (Duffield 2001: 16). The links between conflict, poverty, security and development are now widely accepted by donors and civil society groups (Fitzgerald 2004: 8). The UK House of Commons Committee on International Development in a 2006 report, for example, called this new synergy the securitization of development (UK Parliament 2006: 13). At the UN, Secretary General Kofi Annan, found them mutually dependent. In the 2005 UN General Assembly, he noted: 'Not only are development, security and human rights all imperative, but they also reinforce each other' (UN Secretary-General 2005: 5). Still, the nexus between development and security has moved beyond the basic premise of social economic development, to include areas like human rights, arguably following a World Bank-commissioned study 'Voices of the Poor'. The study concluded that:

> The first priority for people living in impoverished areas was security, which was ranked just as high, and in many cases higher, than access to both food and shelter'. (Fitzgerald 2004: 7)

Mark Duffield, whose work on the links and convergence of security and development makes a significant contribution to this field and notes that this convergence is not simply a policy matter, but has profound political and structural implications (Duffield 2001: 16). These implications are evident in the day-to-day interactions between communities, the government and third sector or voluntary institutions in post-conflict South Sudan. In fact, social economic development concerns are increasingly important in relation to how security is understood, perceived and implemented (Duffield 2001: 1).[2] As such, in post-conflict countries like South Sudan, social economic development resources must be used to shift the balance of power between groups and even to change attitudes and beliefs (Duffield 2001: 15) especially among those that place the gun at the fore of most interactions. This is South Sudan's litmus test if the country is to successfully demilitarize. The aim of this book, therefore, is not to dispel the importance of other post-conflict interventions at the expense of social economic development, but rather to place the development of livelihoods in particular within the spectrum that informs the post-conflict narrative which culminates in demilitarization.

The arguments here generally engage with the merging of development and security issues and the morphing effects of this on modern-day assertions of security; specifically, the emergence of a new thinking in security that brings together development, defence and diplomacy or '3D' (Fitzgerald 2004). A relatively new term, the 3Ds of security focuses on not only the merging of development, defence and diplomacy, but also on the intricate relationships between them which increasingly informs the international interaction with security, especially in developing and post-conflict countries.[3] This is aimed at developing joined-up thinking, seeking to address security by looking at challenges to social economic development that might contribute to conflict.

Nonetheless, it is the links drawn between conflict and lack of development (Ikejiaku 2009) that subsequently give foundation to the merging of development and security. The reality of researching these links and subsequently coding and utilizing the data is, however, not easy[4] as it can result in contradicting assertions subjective to context and environment. For example, while the World Bank-commissioned study 'Voices of the Poor' stated that security was the biggest concern for people living in impoverished areas over other needs like food and shelter' (Fitzgerald 2004: 7), a study carried out in Eastern Equatoria found the opposite. The household survey by the Sudan project of the small arms survey and the Danish demining group assessing the links between insecurity and underdevelopment argued that:

> Across their entire research sample, respondents ranked education and access to adequate hospital care as their most pressing concerns, followed by clean water. Food was also a top concern in Torit and Ikotos. Security ranked at or near the bottom of overall concerns in all counties'. (Human Security Baseline Survey: Small Arms Survey 2010: 1)

The household surveys highlighted not only the intricate link between insecurity and underdevelopment in Eastern Equatoria, but also how this resulted in a militarization of livelihoods. The data collected over extended periods of fieldwork shows the links between insecurity and underdevelopment and subsequently development and security in the post-independence South Sudan. The chapter begins with the underlying challenge: the long civil war, including the First and the Second Civil Wars and their effect on development. Generally, violent conflict not only causes loss of life and destruction of livelihood support systems, the environment, physical and economic infrastructure and social fabric, it also completely re-engineers communities by displacement. While populations are removed from their homes and often rely on relief supplies (Annor-Frempong and Ojijo 2012), in most cases, they return home and continue with their lives and former livelihoods. In the case where the war was protracted like in South Sudan, the post-war reality can be very different.[5] This book particularly engages with these realities and reflects on the formidable task of overcoming them by reversing the legacy of war through restoring the communal and individual social economic fabric of society.

A history of underdevelopment

The biggest legacy left by war in South Sudan is that of underdevelopment. As such, undoing the legacy of underdevelopment left by not one, but two civil wars is one of the greatest challenges to development in contemporary South Sudan and that is not taking into account the damage from the post-2013 conflict. Hence, South Sudan's troubled history of war and seemingly never-ending cycles of conflict directly relate to its underdevelopment. The performance of the country's economy, like many post-conflict countries, reflects on the magnitude and nature of wartime destruction (USAID 2009: 13). This has serious implications for recovery, taking into account that South Sudan's two long civil wars not only caused great destruction, but also prevented development for almost four decades.[6] In essence, the starting point for post-conflict development in South Sudan is worse than in other post-conflict countries.[7] The livelihoods paradox in South Sudan is thus part of a wider narrative of underdevelopment in Sudan's peripheries that stretches to a period long before the country's independence in 1956.[8] The story of South Sudan's underdevelopment can thus be traced back a long way and entails not only a history of developmental neglect but a total lack of investment in social programmes like education and health in the south. This underdevelopment or marginalization has been the backdrop on which Sudan's wars have been fought; nevertheless, the issues potent to Sudan's wars are discussed in more details in Chapters 2 and 3.

Taking stock – South Sudan's Development Plan

The state of South Sudan's development in the post-2005 period was perhaps better articulated in the South Sudan Development Plan 2011–13 (SSDP). The plan presented the development aspirations of South Sudan in the first three years of independence. However, as development is largely understood as an economic process (Duffield 2001: 38), assessing the state of South Sudan's economy was central not only to the realization of the country's development narrative, but the wider demilitarization narrative as well. The articulation of South Sudan's development in certain terms can nonetheless be a complex process, especially given that the country lacks credible development data.[9] The world development indicator, the United Nations Human Development Index (HDI) 2013, for instance, provided no data for South Sudan. This illustrated part of the challenge in quantifying development in the country pre-December 2013. Similarly, the African Development Bank strategy for South Sudan raised the same concerns stating that:

> South Sudan has a very high degree of socio-economic fragility, especially in terms of weak institutional and human capacities, limited baseline information and statistics and one of the worst social development indicators. It is worth noting at this stage that the preparation of South Sudan's interim country strategy paper was fraught with problems, including in particular limited data and statistics across all sectors, which explain on occasions the absence of most of the conventional figures. (ADB 2012: 7)

Still, some countrywide data did exist with South Sudan's National Bureau of Statistics (SSNBS). This data was, for example, presented and used in the South Sudan Development Plan (SSDP). Even then, there was no consensus on the data, which presented 51 per cent of the country's population as poor, 80 per cent as dependent on agriculture and education and health indicators in the country as among the worst in the world (South Sudan Development Plan 2011–13: xxi). Apart from the SSNBS, the World Bank also provided some data in its Gross National Income per capita index summarized here in Table 7.1.

Table 7.1 World Bank – World development indicators 2012

Country	Income level	GDP (current US$) (billion 2011)	Population (million)
Ethiopia	Low income	$30.25	84.73
Central African Republic	Low income	$2.195	4.487
Sudan	Lower middle income	$64.05	34.32
South Sudan	Lower middle income	$19.17	10.31
DRC	Low income	$15.65	67.76
Uganda	Low income	$16.81	34.51
Kenya	Low income	$33.62	41.61

Source: World Bank report 2012, accessed February 2013.
DRC = Democratic Republic of Congo.

The data summarized in the table above ranks South Sudan as a lower middle income country on a calculation of gross national income in relation to its population. This placed South Sudan above all its neighbours with the exception of the Republic of Sudan which is also classed as a lower middle income country. While this ranking implies that South Sudan's income per capita was higher than neighbouring countries, it did not, however, reflect on the country's development[10] where South Sudan's development indicators remained among the worst in the world.[11] What it did indicate, though, was that the country had the potential to develop and had the capital to drive the development internally. Still, South Sudan's micro-economy and, to a large extent, its macro-economy were in the hands of external players, either international partners i.e. donors and international aid agencies[12] or regional businesses. South Sudan's economic indicators provided by the African Development Bank also showed an over-reliance on the oil sector which accounted for the high Gross National Income (GNI) that made South Sudan a lower middle income country. The African Development Bank put South Sudan's economic and growth indicators more into context as illustrated in Figure 7.1 below.

While the reality of South Sudan's post-2005 economic context and growth drivers reaffirm oil as the largest contributor to GDP in 2010, it also pointed at subsistence agriculture, forestry and fisheries as the most promising non-oil sector accounting for 14.5 per cent of GDP in 2010. However, no matter what the figures looked like in South Sudan, the greatest challenge perhaps remained in reconciling the theory of economic growth and its practice in a post-conflict country like South Sudan. The country's development plan is an example of this

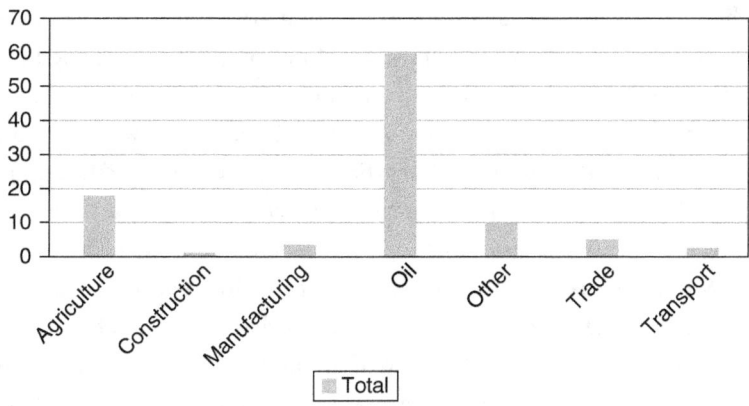

Figure 7.1 South Sudan GDP shares in 2010.
Source: South Sudan National Bureau of Statistics.

gap between aspiration and realization. This is where the approaches to South Sudan's development, but also the wider post-conflict exercise, have gone wrong by pursuing rigid, generic, liberal peacebuilding programmes, out of touch with the country's needs and realities. As such, rethinking the development approach in South Sudan to reflect the country's empirical complexities offers the country not only a path to economic prosperity, but also reaffirms a viable component in its demilitarization. That social economic development is therefore an important part of the demilitarization jigsaw, and in South Sudan that jigsaw starts with addressing the militarized livelihoods constructed in the war years.[13]

This gun is our food – militarized livelihoods

'This gun is our food' was the title of a paper by Arnold and Alden (2007) looking at demilitarization of a militia operating in the Upper Nile region of South Sudan. Although its premise and content were different for the scope of this chapter, it captures the intricate and interwoven relationship between the gun, people's sense of security and their way of life which all culminates in what this chapter calls militarized livelihoods. This is widely used to mean different things, mainly in understanding the factors that influence people's lives and well-being (Bernstein et al. 1992; Carney 1998; Davies 1996; Rennie and Singh 1996). However, this book uses the term livelihood in its most basic form; that is to mean a person's or community's means of securing the basic life necessities of food, water, shelter and clothing. By militarized livelihoods, therefore, this research refers to the use of the gun and military means and violence that has accumulated over the various civil wars, not only to achieve the basic life necessities, but also to protect and safeguard them.

The idea of militarized livelihood in South Sudan is, however, a complex interaction of South Sudanese everyday lives and the harsh reality left behind by the civil wars. This, the head of development at the Lafon County headquarters in Imehejek says, means that people are used to herding their animals with a gun as opposed to a stick, that children learned to shoot birds rather than trap them and that women and girls only cultivate crops when it is considered safe to do so for fear of abduction by armed neighbouring, warring communities. The challenge in post-conflict South Sudan, therefore, seems to be that of removing the gun from the centre of everyday life. This was witnessed during the fieldwork period in Iboni (Lafon County), in Mogos (Kapoeta County), in Kimatong (Budi County) and Imuyale (Ikotos County) where villagers attending an agriculture and livelihood training session and demonstration came armed with their AK-47s but brought no farming tools (see Figure 7.2).

The carrying of firearms to social gatherings, including training sessions on farming methods, is not uncommon in rural South Sudan and points at the extent to which firearms are interwoven into everyday life and thus, by extension, livelihoods in the countryside. It is also worth noting that the degree and extent of the socialization and the normalization of firearms' use in everyday life in the country varies across different cultural contexts.[14] In Eastern Equatoria, the research area, this was more pronounced and the idea of militarized livelihood

Figure 7.2 Residents of Mogos – Kapoeta East County 19 July 2011.
Source: Nyambura Wambugu.

across the different administrative and ethnic boundaries is also more localized.[15] On this, a senior government official working with the youth added that 'the militarization of livelihoods in South Sudan tends to be primarily in areas where cattle are thought to be the main source of livelihood'. He particularly argued that the use of firearms is also more associated with the cattle sector than with the other sectors, so it is more prevalent in cattle-keeping communities than in farming communities. This was reflected in the fieldwork in Magwi County where the community did not keep cattle and there was a less obvious reliance on firearms in their everyday lives.[16]

The interlocking relationship between communities and their firearms and the then translation of these firearms into everyday tools is what sets South Sudan apart. Firearms are used to access livelihoods like food: when young men hunt by shooting game meat, be it wild pigs or dik-diks, when young boys shoot birds or when the firearms are perceived to be the most secure way for a community to protect their cattle. These interactions have, over the years, translated into a militarization of livelihoods in South Sudan. Although the engraining of firearms into the everyday communal social economic activities is one of the legacies left by the long civil war, it also informs the fear of South Sudan falling into the conflict trap;[17] a fear that came to fruition on 15 December 2013 (Collier and Hoeffler 2004; Collier et al. 2003). Even before the political and military fallout in December 2013, the worry that South Sudan would slip back into conflict had been heightened by rising insecurity in the country, an insecurity primarily born out of armed rebellions in the east and north of the country and against a background of meagre social economic improvements and lack of service delivery in the country (Mayai 2012).

As such, in order to avoid the conflict trap, roll back current conflicts and create an environment in which communities, especially in the cattle-keeping communities in South Sudan can effectively demilitarize, the militarization of everyday social economic interactions must be addressed. This must begin with the demilitarization of livelihood. The resounding logic from the fieldwork is that the farming communities in South Sudan, as was experienced in the research sample of Eastern Equatoria, are less inclined to use firearms and have far less use for them in their day-to-day lives. Arguably, the first step towards demilitarizing livelihoods in South Sudan would be to seek a cultural change from cattle-keeping and the status of cattle in communities, so that this over time would diminish the overreliance on cattle-keeping and perhaps a shift towards farming would eventually take root. This would follow the argument that 'societies must be changed so that past problems do not arise, as happened with development in the past [...] this process of transformation cannot be left to chance but it requires direct and concerted action' (Duffield 2001: 15).

The long road back – demilitarizing livelihoods in South Sudan

The whole idea of demilitarizing livelihoods in South Sudan sits within a larger narrative of a country trying to find the road back from the turmoil and legacy of war. This journey nonetheless underpins the ability of a society to transform itself from a survival economy during the war to a post-conflict economy. The journey of rebuilding livelihood and reasserting people's ways of life is the most basic realization of demilitarization, yet perhaps also its most successful.[18] The role of development in demilitarization thus begins with communities re-establishing their economic viability by rebuilding the country's economy and networks from the bottom up. In South Sudan, this ultimately involves reskilling away from the gun, both at individual and community level. Giving people skills that are economically viable is the surest way of getting them to give up the army and their guns.[19]

However, the placing of reskilling within the liberal peacebuilding framework, especially as a key feature continually embodied in DDR, does present some challenges. Still, in the post-2005 intervention, reskilling or capacity building was arguably relegated to generic copy and past practices from other liberal peacebuilding exercises. This was evident in the multitude of capacity building programmes implemented in the country, few of which were locally conceived.[20] That these programmes were externally funded only perpetuated this. The fieldwork period witnessed more than 20 training sessions associated with these programmes in various areas including: in agriculture, DDR, computers, business planning, organizational capacity, social justice, human rights, women's rights, civic education, elections, water and sanitation, health, girl education, etc. These programmes were run and delivered often by an international NGO worker, South Sudanese diaspora or by regional staff from the region. These trainings, delivered mainly in English and using a classroom approach, raised several questions, particularly in view of South Sudan's extremely low literacy rates, especially in the rural areas at less than 20 per cent.[21]

However, despite these challenges, the importance of helping South Sudan's population acquire new skills cannot altogether be ignored. Still, these challenges again point to a post-conflict recovery strategy that hasn't factored in challenges to the blueprint.[22] As Giordano (2011) puts it: 'For post-conflict development to succeed there must be a collation of a number of principles, at the top of which is understanding context but also promoting "jointness" of action, defining a holistic approach, planning long-term development and including the private sector' (Giordano 2011).

Amidst the challenges of South Sudan's post-conflict development, some of these principles are lacking, especially the 'jointness' of action. To a large extent, the post-conflict intervention in South Sudan exists two-fold: one, at the government level, less conspicuous and almost negligible, and two, at the non-governmental level who dominate the field.[23] Preoccupied with internal and external conflicts, reskilling of the masses seemed less of a priority for South Sudan's government[24] with the two seemingly not working together.

However, while South Sudan presents its own challenges to the realization of some of these principles, most donors and international organizations working in the country broadly plan for them as part of their post-conflict liberal peace interventions. The United States Agency for International Development (USAID), for example, produced a guide for its staff working to implement development and aid in countries coming out of conflict – 'The USAID guide to economic development'. While the guide indicates the significance placed by major donors on post-conflict development, and especially on social economic development, these guides are often set out with a focus and interest in line with unilateral donor national interest and foreign policy. In the case of USAID, the guide focuses on seven specific sectors:

1. Macroeconomic foundations, including both fiscal and monetary policy and institutions.
2. Employment generation.
3. Infrastructure.
4. Private sector development, including the private sector enabling both environment and enterprize development.
5. Agriculture.
6. Banking and finance.
7. International trade and border management.

USAID rationalized the choice of these sectors as the most relevant to post-conflict development and reconstruction stating that 'evidence shows that early attention to the fundamentals of economic growth increases the likelihood of successfully preventing a return to conflict and moving forward with renewed growth. Since 40 per cent of post-conflict countries have fallen back into conflict within a decade, it is critically important to heed this evidence and alter the familiar donor approach, which focuses first on humanitarian assistance and democracy building, with economic issues sidelined to be dealt with later' (USAID 2009).

In this respect, it would be fair to say that in South Sudan, the donor community has broadly adopted the USAID guide. Donor interventions in post-conflict South Sudan have been multi-tracked, incorporating humanitarian assistance, democracy building and economic stabilization.[25] However, in all the sectors mentioned in post-conflict recovery strategies, agriculture is a recurring one. Taking the USAID sectors, for example, all the interventions except agriculture are dependent on intervention at a macro-level. Unlike establishing macroeconomic foundations, generating employment, building infrastructure, developing a private sector, banking and finance or formulating international trade and managing borders, agriculture can be achieved at a micro-level. This can also be built from the bottom up, with little resources and with minimum intervention from the state or donors, yet it is likely to also have a more resounding effect as an economic stabilizer.

This is because agriculture has become a major component in the post-conflict planning of major donors like the World Bank. In its 2012 report, the bank confirmed its support to key post-conflict sectors, especially agriculture, to which it allocated $4.3 billion for the year against $1.7 billion for education and $2.4 billion for health, although infrastructure financing took the largest share with $19.5 billion.[26] In South Sudan, arguments on the importance of agriculture are especially articulated in the Sudan Recovery Fund (SRF) which began in 2008. Administered by the United Nations Development Programme (UNDP) on behalf of international donors, the fund distributed over US$55 million to key development projects throughout Southern Sudan in 2010 with the first phase targeting agricultural production. The question that arises, therefore, is why does agriculture as a sector get so much attention in post-conflict reconstruction and why does this research single it out as a key development component central to the realization of the demilitarization narrative in South Sudan? The answer to this is perhaps to be found in a study on rebuilding livelihoods in post-conflict northern Uganda by Oxfam and Makerere University which concluded:

> Most conflicts in the developing world take place in rural areas, displacing large numbers of civilians and disrupting their agricultural livelihoods. Rebuilding

agriculture is an important strategy for post-conflict reconstruction. Agriculture is well-suited to absorb demobilised combatants, improve food security and enhance livelihoods. To stimulate agricultural production, post-conflict programmes often have to provide agricultural inputs and assets including seeds, tools and livestock that have been lost during the conflict. (Birner, Cohen and Ilukor 2011: 7)

Such arguments have catapulted agriculture to the front of the post-conflict reconstruction agenda with implementation in countries like Mozambique, Namibia, Sierra Leone, Liberia, Bosnia and Kosovo (Tizikara and Lugor 2012). In South Sudan, the realization of agriculture as a viable economic stabilizing alternative has nonetheless been met with a number of challenges, including low skill levels, harsh climatic conditions and militarization.[27] This means that agriculture in South Sudan serves not only as a way of renewing livelihoods and economic stabilization, but also as a tool for demilitarization that would ideally see the firearms traded in for hoes.

The gun for a hoe: agriculture as the answer?

While the idea of the gun for a hoe might sound patronizing,[28] it is a model that has been used repeatedly in various post-conflict recovery strategies, especially those associated with DDR (Pantuliano 2009). In particular, research has shown that agriculture is the sector that can best absorb demobilized combatants (Taeb 2004; USIP and PKSOI 2009). This is informed by the notion that agriculture as a livelihood programme cannot only rehabilitate rural economies, but it also provides a degree of social protection and subsequently a link between relief and development.

Broadly, agriculture-based strategies are best suited for sustaining peace, promoting cooperation among formerly hostile groups, integrating former combatants into the productive economy and helping displaced persons to resume their pre-conflict livelihoods (Birner, Cohen and Ilukor 2011: 7). For South Sudan, there is a strong consensus within the government,[29] that agriculture should be a vehicle for broad-based non-oil growth and economic diversification (Tizikara and Lugor 2012). This is especially taking into account the country's over-reliance on the oil sector[30] which currently contributes about 95 per cent of the national budget.[31] Indeed, the experiences of other countries like Rwanda, Sierra Leone, Liberia and Mozambique have shown that

GDP growth from agriculture has been twice as effective at reducing poverty compared to GDP growth originating from other sectors (World Bank 2008). The 2016 Alliance for a Green Revolution in Africa (AGRA) report "Progress towards an Agriculture Transformation of Sub-Saharan Africa." which reviewed the impact of Agriculture on African economies over a ten-year period drew similar conclusions; that agriculture provided the surest path to producing sustainable economic growth that is felt in all sectors of society in Africa (AGRA 2016).

It is from these assertions that agriculture has gained credence as a core economic sector in South Sudan's post-war development plan. However, like many great policies, the challenge lies not in its formulation but in its realization. In agricultural terms, South Sudan's suitability for crop production is well-documented. The Food Agriculture Organisation of the United Nations (FAO), for example, indicates that most agricultural land in South Sudan is still under natural vegetation (Diao et al. 2009). The World Bank also presents that:

> Only 3.8% (2.5 million ha) of the total land area (64.7 million ha) is currently cultivated, while the largest part of the country (62.6%) is under trees and shrubs. This ratio (crop land to total land) is very low in South Sudan compared to Kenya and Uganda where it accounts for 28.3% and 7.8%, respectively. (World Bank 2012)

While this underwrites the potential for agriculture in South Sudan, its realization remains limited due to armed insurrections, inter-tribal clashes and floods (Tizikara and Lugor 2012: 7). These have particularly affected any realistic prospect for big industrial investment that the government had hoped for.[32] At a micro-level, however, there have been small investments driven mainly by NGOs and donors who view it as a viable economic option. Even so, the role of agriculture in economic development cannot be understated, especially as the majority of people in developing countries still earn their living from it (Ingham 1995: 274). Nevertheless, observations of its realization in South Sudan have highlighted some of the underlying challenges. The thinking of the governments in Juba and in Torit has been that agriculture is likely to be the easiest and most reliable way to stimulate economic growth, especially with a largely non-literate population[33] which possesses minimal skills owing to the long war. The investments in agriculture in South Sudan, a professor of agriculture at the University of Juba asserted, would have to go further than they ordinarily would:

> Investments in agriculture have had to take on the role of teaching people how to dig and plant on top of providing any seeds. Whereas in other post-war

countries, like Sierra Leone, Mozambique, Liberia and Angola, the challenge was in providing seeds and tools, in South Sudan giving tools and seeds has little effect if you don't teach the population what to do with the tools and seeds.[34]

The fieldwork process that involved a two months' attachment with the food security programme of the Catholic Diocese of Torit proved this statement to be true. It also proved the agriculture for development agenda that is common across Africa and especially in post-conflict countries (Giordano 2011: 5) to be valid. This reignited debates of building a micro-economy from the bottom up beginning with the creation of a food sufficient population. Even with changing economies in developing countries with growth in other industries, for example, manufacturing and service industries, it is still the case that agriculture makes up a significant percentage of the economies. This is shown in the table 7.2 below which shows the share of GDP in developing countries taken up by agriculture and the percentage of the labour force working in the sector in most of the pre-independence period.

Although these figures are dated and reflect a period almost 20 years ago, the promotion of African economies depending on agriculture has not changed much.[35] As such, the agricultural sector still plays a key role in economic growth by providing a marketable surplus of agricultural produce which provides a solid income base for the agricultural population (Ingham 1995: 36). This argument is particularly reflected in Magwi County and perhaps it offers a tangible solution to the idea of demilitarizing livelihoods as part of the demilitarization narrative in South Sudan.

Table 7.2 The agricultural sector in developing countries (1965–85)

	Low-income developing countries	Lower-middle income developing countries	Upper-middle income developing countries
Agriculture's share of GDP			
1965	41	29	15
1985	32	22	10
% Change	−9	−7	−5
Agriculture's share of the labour force			
1965	77	65	45
1985	72	55	29
% Change	−5	−10	−16

Source: World Bank Development Report 1987.

Realizing agriculture – the empirical

Magwi County is an example that agriculture in South Sudan can be achieved to profitable levels and it can completely change how communities make a living. For three years, 2008, 2009 and 2010, Magwi is the only county in the country that produced food in surplus. All the cassava that I'm using to teach other communities across EES how to farm has come from Magwi. The World Food Programme is buying seeds from Magwi as well as food and using it to distribute around the country. Because there is food and people have some money, there is also less insecurity in Magwi compared to all the other counties.[36]

This interview was at the beginning of a two months' attachment to the food security programme of the Catholic Diocese of Torit. The programme coordinator, an agronomist from neighbouring Uganda, was embarking on a campaign to teach communities how to farm. This at the time seemed a bit strange based on the assumption that everyone in rural Africa knew how to farm with skills that are passed on from one generation to another. This was definitely the case within my own communities in neighbouring Kenya and in neighbouring Uganda, where the country's subsistence farmers are now the biggest food exporters to South Sudan.

Nonetheless, after a few weeks it became clear that more than four decades of war in Sudan's two civil wars had left the population more conversant with firearms than with the farm hoe. As a result, the populations I came across in the course of my fieldwork had lost their farming skills; lost after decades of life as refugees depending on food aid. As such, the training sessions I attended were basic and involved an introduction to the hoe and how to use it. The training also involved explaining crops and their benefits and especially why they were important in the immediate and foreseeable future. In the village of Imuyalei in Ikotos County, the coordinator explained:

> When you are digging, it is not only the spacing which makes the yields good. It also deals with the depth, how much the hoe enters into the soil. When you are digging [...] if the hoe does not enter deep, the roots will find it very difficult to penetrate and they will not perform well. This hoe, if we have a ruler from the tip to the end is 15 centimetres – I know.
>
> If you have a ruler you'd measure and you will find it's true. When you dig you should let the hoe enter up to somewhere here [...] at least ten centimetres. If you had a ruler you'd see it's ten centimetres which is nearly half a foot. When you dig, dig like this. You dig like this [...] it makes the hoe enter completely in

the ground. Some of the crops I've given you, the cow peas will grow in 17 days. The cassava you can harvest over a long time so there will be no problem of hunger. Also make sure you cover the seeds properly with the soil. These birds are also seeing what we are doing. If you don't cover they will come and eat your seeds.

The training in Imuyalei also shone a light on the links between development and the idea of livelihoods, especially in establishing alternative livelihoods and demilitarization in South Sudan. Although the link is never clear-cut (Tschirgi 2005: 2), the experience in Imuyalei and the other villages visited during this part of the fieldwork including Charakwor, Imehejek, Iboni, Kimatong, Isohe, Hiyala, Camp 15, New Kenya and Katire, all offered great insight into the possible knock-on effect. All these villages raided each other for cattle. It is because of this culture of raiding that communities hold on to their firearms. The cattle subsequently are at the centre of human interactions; they provide milk and cream for the children and are such important tools for women as care-givers. Cattle similarly provide prestige and wealth to the men as a marker of family wealth.

Livestock is also significantly important outside the family setting. In the traditional courts, many cases are adjudicated and settled using livestock. For instance, cattle are used for blood compensation[37] or bail and for settling many other criminal or civil cases. Generally, livestock remains the basis of most social and economic interactions in these communities. It is from this perspective that the efforts by the Catholic Diocese of Torit (CDOT) to provide alternative livelihoods in agriculture can truly be understood, especially in relation to this book's pursuit of demilitarization. For example, in the village of Imuyalei, the village elders explained on arrival to the village that they would ask all the young men known as the Munyumiji – the warrior youth – to attend the training. One elder explained:

> The Munyumiji are all in the village, back from the cattle camps. Because it is rainy season, they have brought the cows closer to the village. There is now a lot of grass around the village. During this period, we are also preparing the initiation of the younger boys into the Munyumiji, so now they can join their brothers in protecting the cows. If you want to teach them how to plant, they are all here so we will send for them.[38]

After the two-hour training and seed distribution exercise, the food security coordinator, on the journey from the village to the next training location, expressed his delight at the high number of the warrior youth who turned up, stating:

> If there is food security in these villages, my hope is that this might encourage the Munyumiji to stay closer to the villages and, with time, perhaps realise they can make some money out of selling their crops. This might stop them from going to the road and robbing vehicles where they shoot people just like that. The vehicle here you see [...] this is a bullet hole. The priest took this to go and say Mass during Christmas in the villages on the other side of the hills over there. On the way back, the car was shot at, and he was saved by lowering his head. You can see here where the bullet went through. It was aimed at the head.
>
> It is these same boys in the village who are doing these things when they are away in the cattle camps. They need some money for cigarettes, they want to buy some soap and now they want to buy some of the local brew. They have no money so they do an ambush on the road and steal or they go cattle raiding and bring some of the raided cows to the market and sell them. It never used to be like this, but now you see a lot of cows in trucks going to Juba. These cows are all raided. People here don't sell their cows so the young men have realised they can raid and keep some and give some to traders for a little money. If we teach them how to grow food, maybe it will encourage some of them to sell their produce in the local market and get some money that way. These changes are possible as I have seen them.

The coordinator insisted that the realization of his vision was attainable because many young men who had come to him in his eight years in CDOT for seeds and advice had managed to make a living out of farming. He identified one such young man in Torit, whom he thought was proof of what young men could achieve if helped to learn how to farm. The food security coordinator was convinced that farming was a viable solution to the problems of insecurity and poverty in Eastern Equatoria. I met this young man during the fieldwork period in Torit. He was selling household goods, plastic cups, plates, sugar, wheat, salt, batteries and other small things in the market. He explained that he had fought in the war from a young age and had stayed with the SPLA until 'peace came'. He, like many others who had been involved in the war, simply went back to the village after the signing of the CPA. After thinking about what to do after the war, he heard that CDOT was giving seeds and tools to farmers in the church. He told me he went to the church, met with the food security coordinator, who gave him seeds and a hoe and advised him on how to plant stating:

After visiting the mission, I went to the area behind the barracks near the Kineti river and started clearing the bush by the river. I dug the place and planted the seeds. After some time they grew very well. I took them to the market and I took some to my wife. After, I went back to the coordinator for more seeds to plant again. He said he wanted to see my area of digging.

I took him [...] and he said I should clear the bush by digging deeper this time and not to plant the crops in the same place as last time. After that he gave me seeds and this helped me again to grow and sell in the market and he also told me that when I sell I should keep two tins to plant next time. Now I plant two times with the rains and one time I get water from the Kineti and pour on the garden. With the little money from the garden, I bought a boda boda and I worked with it until I got something small to buy little things to sell on the market stall. Now I still plant, but I got someone else to do it for me and I pay them; my brother is also working on the boda boda and I'm on the stall in the market.[39]

While this is just one case, it is one that perhaps best articulates the possibilities that exist for success in agriculture as a social economic stimulus from the bottom up. This personifies the general case that agriculture's share of employment is usually greater than its share of national output (Cervantes-Godoy and Dewbre 2010; Lanjouw and Murgai 2009). It especially indicates the direct link between development and demilitarization by offering an alternative means of livelihood, particularly away from the cattle sector which heavily relies on firearms for protection and sustainability, thus presenting the biggest obstacle to demilitarization in South Sudan.

On the whole, though, the links between firearms and livelihoods in Eastern Equatoria were especially visible in the different counties in the state. Arguably, the lack of cattle in Magwi County and the lack of militarism that surrounds cattle-keeping in the other counties, illustrates that there is some truth in the parallels drawn between the cattle sector and militarism in South Sudan. The sense of security in Magwi and the absence of increased violence in the county, as well as the engagement of young men who otherwise would be the Munyumiji – the warrior youth – in agriculture, could thus explain Magwi's standing as the first and only county to achieve a surplus in domestic food production in South Sudan in 2009, 2010 and 2011 successively.[40] This surplus has put the county on the World Food Programme map as a supplier of seeds and planting material for other counties in EES, including those used by the CDOT food security coordinator in Imuyalei and other villages.

Although the realization of the agricultural success in Magwi and the subsequent evolution of agriculture as a lucrative social economic activity offers great hope to the 'gun for a hoe' book, it remains largely idealistic. Nevertheless, its promoters argue, it is still the surest way to breathe life into the rural economies and at the same time force communities to rethink their way of life. If agriculture as an alternative means of livelihood succeeds, regardless of the degree of success, it would amount to a success in the wider narrative of realizing demilitarization through development in the country.

Conclusion

South Sudan's militarized livelihoods as part of the country's post-conflict social economic development is arguably the final component in South Sudan's demilitarization narrative. By exploring the overlapping links between security and development, it's clear that 'both development and security are extremely broad and elusive concepts that often puzzle attempts to integrate them' (Tschirgi 2005: 2). As such, the question of development (perceived in view of livelihoods in this book) as a component of demilitarization is approached with caution and the realization that although the security and development nexus continues to grow and evolve, especially within liberal peacebuilding, its outcomes remain unclear. This is particularly the case in complex post-conflict scenarios like South Sudan. As such, the work here reflects on the Necla Tschirgi (2005) work on untangling the relationship between security and development policies in which she argues:

> Only some 15 years ago it was unusual for policymakers to talk of development and security policies in the same breath. Today the reverse is true [...] the United Nations, the European Union and the African Union, among others, all profess the necessity for integrated security and development policies. Yet behind the current security development nexus proposition, there are multiple layers of confusion, contradictions and policy dilemmas. (Tschirgi 2005: 2)

Against this background, this chapter set out to present and explore the role and relevance of development and especially social economic development in South Sudan's demilitarization. Firstly by disentangling development from security and the broader liberal peace pursuits and focusing on South Sudan's specifics and how to effectively stimulate and sustain social economic development at the micro-level amidst the multitude of empirical challenges. It explored the role of agriculture in attaining this against a body of literature that perceives agriculture as a viable post-conflict development stimulus. Even in countries that are not coming from conflict in Africa, agriculture is widely perceived as the most effective way of driving social economic development as articulated in the African Union Maputo Declaration of 2003. As such, that the largest share of the working poor are engaged in agriculture in Africa gives even more credence to its development as a major contributor to improved welfare and livelihoods in the continent.

Despite the promise offered by agriculture as a social economic stimulus that can begin to develop the South Sudan micro-economy from the grassroots, the parallel challenge of the lack of infrastructure and the inaccessibility of most of rural South Sudan dampens this hope. A recent study on sub-Saharan Africa shows that the realization of agricultural potential depends on access to markets (Dorosh et al. 2009). Specifically, that an area nine hours away from a market, for example, realizes only 8 per cent of its agricultural potential, compared to an area only four hours away which realizes 46 per cent. Thus, to realize agricultural potential in South Sudan, it is imperative that public investments are made to 'reduce the distance' between production and consumption areas (Tizikara and Lugor 2012: 7). It is this assertion that perhaps best articulates the challenge of presenting agriculture in South Sudan as a viable development option in efforts to demilitarize livelihoods currently revolved around the cattle sector and the militarism that surrounds it.

This reaffirms what Tschirgi (2005) argues to be gaps in the realization of the security development nexus; gaps that she argues exist between knowledge and policy, between policy and practice, and between policies and politics (Tschirgi 2005: 15). In South Sudan, this gap exists between the government's aspirations for development on the one hand, the third sector constructions on the other and severe underdevelopment. The Government of South Sudan's aspirations for agriculture exist in the way of agribusiness, while in the third sector, agriculture falls behind more popular development programmes like community empowerment, gender-based violence, child protection, human rights and civil societies. Food security in terms of agriculture is at the bottom of the list of both local and international nongovernmental organizations.[41] Where it does exist, though, it's more of a lip service than a reality.[42] In the Government of South Sudan portal, for example, the Ministry of Agriculture approaches the country's agricultural potential in terms of agribusiness and in relation to South Sudan's vast land mass and water supply but does not mention small-scale agriculture or plans to encourage the local population to practise smallholding agriculture.

This illustrates the difficulty in realizing demilitarization through development in South Sudan; that despite being a signatory to the Maputo Declaration (2003), the GOSS seemed broadly oblivious to the potential for improving life at the micro-level through rural and small-scale agriculture. This is evident in the national Ministry of Agriculture's leaning towards agribusiness and mechanized farming despite the lack of an actual realization plan for this aspiration.[43] It is the case that although there is great acknowledgement, especially within senior government circles that agriculture and farming is one way of 'engaging the youth in South Sudan to be productive',[44] the challenge is in the translation of this acknowledgement into reality. Although this illustrates the challenges facing not only agriculture, but also other areas of development in South Sudan, that of matching rhetoric to action, this research suggests that despite these challenges, this might be the more sustainable way of demilitarizing livelihoods in the country.

They do, however, also illustrate the empirical complexities associated with South Sudan. This chapter's focus on agriculture is mainly based on this complexity and is informed more broadly by the research theoretical and contextual framework which asserts a case-specific approach to demilitarization and its components. Although there is no concordance on how to approach South Sudan's post-conflict development among both local and international actors, something that's evident in the country's social economic stagnation, its importance to the wider pursuit of a stable and secure post-conflict security in the country cannot be overstated.

Although most conflicts tend to be fuelled mainly by ethnic rivalries, disputes over land and cattle, the spread of arms, the presence of militias, high levels of youth unemployment and the huge gap between the expectations of the population in the post-independence era and the challenging social reality on the ground (ADB 2012: 8), in South Sudan a militarized youth and livelihood perhaps presents the biggest threat. It is specifically because of this reality that this chapter is an integral part of this book and the demilitarization narrative in South Sudan. Broadly speaking, ethnic rivalries and the proliferation of small arms in South Sudan are at the heart of conflicts and inter-communal violence. Social economic development offers a break from this by becoming a technology of security that is central to the country's realization of demilitarization (Duffield 2007: viii). Beyond the challenge of the untangling of South Sudan's militarized livelihoods, social economic development driven by agriculture in South Sudan promises to help steer the country away from its presumed conflict trap. However, in a landscape dominated by both internal and external threats, this seems like a tall order but agriculture can offer a way forward if conceived locally to be case-specific and sensitive to the country's empirical realities.

8

Conclusion

Is peace possible in South Sudan and, if so, what kind of peace? This book has attempted to answer this question by examining the post-2005 peacebuilding effort in the country. It asserts that South Sudan's return to conflict marked it as yet another failure in a basket already full of failed liberal peacebuilding examples, not only in Africa but across the world. Peace has been elusive in the country despite massive international, regional and local investment, mainly because of the type of peace pursued and how it was pursued, mainly through the adoption of liberal peacebuilding.

The period following the signing of the 2005 peace agreement in Sudan between the government in Khartoum and the rebels in the south (SPLA/M) provided for a period of relative peace. This subsequently allowed for the 2010 national elections and the 2011 referendum on independence to take place, although the peace that emerged did not last nor was it total. This book has examined what went wrong in the post-conflict intervention that followed the signing of the 2005 peace agreement in South Sudan and questions whether the circumstances that led to the country's return to war in 2013 could have been avoided.

Although 99 per cent of South Sudanese voted to secede from the north[1] on 9 January 2011, the new civil war necessitated some difficult questions and conversations within South Sudan, both regionally and internationally. Some of these conversations included a forum by the Rift Valley Institute[2] in January 2014 which questioned not only the viability of peace in South Sudan, but that of the country's independence as well. The forum, which took place three weeks after the start of the December 2013 fallouts, highlighted the fierce divisions emerging between supporters of former vice president Riek Machar and President Salva Kiir.

The forum tackled some of the questions raised in the application of liberal peacebuilding in the country; specifically that liberal peacebuilding was arrogant, top-down, externally driven and treated local agency and structures with contempt. One South Sudanese panellist, who had worked as a senior government official, questioned an intervention that saw young, recently graduated undergraduates from Europe or the USA with little experience posted to government ministries in South Sudan as technical experts.

The points he made were familiar and his arguments were not dissimilar to other critiques of liberal peacebuilding as a predetermined formula rolled out by international backers with little regard to local conditions or suitability. The participant argued that this approach was, in part, why the international intervention in the country had failed to deliver on the liberal peace it had promised, leaving instead a country fragmented along tribal lines and in the midst of a new civil war.

Subsequent assessment of South Sudan's descent into conflict points to a post-conflict liberal state that was dysfunctional; also one where democratic aspirations were swapped for patronage and rent-seeking systems. These ultimately led to the power struggle within the ruling Party SPLM and to the December 2013 conflict. Fighting between different factions of the presidential guard on the night of 15 December 2013 not only snowballed into the country's new civil war,[3] but it also marked the failure of liberal peacebuilding in South Sudan.

Beyond December 2013

The structures set up in the liberal peacebuilding intervention in the country also proved unhelpful in the post-December 2013 conflict. To some extent, the liberal state set-up proved to be more of a problem, especially the 'winner takes it all' parameters of the electoral democratic norms adopted in the new multi-party state. As the main party, the SPLM was, in 2013, gearing towards general elections which were scheduled to be held by 9 July 2015. The party was required to front a presidential candidate to be its flag-bearer who, given the SPLM dominance, would almost certainly be elected president. The president then accessed and controlled the country's patronage systems that run through the various institutions, thus making politics, elections and ultimate access to power in the country a zero-sum game. As such, even amidst numerous discussions on what went wrong following the 2013–14 crisis, it was clear that neither side in the new conflict was willing to compromise. Agreements on cessation of hostilities were broadly ignored by both sides who continued to fight, hoping for a military victory.[4]

This made peacemaking between the two sides seem precarious and, arguably, pointless prior to victory or war exhaustion (Cooper 2006). The characterization of South Sudan as a militarized society and its history of protracted civil wars made this even more difficult. At the beginning of the post-December 2013 conflict, it became clear quite quickly among observers that what might have started as an SPLM political party dispute had morphed into not only an ethnic conflict, but one primarily aimed at gaining control of South Sudan's oil revenues.[5] This was illustrated by the focus both sides in the conflict paid to the defence and attack of the oilfields in the Greater Upper Nile region. More than three years into the conflict, its changing dynamics completely redefined inter-community relations in the country, fostering divisions and wounds that may take generations to heal.[6]

The peace agreement that emerged from negotiations in August 2015, therefore, proved ineffective on many levels. It stuck, however, to the liberal peace formula and cleared a path to reconstruction that involved a transitional government and a transitional period culminating in an election. To a large extent, the agreement on the resolution of conflict in the Republic of South Sudan, like the 2005 CPA before it, provided the basis for a post-conflict intervention based on liberal peacebuilding. With hindsight, South Sudan's post-August 2015 intervention should have learned from the mistakes and shortcomings of the previous post-2005 CPA intervention.

Contextualization of the South Sudan liberal peacebuilding experience

This book contends that liberal peacebuilding specifically did not deliver what it promised. It did not build a liberal peace underwritten by a liberal democracy, liberal democratic institutions, multipartism and parliamentary politics, all of which should have been able to prevent a political party power struggle from turning into an armed rebellion. The contextualization of South Sudan's liberal peacebuilding experience, therefore, paints a complex web of realities that led to the failure of its implementation. On the one hand, the arrogance of liberal peacebuilding and its practitioners in dismissing alternative approaches to post-conflict reconstruction; on the other, the obsession of liberal peacebuilders with elections, institutionalization, and the building of a liberal order in South Sudan that blinded them to obvious challenges and obstacles in the attainment of a liberal peace in the country.

Still, the most resounding critique remains, that liberal peacebuilding prescribes rigid generic liberal solutions to complex societies; that liberal peacebuilders set out to implement these solutions with little regard to the host communities. As such, more often than not, where liberal peacebuilding intervenes to solve one 'problem', it creates two more.[7] The tunnel vision employed by international actors in 'stabilizing' a country, therefore, sometimes overrides the bigger picture. According to Newman (2011):

> When international stability becomes the priority, rather than addressing local conflict or demands for justice, international peacebuilding tends to rely on top-down mediation among power brokers and on building state institutions, rather than on bottom-up, community-driven peacebuilding or the resolution of the underlying sources of conflict. (Newman 2011)

Since the beginning of the post-December 2013 crisis, descending voices of liberal peace have become louder. They critique the international approach to South Sudan's post-conflict reconstruction and argue that 'in South Sudan, the Western "nation-building" system was as chaotic and dysfunctional as it was in Iraq, Afghanistan, Somalia, Yemen, Libya and East Timor'.[8] However, whereas the never-ending cycles of conflict in South Sudan epitomize the failing of the liberal peacebuilding approach in the country, the underlying causes of the failure can be found in the country's history.

In 1955, before the independence of the Sudan, Southern Sudanese struggled for a political stake after independence ended up with the Torit Mutiny on 18 August. This marked the beginning of a long history of civil war. Since 1955, the politics of the south, like those in the north, have been a curious mix of military interventions, regional blocking and religious artifices that blurred lines between politics and the military in not only South Sudan, but Sudan as well. In South Sudan, the overlapping relationship between politics and the military is at the centre of the complex realities that beset the country. This is embodied by the relationship between the SPLA and the SPLM and the socio-cultural attachments to the SPLA/SPLM brand that even new rebellions keep the name. In the immediate period following the December 2013 crisis in South Sudan, the former vice president Riek Machar announced that:

> We decided to organise a resistance against the regime, so, yes, if you heard troops in Upper Nile, in Jonglei, in Unity State, in Equatoria saying what I am saying, yes, we are now an organised resistance against the regime, we call ourselves SPLM/SPLA.[9]

That the post-2013 armed opposition/rebellion maintained the same name as the ruling party and national army derived from the former liberation movement was curious. However, it illustrates the intricate relationship between the political, the military and the legacies of militarization in the country that are embodied and personified by the SPLA/SPLM name. These are reflected across politics and social economic realities in the country. The contemporary analysis of South Sudan's politics and social economic realities, for example, reflect an ethnically divided national politics. This is littered with a multitude of private tribal militias who collate into a national army through various persuasions, but all linked to the liberation movement SPLA/M by a sense of nostalgia.

As such, politics is epitomized by a constant jostling for power, livelihoods and crumbs from the oil revenue and aid industry tables.[10] The evolution of South Sudan's post-conflict politics is therefore based on the pursuit of self-preservation and alliances that not only seek out but nurture private 'militias' as the most reliable, tested and proven way to access power. The trajectory of South Sudan's post-conflict politics is perhaps more of a hindrance to the country's demilitarization, despite the urgent need to resolve the vicious cycles of violence, stability and instability.

This would necessitate a re-evaluation of the links between demilitarization, post-conflict security and the broader South Sudan specific realities. Some of these include a look at some critical issues like illiteracy and, specifically, whether it is possible to pursue liberal peacebuilding in a society that's widely illiterate and non-urban. To a large extent, for liberal peacebuilding to be effectively realized, the recipients of the intervention must have a sufficient grasp of liberal principles and constructions and aspirations. These include an understanding of the principles of democracy with elective and representative politics, assertion of rights and freedoms alongside the burden of citizen responsibility, the promise of equality before the law, constitutionalism and universal adherence to the rule of law.

The empirical evidence illustrated that many respondents had little or no comprehension of simple liberal principles like elections, voting, government, what they mean and even aspire to achieve. From the focus groups' data in Appendix 2, it was clear that while there was an element of language recognition of terms like government, voting, elections etc., there was no language comprehension for many of the respondents in the villages. This was evident in answers to questions like 'What is government?' where answers included: 'Government is everybody who has gone to school. Government is people who know how to read and write so that if there are visitors they can talk to them.'

This is not, however, a measure of a community's lack of knowledge but rather a lack of understanding of a system foreign to them. In Iboni, one of the research sites, for example, the communities already had an elaborate system of traditional government. This reaffirmed Mahmood Mamdani's observations and assertions on the effect of the settler vs. the native in the construction of the post-colonial African state (Mamdani 2005), with the settler in this case embodied by the Government of South Sudan. More recent work by Leonardi et al. (2011), Leonardi and Abdul (2012) and Diehl et al. (2015) also highlights the interactions and intricate relationships between 'new' state authority and traditional authority in South Sudan.

Although the villages visited in the fieldwork had little recognition for GOSS, they did function and had social, political and cultural systems in place that had been in existence for generations. While their egalitarian systems may seem at odds with those of the emerging nation state, the research conducted for this book asserts that they are not entirely incompatible. However, their compatibility, this book argues, is not a matter of choice but rather of necessity if the new South Sudanese state has any chance of rising beyond its current limitations. Generally, the traditional, socio-cultural and political structures required no literacy, no written constitution and, as such, no access to formal education. The disruptions of the protracted civil wars in the Sudan, therefore, had no effect on these social political structures, which adequately adjusted to accommodate the military governance and CANS that came with the war.

However, the nature of South Sudan's egalitarian systems at the dawn of an emerging nation state became the litmus test to the country's post-conflict existence. The disparities between South Sudan's alarming 73 per cent illiteracy[11] statistics and the aspirations of post-conflict liberal peacebuilding are nevertheless daunting. For the most part, the emergence of the liberal state, with a formal written constitution and laws in English and Arabic, requires a population to be literate to not only contextualize and understand the new 'rules', but also to actualize them. In the absence of this, what exists in rural South Sudan are communities caught between the reality of their past, the shock of their present and the demands and aspirations of the future. Hence the question: 'Is it possible to achieve post-conflict societal transformation with an illiterate and non-urban population?' So far, such realities have resulted in a liberal peacebuilding that has been unsuccessful in South Sudan. However, for liberal peacebuilding in South Sudan to escape the criticism of a lack of local ownership, then all the processes and actors must concede the challenge presented by the country's illiterate and rural inaccessible communities and adopt a peacebuilding approach that accommodates these challenges.

Despite the impact that illiteracy and the non-urban and isolated communities have had, not only on demilitarization but on the wider international post-conflict engagement in South Sudan, there are questions to be asked as to why these issues have not been at the fore of discussions on construction of the post-conflict South Sudanese state. When this question was raised to many stakeholders of the post-conflict endeavour in post-2005 South Sudan, both locally and internationally, there was a consensus that in the light of everything that needed to be done, the fact that populations are illiterate and that many do not live within the bounds of the authority of the emerging state was not on the list of priorities.

Demilitarization, therefore, unlike liberal peacebuilding, may offer a better chance of providing South Sudan with a more appropriate peacebuilding approach that includes constituents otherwise excluded by liberal peacebuilding. Demilitarization's focus on securing a stable post-conflict security as the premise of all other post-conflict reconstruction, this book asserts, is more likely to deliver on a peacebuilding experience that works for South Sudan. The restructuring of governance, securing of sustainable livelihoods and the restructuring of security are all intertwined in arriving at a comprehensive approach to post-conflict security.

Reviewing key themes

Security

The key question is essentially: 'How do you start to restructure and reform security in a country that has had two major civil wars, a third one post-independence and countless rebellions?' What are the priorities, what is the strategy and, more importantly, what is the yardstick upon which success is measured? This book concludes that the restructuring and reforming of security post-conflict is an essential part of addressing post-conflict reconstruction. It specifically engages with different processes in South Sudan's post-conflict restructuring and reforming of security, the principles of which were written into the CPA.

Despite the mapping out of most of the post-conflict security arrangement in the peace agreement, empirical enquiry in this research showed that there was little synergy between the contextualization of post-conflict security restructuring and reform and its realization. By examining the prevailing approach to South Sudan's post-conflict security as part of the international liberal peacebuilding engagement in the country, this book questions the appropriateness of liberal peacebuilding in securing long-term peace and explores the gaps between theory and practice in realizing post-conflict security reforms and restructuring. Prevailing liberal peacebuilding approaches to security embodied by the onset of SSR and DDR have been at the core of an externally formulated peacebuilding process that often overlooks empirical differences in their application. In post-2005 South Sudan, this led to the failure of SSR and DDR having any real effect on the country's post-conflict security architecture beyond the cosmetic. South Sudan's 2013 slide back into war is an extension of this failure.

Still, the processes set in motion by the SSR and DDR engagements in the country did achieve some degree of success, if only in putting in place the structures and frameworks necessary for reform and reorganization of security. The failure of these successes to go beyond the surface and to reach the militarized youths of rural South Sudan is nevertheless indicative of the chronic gap between the macro and the micro of SSR and DDR. Here, the macro is represented by the international engagement led by the UN mission in South Sudan (UNMISS) and other international partners working with government institutions and departments at a policy level. The micro represents the filtering of policies to practitioners and local stakeholders for implementation by both local and international agency.

This book asserts that there is a disconnect between the realization of SSR and DDR at macro- and micro-levels emanating from language recognition of SSR/DDR lingua without the corresponding language comprehension. This presents its own set of challenges to the reform and restructuring of post-conflict security in South Sudan. The fieldwork specifically indicated that although practitioners of SSR and DDR broadly understood the aspirations of the terms, there was little effort in defining the precise understanding of SSR and DDR in their use in South Sudan. Chapter 4 specifically addresses the challenges resulting from this. In particular, it argues that there is an ambiguity surrounding definitions of especially SSR, which can be directly associated with the ambiguity found in its implementation. Interviews with both local and international agency also illustrated that DDR did not fare any better, especially in the chapter's examination of the scope, breadth and mandate of the South Sudan DDR Commission.

The challenges resulting from broad language recognition but no language comprehension and ambiguity in definitions have a direct effect on the design of any intervention, coming from the premise that how a problem is defined ultimately informs how it is solved. As such, ambiguity in the definitions of SSR and DDR has resulted in ambiguity in its attempted resolution. Similarly, in the initial stages of researching this book, the very term demilitarization was met with great suspicion as it was understood in a liberal peace context to mean the disarming of the military and the declaration of demilitarized zones. Most notably, in an interview with the national head of DDR in South Sudan during the first fieldwork period in 2011, he strongly questioned my motives. 'What do you mean demilitarisation [...] young girl, do you know what demilitarisation means [...] you are talking of disbanding our army, and our military capability. Demilitarisation was only done in Germany and nowhere else. Your research is very misguided!' While his reaction to the initial research title 'demilitarizing South Sudan' was the strongest encountered, his perception of demilitarization was based on his definitions of the term in line with a post-World War construction of the term.

This reaction to the term demilitarization again illustrated the challenge of the language recognition – a language comprehension paradox in perceptions of security. Arguably this has a part to play in shortfalls in the realization of post-conflict restructuring and reforming of security in South Sudan. The book, therefore, through a focus on demilitarization, reassesses the constructions of South Sudan's post-conflict security and argues that a legacy of war in the country makes its realization more challenging. It therefore concludes that for South Sudan to achieve a stable and secure post-conflict security, it must approach its restructuring and reform of security pragmatically, especially in the post-August 2015 reconstruction; that the pursuit of an electoral democracy where the winner takes all may contribute to its volatility rather than its stability. Demilitarization as an alternative approach, based on a case by case assessment of individual empirical realities, is thus ideal. In South Sudan, this would take into account the legacy of civil war and militarism in the country. Specifically, demilitarization would offer an intervention based on need and not dogma or a romanticized ideal.

Governance

Like security and development, governance in post-conflict South Sudan is not a straightforward matter and can be a double-edged sword. On one hand, whose instruments and processes are at the heart of a liberal peacebuilding approach to post-conflict reconstruction that thrusts a country, with both systemic and institutional immaturity, into the snake's pit of liberal democracy, resulting in a revolving door to conflict. On the other hand, one that cuts across the militarized culture of governance in South Sudan and the promise of democratic governance aspired to through universal suffrage and delivers governance that is bound by limitations of law and civil duty. This book presents that, for the most part, South Sudan finds itself transient between the two as illustrated by various debates among the southern elite on the form of liberal democracy that best suits their new country: a federal state or a unitary decentralized state?

These debates are especially relevant in view of South Sudan's post-December 2013 return to conflict, especially as South Sudan's TGoNU implementing the August 2015 peace agreement and international partners once again wrestle with the broader issues of post-conflict governance. This book and specifically Chapter 6 does not contest the importance of governance in post-conflict consolidation of peace and security. Where this book raises questions is in the pursuit of a liberal peace through the creation of a liberal state and principles of liberalism as the ultimate outcome, irrespective of the consequences. This book's key argument and contribution to the existing post-conflict thesis, especially with regards to post-conflict security, is that each country should map out its own path; that each post-conflict experience is different and informed by individual country realities. The conceptual frameworks explored in this book particularly offer the basis for this argument and conclude that for a post-conflict country to realize a stable and secure post-conflict security, the answer lies in finding an agreeable middle ground between the country's military and armed groups, the political elite and the citizenry on the kind of peace and relations they perceive and seek for themselves. Generally, therefore, a post-conflict setting that negotiates its own relationships between its military and its civil offers the best chance for a stable and a secure post-conflict security, reconstruction and sustainable peace for development.

Such an approach would not only have foreseen some of the challenges that beset the post-2005 CPA intervention in South Sudan, but might have been able to avoid some of them. However, this is not to say that there have been no gains in the liberal peacebuilding pursuits of governance in South Sudan, as gains, especially in structure and institutional building, cannot be ignored. Still, even with considerable gains in the building of structures and institutions, the biggest setback and prevailing challenge remains in their functionality. This illustrates some of the challenges to liberal peacebuilding, especially that although institutions and structures built as part of liberal peacebuilding are applauded in public, in private they are perceived as donor inconveniences that must be managed. This was the case in the post-2005 intervention as a senior army official explained:

> The generals are still in charge; they might be in suits and some are in the barracks, but they are in charge. They seem to have an understanding with parliament; you leave us alone, we leave you alone. If the generals want something, they take it to parliament, it's passed, maybe they do some manoeuvre during the night, some people meet and make arrangements and tomorrow the thing is passed. After all, they were all in the bush together. They know each other.[12]

While this ineffectiveness appears to be an open secret in South Sudan, there is also the feeling that:

> ... a journey of a thousand miles starts with one step. Yes, things don't work as well as we would like them but at least there is a parliament, there is a judiciary and there is an executive. Right now, that's good enough and maybe one day they will get better.[13]

However, with the re-emergence of conflict in December 2013, it was evident that things had not got better, raising questions yet again as to the merits of liberal peacebuilding intervention in the country. This also gave empirical credence to some of the critique of liberal peacebuilding as a self-sustaining approach that falls short of recognizing its own limitations and addressing them. The interview above further illustrated a common attitude among liberal peacebuilding practitioners – an acknowledgement of its shortcomings but a 'conspiracy of silence' that ignores these shortcomings, resulting in a cycle of repeated mistakes and the same unsatisfactory outcomes[14] that are now characteristic of liberal peacebuilding. While South Sudan as a case study conclusively illustrates the shortcomings of liberal peacebuilding, especially in regards to issues of governance and the pursuit of institutions and processes akin to especially democratic governance, the lesson not only from South Sudan, but more generally, is to learn from the failings. With the degeneration of the South Sudanese state witnessed post-December 2013, looking at the failings of liberal peacebuilding is not only paramount but it also offers the opportunity to look at an alternative approach which this book presents in demilitarization. The experiences of South Sudan should therefore not pass as just another blip in the liberal peace progress chart, but should be used to fundamentally carry on the broader approach to post-conflict reconstruction.

Arms and livelihoods

Social economic development is the other key component to the successful attainment of a stable and secure post-conflict security. However, this book engages with the paradox of post-conflict social economic development in South Sudan by focusing on the complex relationship between arms and livelihoods in the country. It concludes that the links between arms and livelihoods are part of an even more complex relationship between the state, international agencies and donors and the aspirations for the general social economic well-being of the South Sudanese people. Chapter 7 especially illustrates these complexities by exploring the paradox of the country's history and legacy of underdevelopment concurrent to that of militarism.

Together, the history and legacy of underdevelopment and militarism are entrenched in the social economic dependency on firearms explored in Chapter 7 on arms and livelihoods. This is a key point in the attempt at demilitarizing South Sudan and redressing the country's post-conflict security, especially with a view to disarming the civilian population. Nevertheless, despite the importance that this book places on social economic development, empirical evidence from extended fieldwork periods illustrates some deficiencies in prevailing approaches. Some of these deficiencies can be directly attributed to the prevailing liberal peacebuilding programmes applied to post-conflict South Sudan which can be traced back to externally constructed programmes that fall short of the empirical need and expectations and, as such, have little real effect.

This book especially questions the constructions of development in post-2005 CPA South Sudan. For the most part, the development sector that emerged in post-war South Sudan as an extension of the war years' aid efforts (Operation Lifeline Sudan) may have contributed to the weakening of the emerging South Sudanese state. This book presents that the development sector that emerged in post-war South Sudan largely took on microeconomic factions that are and should have been the preserve of the local government. This would have allowed local government to develop a meaningful social economic framework independent of aid patronages and the subsequent trusteeship relationships that emerge from them.

The crisis that followed events of 15 December 2013 especially highlighted this and also the profound influence of aid and development players in South Sudan and the complex relationship between them, the South Sudanese state and its populace. However, the status quo in this relationship changed with the post-December 2013 conflict. The South Sudanese president Salva Kiir, for example, accused the United Nations of running a parallel government in his country at the height of the 2013–14 crisis, raising familiar questions for the liberal peacebuilding critique. Essentially, did the liberal peacebuilding efforts in the country overstep their mark, and did the UN and the international partners create a neo-trusteeship in South Sudan? On this, one of the many analyses that emerged in the post-December 2013 period asserted that:

> In light of a near complete absence of infrastructure in the country, the UN has indeed taken on roles and duties that are more traditionally provided by the state. On the UNMISS website, take a look at the core functions of the mission: child protection, disarmament and reintegration of militia groups, human rights protection and peacebuilding. In addition, other UN programmes oversee massive efforts to roll out food and healthcare to some of the nation's most vulnerable. Government officials even have to beg rides on UN planes to get to the more remote parts of t3heir own countries. Should South Sudan's government be providing these services instead? Absolutely. Can it? No. That's where Kiir gets it wrong. Instead of criticising, he should be praising an institution which has relieved him of several of the burdens of governance; that has, in fact, masked the inadequacy of his own rule.[15]

The question as to whether the liberal peacebuilding exercise in South Sudan ended up weakening the same state it was supposed to be helping is a valid one. There are, however, no easy answers to this question and the subject indeed needs further investigation. Still, it does raise a few relevant points, like what exactly should be perceived as development in a post-conflict country and where is the line between development assistance and taking over a country's microeconomic structures? More importantly, with President Kiir vocalizing arguably widely held sentiments by many South Sudanese civilian and government officials interviewed for this book, what next for GOSS and its development partners, especially in the next phase of reconstruction? In light of the current crisis, there were concerns in the talking shops that followed the 2013–14 crisis that social economic development had been neglected in the list of priorities that included politics and ethnicized violence.[16] Yet, as this book has illustrated in Chapter 7, the militarized nature of South Sudanese society, coupled with the lack of social economic development, is likely to be a continued source of instability and insecurity.

With this in mind, this book approaches development from a pragmatic standpoint and as part of demilitarization. Chapter 7 specifically steps away from big-themed development characteristics of South Sudan's liberal peacebuilding development programmes and takes a bottom-up approach. This approach is especially aimed at changing societal and especially youth associations and overreliance on firearms as the main socio-economic determinant, especially in South Sudan's hinterlands. In view of South Sudan's social economic statistics and projections which are dire, irrespective of source and scope, this book argues that the prevailing top-down approach to social economic development in the country is unlikely to impact the kind of change needed to ascertain a stable and secure post-conflict security. This is reaffirmed by statistics which indicate that 70–75 per cent of South Sudan's population is under the age of 30, of which about 80 per cent, as of December 2013, were classified as unemployed and, as such, were excluded from the gains of independence.[17]

Any attempts at redressing the shortcomings of South Sudan's post-2005 CPA existence must therefore strive to include this large and versatile section of the population. Specifically because this group predominantly makes up the raiders, militias and rebels, they epitomize South Sudan's unstable and insecure state. The greatest challenge for South Sudan, therefore, lies in how to provide sustainable social economic development to a militant, armed, largely illiterate youth as a testament to their inclusion in the nation-building process. This book argues for a developmental path set alongside the African Union Maputo Declaration, one of the many international treaties and agreements South Sudan has ratified since its independence on 9 July 2011. The Maputo Declaration specifically presented a development path through agriculture. Arguably, agriculture is a tried and tested bottom-up microeconomic performer across Africa and was already tried in South Sudan as illustrated by successes in Eastern Equatoria's Magwi County.

Conclusion

The success or failure of peacebuilding should not hinge on any theoretical underpinning or a school of thought, but be about the actualization of peacebuilding that is suited to the country in question. The failure of liberal peacebuilding in South Sudan can be traced to the preoccupation with building a liberal order in a country less suited to it. In South Sudan, a peacebuilding underpinned by a narrative of demilitarization might still have the best chance of succeeding in achieving a sustained peace that is locally legitimized and owned.

This book in its totality explores and examines the state of South Sudan's post-2005 security and concludes that the prevailing approach of liberal peacebuilding adopted in the country failed to deliver the liberal peace it promised. The

December 2013 crisis and the civil war that followed an internal political party dispute add to this book's questioning of the international engagement in South Sudan at the end of the north-south war in 2005.

In so doing, this book offers demilitarization as an alternative approach in peacebuilding and concludes that with demilitarization, some of the failings witnessed in post-CPA South Sudan could have been avoided. The book adopts Eboe Hutchful's construction of demilitarization as a concept involving different components and focuses on three areas in South Sudan's demilitarization: security, governance and social economic development conceived through livelihoods.

Through an in-depth look at the country's post-conflict restructuring of governance, security and redressing of post-conflict livelihoods, these are the most relevant components in South Sudan's post-conflict reconstruction. A peacebuilding intervention based on demilitarization would not only have avoided the pitfalls experienced by liberal peacebuilding but would have been more flexible in allowing for an illiberal peace if needed.

As such, this book makes a significant contribution to existing debates through its extensive fieldwork data. However, it is also the case that any progress made by this book in moving peacebuilding debates forward is not exhaustive. There is scope for further study of the issues raised and themes addressed in relation to post-conflict reconstruction and the presentation of demilitarization as an alternative approach to peacebuilding in complex cases like South Sudan with deep-rooted militarism and that have experienced prolonged civil wars. As such, this book aims to open the door and evoke interest in further research on not only South Sudan, but in empirically grounded studies of post-conflict security and peacebuilding based on demilitarization.

Appendices

Appendix 1: New South Sudan Administrative Divisions – December 2015

Among the 28 states, with their capital cities, decreed by President Salva Kiir Mayaardit are:

Regions	New States	Capital
Greater Equatoria	4-1: Imatong	Torit
	4-2: Namurnyong	Kapotia
(8 states)	4-3: Maridi	Maridi
	4-4: Amadi	Nimule
	4-5: Gbudwe/Bodudwe	Yambio
	4-6: Juba	Juba
	4-7: Terekeka	Terekeka
	4-8: Yei River	Yei
Greater Bhar el Ghazal	4-9: Wau	Wau
	4-10: Aweil	Aweil
(10 states)	4-11: Lol	Raja
	4-12: Aweil East	Ruwengjo*
	4-13: Twic East	--
	4-14: Gokrial East	Kwajok
	4-15: Tonj	Tonj
	4-16: Eastern Lake	Yirol
	4-17: Western Lake	Rumbek
	4-18: Gok	--
Greater Upper Nile	4-19: Northern Lich	Bentiu
	4-20: Southern Lich	Leer
(8 states)	4-21: Ruweng	Pariang
	4-22: Eastern Nile	Malakal
	4-23: Jonglei	Bor
	4-24: Western Nile	Kodok
	4-25: Western Bieh	Ayod
	4-26: Eastern Bieh	Akobo
	4-27: Latjor	Nasir
	4-28: Boma	Pibor

28 states for South Sudan decreed by President Kiir, Oct. 2, 2015

Appendix 2: Questionnaire – Perceptions of Demilitarization and DDR in South Sudan

Field Number [Researcher use only]:

Respondent Number [Researcher use only]:

Name:

Age:

Sex:

Nationality:

Current occupation:

How many years have you done your current job?

Previous job:

How many years did you do your previous job:

Questions Set 1:
S1a. What is demilitarization?
S1b. Do you know of any country where there has been demilitarization?
S1c. Can demilitarization be applied in South Sudan?
S1d. How can demilitarization be applied?

Questions Set 2:
S2a. What is DDR?
S2b. Do you know of any country where there has been DDR?
S2c. Can DDR be applied in South Sudan?
S2d. How can DDR be applied?

Appendix 3: Questionnaire – Restructuring Security

Field Number [Researcher use only]:
_____
_____

Respondent Number [Researcher use only]:
_____
_____

Name:
Age:
Sex:
Nationality:
Current occupation:
How many years have you done your current job?
Previous job:
How many years did you do your previous job:

Questions Set 1: Chapter 4 – Restructuring Security What does security mean in South Sudan?
Who are the main players in security in South Sudan?
What do you think of the restructuring and reform of security in South Sudan after peace?
What does/would restructuring security in South Sudan entail?
How do you rate security in South Sudan before the CPA?
How do you rate security in South Sudan after the CPA?
How do you rate security in South Sudan after the referendum?
How do you rate security in South Sudan after independence?
What should be the country's priorities in addressing its security?
What are the various divisions in the security services in the country?
The police?
The intelligence?
What are their functions?
What do you think of the police?

Do you think the former militias have a role to play in South Sudan security?
What is professionalizing security?
Has security failed in South Sudan?
Why?

Appendix 4: South Sudan Armed Rebellions: Date of Compilation February 2013

Name/Leader	Organization	Area of Operation	Reason and Demand	Current Status
George Athor	South Sudan Army South Sudan Democratic Movement (SSDM)	Jonglei State Upper Nile States	Launched a self-proclaimed armed rebellion against the Government of South Sudan (GOSS) in the aftermath of the April 2010 elections. George is considered the most powerful of the post-election insurrectionists. He claimed to have been uniting the other rebellions under him. He was killed on 19 December 2011 in Morobo County in Equatoria State.	Killed 19 December 2011
Peter Gatdet	South Sudan Liberation Army	Unity State April 2011	The government has failed miserably. It must go. Gatdet accused the southern government of tribal nepotism, corruption, undemocratic rule and mismanagement of the military.	
David Yau Yau		Jonglei State	Yau Yau rebelled against SPLM after the elections – in April 2010 when, as an independent candidate, he lost his campaign to represent the Gumuruk-Boma constituency in Pibor County at the Jonglei State Assembly.	Ongoing rebellion in Pibor County, Jonglei State

Name /Leader	Organization	Area of Operation	Reason and Demand	Current Status
Gatluak Gai		Unity State May 2010	Aspired to be Koch County commissioner prior to Taban Deng Gai's appointment as governor following the 2008 Sudan People's Liberation Movement (SPLM) convention. Joined Campaign of Angelina Teny (wife of Vice President Riek Machar) for Governorship of Unity State with the hope he would gain the county commissionership if she became governor. When she failed – he launched the rebellion.	Killed 23 July 2011
Gen Bapiny Monituel		Unity and Upper Nile States	A former Nuer militia leader loyal to Paulino Matip. SAF Brigadier General after the CPA, refusing to join the SPLA after the 2006 Juba Declaration.	
Gabriel Tang Gatwich Chan aka Tang-Ginye (Long Pipe)		Upper Nile State	A Nuer from Fangak County in Jonglei State. A key figure in the brutal chapter of north–south violence which resulted in some of the worst atrocities committed during Sudan's Second Civil War (1983–2005). A militia leader who joined the Joint Integrated Units from the Sudan Armed Forces (SAF) side after the CPA. His forces are said to have been responsible for the SPLA / SAF crushes in Malakal during the interim CPA period. After the signing of the Juba Declaration he lost about 70 per cent of his forces who joined the SPLA under Brig John Both. Offered the position of Commissioner of Fanjak in June 2006 by the SPLM/A in exchange for his loyalty (didn't take it). As late as 2011, his forces have been involved in clashes with the SPLA. Currently under 'house' arrest in the capital Juba	

Appendix 5: Archive document – staff list for SSRC in 2004

SUDAN RELIEF & REHABILITATION COMMISSION (SRRC)
NAIROBI / KENYA
OFFICE OF THE COMMISSIONER · SRRC

P.O. Box 39892
Nairobi, Kenya

Our Ref: SRRC/UN/1-A-1

Your Ref: ....

Date: 6th April 2004

OFFICE OF THE UNICEF
OLS COORDINATOR
NAIROBI.
20 APR 2004
RECEIVED
TIME:..........................

Bernt Aasen
Deputy Humanitarian Coordinator OLS
Southern Sector
Nairobi.

RE: SRRC UPDATED STAFF LIST FOR APRIL 2004

Here below is the SRRC updated Staff List effective April 2004.

S/NO.	NAMES	POSITION
A)	**RUMBEK HEADQUARTERS**	
1	Mr. Elijah Malok Aleng	Commissioner SRRC
2	Mr. Thomas Dut Gatkek	Director General SRRC
3	Mr. Matur Ajac	Administrator SRRC
4	Mr. Gabriel Otor	Chief Administrator - Ramcell
5	Mr. Joseph Awan	Chief Water Coordinator
6	Mrs. Mary Baranaba Akec	Resource Centre and Finance
7	Mr. Rex Abdallah	Office Secretary
8	Mr. Mabior Deu Awuol	Training Officer
9	Mr. William Ajal Deng	Legal Advisor
10	Mr. Abraham Mayom Makuac	Field Officer
11	Mr. Abraham Jok Aring	Coordinator for Disabled
12	Mr. Yel Deng Nguel	Humanitarian Monitor
13	Mr. John Mandeng	Humanitarian Monitor
14	Mr. Rex Olum	Humanitarian Monitor
15	Mr. Alex Lual Nikanora Aciek	Information
16	Mr. Santino Agany	Field Assistant
17	Mr. Paul Hakim Makoi	Field Assistant
18	Mr. Luka Boy	Field Assistant
19	Mr. Deng Kando	Field Assistant
20	Mr. Mayak Anyang	Field Assistant
21	Mr. Dau Atem	Field Assistant
B)	**LOKICHOGGIO.**	
a)	COORDINATION OF EMERGENCIES	
1	Mr. Gathon Jual Riek	Senior Field Coordinator
2.	Mr. Abdalla Nyiker	Deputy Field Coordinator

TEL: 254-20-4440156 / 4448075 • FAX: 4440078 NAIROBI

Source: OCHA.

Appendix 6: South Sudan National DDR Commission composition

Presidential Decree on DDR Council

Composition of the NDDRC Council

The Presidential Order Number 31/2012 for the establishment of the National Demobilisation, Disarmament, Re-Integration Commission Council, 2012 A.D, which came into force on 12th October 2012, stipulated the council to comprise 24 persons as follows:

1. The Vice President of the Republic of South Sudan (Chairperson)
2. Minister in the Office of the President
3. Minister for Defence & Veteran Affairs
4. Minister for Foreign Affairs and International Cooperation
5. Minister for National Security
6. Minister for Interior
7. Minister for Justice
8. Minister for Finance & Economic Planning
9. Minister for Labour, Public Service & Human Resources Development
10. Minister for Health
11. Minister for Information & Broadcasting
12. Minister for Agriculture and Forestry
13. Minister for Transport
14. Minister for General Education & Instruction
15. Minister for Higher Education, Science and Technology
16. Minister for Environment
17. Minister for Housing and Physical Planning
18. Minister for Gender, Child and Social Welfare
19. Minister for Humanitarian Affairs and Disaster Management
20. Minister for Water Resources & Irrigation
21. Minister for Wildlife Conservation & Tourism
22. Minister for Animal Resources & Fisheries
23. Minister for Commerce, Industry and Investment
24. Chairperson of the Demobilisation, disarmament and Reintegration Commission (Secretary)

Mandate of the NDDRC Council

The council shall discharge the following responsibilities, for which it shall be accountable to His Excellency, the President of the Republic of South Sudan:

- To provide strategic political direction for the National DDR Programme.
- To review and approve various policies and guidelines for operation of the National DDR Programme.
- To ensure the coordination and active participation of the all relevant national line ministries in the National DDR Programme.
- To mobilize flexible multi-year funding from government, private sector and international development partners for the National DDR Programme.
- To review and approve the National DDR Programme annual as well as supplementary programme work plan and budget requests to the Ministry of Finance & Economic Planning.
- To endorse the semi-annual, annual and final NDDRP narrative and financial reports submitted by the Commission.
- To decide on the NDDRP launch, suspension, termination and closure, including dates they become effective.
- To oversee the performance of the Commission in executing its constitutional mandate.

Source: GOSS.

Appendix 7: Press Statement President Salva Kiir on 16 December 2013

Press Statement

H. E. Gen Salva Kiir Mayardit
President of the Republic of South Sudan

December 16, 2013, the State House J-1, Juba
Fellow compatriots, Citizens of South Sudan, Good afternoon,

The purpose of this press statement is to inform you about the events that unfolded last night on 15 December 2013 which continued until this morning 16 December 2013 in Juba city, which raised some fears and confusion, amongst the citizens of our beloved nation.

Yesterday at about 6:30 pm, during the closing of the SPLM National Liberation Council (NLC) meeting, an unidentified person near Nyakuron Cultural Centre released gunshots in the air and escaped. This was followed later by an attack at the SPLA HQ's near Juba University by a group of soldiers allied to the former vice president Dr Riek Machar Teny and his group. These attacks continued until this morning. However, I would like to inform you at the outset that your government is in full control of the security situation in Juba. The attackers fled and your forces are pursuing them. I promise you today that justice will prevail.

Fellow citizens,

Let me reiterate my statement during the opening of the NLC meeting a few days ago in which I said that my government will not allow the incidents of 1991 to repeat themselves again.

This prophet of doom continues to persistently pursue his actions of the past and I have to tell you that I will not allow or tolerate such incidents once again in our new nation. I condemn these criminal actions in the strongest terms possible.

Fellow citizens,

Your government led by the SPLM has articulated the ideals of democracy in the party as well as in the government and I will never deviate from them at any cost. The SPLM is fully committed to the peaceful and democratic transfer of power and will never allow political power to be transferred through violence.

Fellow citizens,

In response to the criminal acts of yesterday committed by this disgruntled group, and for the sake of the security and safety of our citizens, I declare a curfew in Juba is to be observed from 6:00 pm to 6:00 am with immediate effect from today, 16 December 2013 until further notice. Security organs are hereby directed to allow the residents of Juba to go about doing their normal work and move freely during the daylight hours. The security organs will also undertake a full investigation into these incidents and the government will ensure that the culprits answer for their crimes before the appropriate law institutions.

Fellow Citizens,

Rest assured that the government is doing all it can to make sure the citizens are secured and safe.

Long live SPLM/SPLA.

Long live the unity of our people.

Long live the Republic of South Sudan.

Thanks and God bless South Sudan and you all.

Appendix 8: South Sudanese reactions to 15 December 2013 – Dr Jok Madut Jok, Loyola Marymount University, California

(Posted on Facebook: 18 December 2013)
(Accessed: 19 December 2013)

Last week I posted a piece in this space praising South Sudanese leaders for what appeared to have been a willingness on their part to debate and dialogue on the political challenges facing the country without opting for violence, something that would have been a true sign of the nation's political maturity. I was writing from Los Angeles at the time, but I came to Juba on Saturday afternoon. Well, obviously I had spoken too soon, perhaps even jinxed it, in the light of the events of 15–18 December in Juba, when members of the Tiger Battalion of the Sudan People's Liberation Army (SPLA), the nation's defence forces, split and engaged in atrocious fights against one another. The fight broke out at two locations on Sunday night, the army command centre located south-west of Juba town and Bilpam army barracks to the north of Juba International Airport, before it spread to other areas within the city limits. By Tuesday afternoon, the fighting had reached the state house and the residence of the president, triggering the heaviest artillery fight when a number of soldiers climbed to the top of the high-rise buildings and launched fire into the president's compound.

The government claims that this was part of an attempted coup orchestrated and led by the former vice president, Riek Machar Teny, and which the government is said to have successfully foiled. According to official counts, the fighting has resulted in the death of 190 soldiers and 110 civilians, the latter of whom died in the crossfire, including people who died inside their homes from gunshots and were crushed when tanks rolled over their bodies. Further reports suggest that the final count in the next few days will most certainly reveal a much higher death toll, injury and damage to property.

This is arguably the most devastating politically motivated incident since 2005 when the comprehensive peace agreement (CPA) was signed to end the north-south war of the old Sudan. Most residents of Juba that we interviewed during the second day of fighting spoke of being heartbroken that South Sudanese citizens should continue to die at the hands of their own leaders, even in times of supposed peace and freedom. Thousands of people had to flee their homes and sought refuge inside the United Nations Mission camp, church and mosque grounds, with their relatives who were further away from the areas of fighting or fled the city altogether. Normal life, if there is such a thing in South Sudan to begin with, was disrupted at a time when people were preparing for Christmas and praying for this year to end peacefully and the next to usher in hope and promise.

The scenes of devastation have been turning my stomach. Dying men in hospitals that cannot be saved due to the lack of blood and no antibiotics, dead bodies piled up to rot, as relatives were too scared to move out to look for their loved ones. The displaced, especially children who suddenly found themselves without a roof over their heads and no food to eat, as the shops remained closed. All the while, sounds of gunfight, traversed with heart-shaking mortar and tank blasts, and which have continued sporadically well into today, Wednesday morning, have all spread fear in the population, leaving them hostage to the madness of a few power-hungry men.

The damage of this incident on future national cohesion, the image of the country and its efforts to encourage investment from outside will be far greater. International flights to and out of Juba were already cancelled for two days of the fighting, businesses were already shut for the same time and a curfew was imposed, all of which must have had serious consequences for business, the cost of which has yet to be tallied. Also uncertain is the fate of political stability in the whole country, especially in light of the accusation of so many political leaders as the ringleaders of the botched coup, some of whom have been arrested and others remain at large. Of these leaders currently detained, the government has confirmed the following:

1. Kosti Manibe Ngai, former Minister of Finance
2. Deng Alor Kuol, former Minister of Cabinet Affairs
3. Pagan Amum Okiech, former Secretary General of the SPLM
4. Cirino Hiteng Ofuho, former Minister of Culture, Youth and Sports
5. John Luk Jok, former Minister of Justice
6. Oyai Deng Ajak, former Minister of National Security
7. Chol Tong Mayai, former elected Governor of Lakes State, fired before end of his term
8. Madut Biar Yel, former Minister of Telecommunications and Postal Service
9. Gier Chuang Aluong, former Minister of Roads and Bridges
10. Majak D'Agoot Atem, former Deputy Minister of Defence and Veterans' Affairs

11. Ezekiel Lul Gatkuoth, former head of South Sudan Liaison Office in Washington DC, USA

Those still at large and being searched for are the following:

1. Riek Machar Teny, former vice president of the Republic and leader of the pack and who has been described as the architect of the attempted coup
2. Taban Deng Gai, former elected Governor of Unity State, fired before end of his term
3. Alfred Lado Gore, former Minister of the Environment

While the fighting within Juba town has calmed, there remain serious concerns, including the mistaken idea among some Dinka SPLA soldiers and rogue security agents that this is a Nuer-Dinka conflict, taking rather ghastly acts of revenge against Nuer. Innocent Nuers have already been killed in the neighbourhoods, stoking what might escalate into tragic acts of ethnic cleansing. Some really heart-wrenching acts have already occurred where Nuer soldiers have been attacked and killed, along with Nuer government officials, even those serving in the offices of Nuer ministers, and ordinary citizens suspected of having participated in the fight against the government. One Nuer officer I happened to know personally, who had been fighting on the SPLA side until Tuesday when there was a lull in the fighting, and had taken permission to go and check on his family, was found at home killed by his comrades, simply because he was Nuer and they mistook him for the enemy. There are many stories of this kind and such is the stuff of which the collapse of a state is made.

Other developments that are currently a source of worry are the reports that the situation is growing into a rebellion in many parts of the country. The most serious of these developments is the revolt in SPLA's Division 8, which is stationed in Jonglei State and commanded by one Peter Gadet, who has a long record of rebelling against the state. He has now reportedly done it again and has taken over some places in southern parts of Jonglei and is rumoured to be planning to meet up with Riek Machar Teny, who is also reported to have headed in that direction. If the SPLA engages Gadet and possibly Machar and Taban, then we will have an all-out civil war in South Sudan, a mere two years after independence, and making good all the predictions by outsiders that the South Sudanese will have limited capacity to build a peaceful nation.

Appendix 9: South Sudanese reactions to 15 December 2013 – Prof. Samson Wassara, University of Juba

Predictable Causes of the Current Political Crisis in South Sudan and Prospects

Introduction

The political crisis of 15 December 2013 is the tip of an iceberg that remains to be dealt with in the immediate future or over a relatively longer period of time. The causes of the crisis are rooted in historical legacies of the long civil war that seemed to have been ended by the signature of the Comprehensive Peace Agreement (CPA) in January 2005. However, the cosmetic reconciliation between the SPLM/A and the GOS, leading to the signing of the CPA, did not heal the wounds of the 1991 rift. Origins but not causes of the current crisis can be traced back to the event. But causes of the current crisis are associated with the past. What is significant is that the indifference of third parties, both national and international, contributed to the outbreak of untold violence in Juba that is spreading rapidly in the Greater Upper Nile region.

The issue

In the first place, failure of institutionalization of the political system and disregard for the rules of the game are the immediate foundational cause of the crisis. The Government of South Sudan (GOSS) was established on a weak foundation. The establishment of institutions was based on ethnic aggregation and personality cults. The political system was entrenched in institutionalized mistrust, where political leaders had much faith in ethnic protégés rather than in national institutions enshrined in the Transitional Constitution of the Republic of South Sudan (TCRSS). Established institutions were highly politicized without taking due note of the rules and regulations governing them. Conversely, where there were such rules and regulations, they were relegated to the margins of the *modus operandi*. These structures were inherited by the Government of South Sudan at independence on 9 July 2011. Furthermore, little attention was paid to national reconciliation. Political leaders missed the opportunity to promote post-conflict peacebuilding among people and institutions after the unity of South Sudan demonstrated during the referendum vote of January 2011.

Another element of discord in the process of state-building is the impact of the 2010 elections on the relationships among SPLM political contenders in South Sudan. The aftermath of the elections witnessed cracks in the ranks of SPLM members. Less attention was paid to the problem of the SPLM and independents, even when some members of the party resorted to violence and mini-rebellions. The logic of militarism dominated the attitudes of actors on the political stage such as 'those who are not with us and have taken up weapons should be crushed militarily'. The logic of militarism dominated political discourses with strong support for political groups in the absence of active and effective civil society organiations (CSOs) in the country.

The weak nature of opposition has its role in the perpetuation of instability in the country. With the exception of the numerically weak SPLM-DC, their voices were rarely heard. Many of the so-called opposition political parties engaged in unnecessary disputes that tore them apart. If they were in power they would have divided the country as what we are witnessing today. So, the absence of alternative views nurtured intolerance in the ranks of the government and the party. Therefore, the society adopted resignation and the attitude of 'wait and see'. This situation of indifference did not the help the cause of state-building and to applying corrective measures to the policies of the fragmented ruling party.

Structural problems in the formation of political institutions add another dimension to the current crisis. The end of a long civil war witnessed the integration of multiple strata of civil and military organizations into political units like the civil service, political parties and security sector institutions. These institutions were composed of blocks of wartime groups whose attitudes and behaviour structurally undermined nation-building processes. This could clearly be seen in entourages of people holding top national executive positions. They recruited armies of bodyguards from their family members, clans, tribal or regional clusters. This fact demonstrates the composite of the fragile political system before and after the independence of South Sudan.

The foundation of democracy consists of political parties. The Sudan People's Liberation Movement/Army (SPLM/A) was by far the most dominant political institution in the political system of South Sudan. Relations between the party and the army remained, nevertheless, blurred. The function of national defence was constitutionally conferred on the SPLA while the role of governance became the responsibility of the SPLM as the majority party in the National Legislative Assembly (NLA) and the Council of State (CoS). The composition of the SPLA lacked an integrated structure for national defence. Allegiance of the army was divided between political factions of the SPLM and its leaders to the extent that neutral political observers regarded the army as an instrument of individuals in the party. The policy of rewarding rebel groups with integration into the army created serious imbalances in the structure of the SPLA at the expense of peaceful regions in other parts of South Sudan. Has this policy contributed to the current crisis? This question remains a researchable one. Hence, personal and structural disputes were developing into dangerous levels to the extent that people began to speculate about the bitter end of squabbles within the SPLM/A.

Brief analysis

The event of 15 December 2013 just justified these assumptions which were held by many political analysts. Schisms began to develop within the SPLM after April 2013 when the deputy chairperson of the SPLM and vice president of South Sudan declared his intention to run for the chairmanship of the SPLM Convention expected in May 2013. The declaration of Riek Machar, the deputy chairperson of the SPLM, sparked an aggressive power struggle within the party and it spilled over into the government. The dissolution of the entire Cabinet was a landmark in the march towards political instability that the party, CSOs and faith-based organisation (FBOs) ignored. Even the AU, IGAD and the UN remained unconcerned witnesses until violence flared up. This political development culminated in the fragmentation of the national army along regional and ethnic lines, emanating from political discourses during the National Liberation Council (NLC) deliberations.

If there were to exist effective civil society organizations, a credible national army and proactive regional and international communities, they would have prevented the destructive pattern of political discourses in the political party and taken appropriate actions regarding the party's political bigotry. One, and many others, could argue that the political crisis was not an abrupt phenomenon, nor did it take people by surprise. It was preventable. The region's shuttle diplomacy taking place now is just the traditional reaction of members of the international community to national and international crises threatening peace and security. They always wait until fire breaks out before they engage in a fire brigade approach to dealing with flames instead of preventing them when a smokescreen forms.

Inconclusive conclusion

This piece is concluded with a question. From here, what is next? Do we continue to play the ostrich after this unprecedented event? How do we engage the citizens (not only intellectuals) to enable them to articulate their perceptions of political parties and governance of their nation? These questions relate to issues that call for debates in the short and medium term. Everybody agrees that the immediate policy priority is to stop the senseless violence taking place now. Then, what is important is to learn lessons from the crisis. Learning lessons from the past alone may not be enough, but applying outcomes of such lessons to substantive national questions is of real significance. Institutions of the state need serious reforms instead of transformations. National political institutions and structures should be put under the powered microscopes of political analysis. It is time for us to reflect on what is subject to reform in the political system, and how and when they should be pursued. The debate continues.

Source: With permission from the author.

Notes

1 Introduction

1. In this book, liberal peacebuilding is used along the Newman et al. (2009) definition of liberal peacebuilding as 'the promotion of democracy, market-based economic reforms and a range of other institutions associated with "modern" states as a driving force for building peace'.
2. Security as used in this book reflects its multifaceted and complex nature as well as difficulties in defining it but stays close to Buzan's definition of security as the pursuit of freedom from threats (Buzan 1991: 18).
3. Tziarras (2012), accessed April 2016: https://thegwpost.files.wordpress.com/2012/06/liberal-peace-and-peace-building-zenonas-tziarras-20123.pdf.
4. The Intergovernmental Authority on Development (IGAD) was created in 1996 to succeed the Intergovernmental Authority on Drought and Development that was founded in 1986 to deal with issues related to drought and desertification in the Horn of Africa. IGAD's mission is to assist and complement the efforts of the member states to achieve, through increased cooperation: food security and environmental protection, peace and security, and economic cooperation and integration in the region. The member states of IGAD are: Djibouti, Ethiopia, Eritrea, Kenya, Somalia, the Sudan, South Sudan and Uganda.
5. South Sudan, the world's newest country, is too poor to celebrate its independence day by Adam Taylor, accessed 24 December 2016: http://www.independent.co.uk/news/world/africa/south-sudan-worlds-newest-country-poor-independence-day-celebrate-a7113126.html.
6. Legitimacy, exclusion and power – Taban Deng Gai and the South Sudan peace process (Small Arms Survey, November 2016), accessed 20 December 2016: http://www.smallarmssurveysudan.org/fileadmin/docs/issue-briefs/HSBA-IB25-Taban-Deng-Gai-Dec-2016.pdf.
7. Community Consultation Report: Eastern Equatoria State, South Sudan UNDP, accessed December 2016: http://www.ss.undp.org/content/dam/southsudan/library/Documents/CSAC%20Reports/Eastern-%20Equatoria-Consult-May-12.pdf.
8. Various News Media outlets on 20 January 2014, accessed 23 January 2014: http://www.presstv.ir/detail/2014/01/22/347035/south-sudan-president-hits-out-at-un/, http://www.voanews.com/content/south-sudan-unmiss-ban-salva-

kiir-accuses-takeover/1834728.html, http://www.bbc.co.uk/news/world-africa-25826598.

2 South Sudan

1. Word used to refer to Egyptian military officers and administrators in Sudan during the Anglo-Egyptian Condominium.
2. Slavery in Africa Is Alive, Well and Ignored, accessed December 2016: http://www.huffingtonpost.ca/diane-bederman/slavery-africa_b_3975881.html.
3. See: Fox Report (2001), accessed December 2013: http://www.foxnews.com/story/2001/07/11/in-sudan-ancient-and-evil-slave-trade-persists/.
4. See: CNN Report (2012), accessed December 2013: http://www.youtube.com/watch?v=pOPD7_SCFNA.
5. See: BBC Four – *Lost Kingdoms of Africa* – Nubia, accessed September 2013: https://www.youtube.com/watch?v=EasSs1VED8w.

3 History of militarization

1. Conversations emanating from the transitions – international interdisciplinary conference at the University of Sussex in May 2009, accessed September 2013.
2. The Turks and Egyptians established the slave trade routes to the South mainly as a means of raising financial resources for their rule (Holt 1961).
3. The Mahdists in the Sudan refer to followers of the Al-Mahdiyyah, religious movement in the Sudan (1881–98) which was established by Muḥammad Aḥmad ibn Abd Allāh al-Mahdī. The movement succeeded in overthrowing the unpopular Turco-Egyptian rule in the Sudan and established a Mahdist state (1885), accessed January 2017: https://www.britannica.com/topic/al-Mahdiyyah.
4. Interview George Kinga Late (August 2006).
5. Tribe in South Sudan used in reference to the 64 distinct groupings of people united by a common language and ties of descent from a common ancestor, community of customs and traditions.
6. The period of colonial rule administered by the British and the Egyptians jointly, otherwise referred to as the Anglo-Egyptian Condominium (1898–1945).
7. Interview with an elderly Southern Sudanese former teacher and Anyanya 1 army officer.
8. Interview former parish priest Lowoi (December 2010).
9. The Nasir Declaration took place in August 1991.
10. Interview former SPLA soldier – Upper Nile region 1983–8 (June 2013).

11 Interview with Catholic priest St Patrick's Missionaries, Riwoto (June 2011).
12 Depopulisation for oil was a programme adopted by the Sudan government to drive villagers in Southern Sudan's Bahr el Ghazal and Upper Nile regions out of their homes to make war for oilfields. Villages were attacked by men on horseback known as the Mujahadeed or Murahaleen: Sudan, Oil, and Human Rights, Human Rights Watch accessed February 2014.
13 IGAD is a regional body in the Horn of Africa region.
14 Juba Declaration has collapsed, accessed 7 October 2013: http://www.sudantribune.com/spip.php?page=imprimable&id_article=14974.
15 Paulino Matip press conference in Khartoum on 31 March 2006 – accessed 4 October 2013.
16 The Countdown, accessed 2 October 2013: http://www.enoughproject.org/publications/sudan-countdown
17 United Nations Security Council Resolution 2046 was unanimously adopted on 2 May 2012. Called for immediate halt to fighting between Sudan and South Sudan. Obliged the AU to find a solution to underlying disputes.
18 Interview with executive director of the Sudd Institute (February 2014).

4 Contextualizing security restructuring and reforms

1 Interview former SPLA commander now a minister (February 2013).
2 Interview retired British Army brigadier (August 2013).
3 The Integrated DDR Standards IDDRS proposed as the blueprint for post-conflict reconstruction in South Sudan. Interview UNDP peacebuilding officer South Sudan April 2010.
4 Interview country director Caritas Switzerland (December 2013).
5 Kawaja is the term used to refer to 'white people' in South Sudan and collectively used to refer to the expert community and INGO workers.
6 Interview with major general – Army training and transformation (June 2013).
7 Interview Swiss Army officer working on SSR.
8 Interview SPLA Zone commander June 2013.
9 Interview with major general – SPLA training and transformation (June 2013).
10 Interview senior military official – UN department of Peacekeeping Operations at UNMISS (April 2013).
11 SPLA Defence white paper 2008.
12 August 2015 Peace Agreement – Agreement on the Resolution of the Conflict in the Republic of South Sudan – pp. 6, 26.
13 US Embassy functions in South Sudan are heavily tied to USAID functions in South Sudan (UN – OCHA Senior Official May 2013).

14 Interview US Embassy official (April 2013).
15 UN Handbook on Integrated Disarmament, Demobilisation and Reintegration Standards launched 2006 and first used on South Sudan. Jointly developed by staff from 15 United Nations agencies, departments, funds and programmes and the International Organisation for Migration taking from their post-conflict experiences: http://pksoi.army.mil/doctrine_concepts/documents/UN%20 Guidelines/IDDRS.pdf.
16 Interview Consultant on DDR UNDP (March 2012).
17 Interview senior project officer – Saferworld (May 2013).
18 DDR Coordinator (EES) GIZ – (November 2010).
19 Interview GIZ DDR Coordinator (EES) (May 2011).
20 Part of the HSBA for Sudan and South Sudan series (June 2013).
21 Interview with Senior UN DPKO military official in South Sudan – has worked in Liberia, Sierra Leone and East Timor (November 2012).
22 Interview Col SPLA EES Division (December 2010).
23 Interview UNDP DDR consultant (March 2012).
24 Focus Group Data.
25 Survey of Public Opinion: South Sudan's Greater Equatoria Region (21 May–15 June 2012): http://www.iri.org/sites/default/files/2012%20August%2017%20 Survey%20of%20South%20Sudan's%20Greater%20Equatoria%20Region,%20 May%2021-June%2015,%202012_0.pdf.
26 See: http://www.ssddrc.org/ accessed 2011.
27 Interview senior researcher training at the Sudd Institute (April 2013).
28 http://www.bbc.co.uk/news/world-africa-17218921.
29 Interview colonel SPLA spokesman office (February 2013).
30 Interview with a BCSSAC director (January 2013).
31 Interview with a special UN Secretary General representative (March 2012).
32 Interview liaison officer Kuron peace village (November 2010).
33 See: http://www.ssddrc.org/home.html, accessed November 2013.
34 Empirical observations from 2002 to 2005.
35 See: http://www.ssddrc.org/about-ssddrc.html, accessed November 2013.

5 Realizing security restructuring and reforms

1 Interview with major general – retired South Sudanese Army in SAF (July 2013).
2 Interview retired British Army brigadier SPLA adviser (June 2013).
3 Interview transport commandant (May 2012).
4 Interview retired British major (June 2013).
5 Data from US Embassy – economics department February 2016.

6. Interview senior researcher training at the Sudd Institute (September 2013).
7. Interview Sudd Institute director of research (May 2013).
8. Interview with major general – Army training and transformation (June 2013).
9. Interview Ministry of Defence Bilpham HQ – SPLA officer (May 2013).
10. Convergence of SPLA soldiers in Equatoria for registration in Kiyala – August 2005 (fieldwork).
11. Term often used to refer to the end of the war.
12. Interview lieutenant colonel SPLA HQ (August 2013).
13. Interview senior UNMISS military official – UN DPKO – has worked in Liberia, Sierra Leone and East Timor (April 2013).
14. Interview minister – brigadier general and former SPLA commander (February 2013).
15. Interview executive director – Sudd Institute (May 2013).
16. Interview with major general – SPLA training and transformation (June 2013).
17. Interview with research director Sudd Institute (May 2013).
18. Interview lieutenant colonel SPLA HQ (May 2013).
19. See: The Conflict in South Sudan: The Political Context Testimony prepared for the Senate Foreign Relations Committee: accessed 10 January 2014: http://www.usip.org/publications/the-conflict-in-south-sudan-the-political context?utm_content=buffere8a1f&utm_medium=social&utm_source=twitter.com&utm_campaign=buffer.
20. Interview with major general – Army training and transformation (June 2013).
21. Interview economics professor University of Juba (June 2012).
22. In 2014 the 'National Security Services Bill 2014' was introduced. The bill was controversial and returned to parliament for revision late 2014. The bill became law in 2015.
23. See: Switching Gears from Concepts to Implementation: Defence Transformation in South Sudan By: Stephanie Blair | South Sudan | 14 December 2012, accessed 10 January 2014.
24. See: Key research themes in Policing in Conflict and Post-conflict Societies Durham University https://www.dur.ac.uk/dgsi/research/police/.
25. Interview chairman Red Army Foundation (March 2013).
26. See: Southern Sudan Justice and Security Sectors Interim Review Draft January 2011 PG: 54.
27. Interview with major general – SPLA training and transformation (June 2013).
28. Interview executive director Sudd Institute (October 2012).
29. In December 2015, South Sudan administrative structures changed from ten states to 28 states in law following an earlier Republican presidential decree.
30. See: Southern Sudan Justice and Security Sectors Interim Review Draft January 2011 PG: 54.

31 Interview South Sudan Police Service spokesperson (April 2013).
32 Interview with major general – SPLA training and transformation (June 2013).
33 Interview senior police inspector – traffic (November 2012).
34 Interview SSR project official Swiss Army reservist (September 2012).
35 Interview senior project officer – Saferworld (May 2013).
36 Accessed December 2016: https://www.wired.com/2010/11/ff_ak47/.
37 Interview police commandant SSPS – wildlife (June 2013).
38 Interview with former South Sudanese consultant in the Ministry of SPLA and Veteran Affairs (February 2013).
39 Interview with major general – SPLA training and transformation (June 2013).
40 Interview driver/former fighter Catholic Diocese of Torit (March 2011).
41 Interview chairman Red Army Foundation (June 2013).
42 Interview senior researcher admin Sudd Institute (September 2013).
43 Interview with senior police commandant – March 2012.
44 Interview retired British Army brigadier SPLA adviser (June 2013).
45 See South Sudan VP calls for mass military mobilization: By Ijoo Bosco, *Sudan Tribune*, Thursday 7 January 2014, accessed 10 January 2014: http://www.sudantribune.com/spip.php?iframe&page=imprimable&id_article=49491.

6 Restructuring governance

1 Although the Transitional Government of National Unity (TGoNU) set up in the August 2015 peace agreement presented yet another important milestone in the country's governance narrative, it is too soon for its meaningful interrogation to take place.
2 The UN, World Bank, USAID and European Union are among major donors that support elections in countries coming out of conflict as a norm. In the case of the UN, the United Nations Development Programme pays much attention to governance whilst electoral affairs is now a major part of UN peacekeeping missions, including the UN mission in Sudan and subsequently South Sudan.
3 Interview SuNDE Elections observer (November 2009).
4 Interview with a programme manager with American National Democratic Institute (February 2013).
5 Interview with a senior programme officer with the American National Democratic Institute – NDI 2 (February 2013).
6 Focus Group Discussion 6 with senior national staff of the American National Democratic Institute (February 2013).
7 Interview Caritas Switzerland (November 2009).

8   See Appendix 4 SRRC officers list sent to the UN operation life Sudan (2004).
9   Extract from NDI 5 and NDI 2 in interviews with South Sudanese staff of the American National Democratic Institute in Focus Group Discussion 6 (February 2013).
10 Interview CEO MatMedia Ltd (April 2012).
11 CANS: referred to civilian structures in SPLA/M-held areas. CANS – Civil Authority of New Sudan was established at the lower levels of Government (County, Payam and Boma (Rolandsen 2007: 5).
12 Interview senior civil servant Ministry of Justice (October 2012).
13 Interview with Irish Catholic missionary who has worked in Sudan (South) for 30 years (November 2010).
14 Interview project official Swiss Army officer (July 2011).
15 Interview with assistant administrator Catholic Diocese of Torit / Misereor Germany who has worked and lived in the south since 1976 (November 2010).
16 Extract from Focus Group Discussion with NDI senior staff.
17 Interview NDI Senior Programme Officer – NDI 2 (February 2013).
18 Interview with South Sudanese consultant for the Chinese government (November 2010).
19 Interview Nigerian naval captain attached to the UN mission in South Sudan (September 2011).
20 Interview NDI senior programme officer – NDI 4 (February 2013).
21 Interview NDI senior programme officer – NDI 2 (February 2013).
22 Most of the participants attending the public forum titled 'Participatory democracy: the role and position of young leaders' were students from the University of Juba or in other colleges in the capital.
23 Interview NDI programme assistant – NDI 3 (February 2013).
24 Interview NDI senior field manager – NDI 1 (February 2013).
25 Interview NDI senior field manager – NDI 1 (February 2013).
26 See full speech by Uganda President Yoweri Museveni 15 January 2014, accessed 16 January 2014: http://chimpreports.com/index.php/mobile/people/blogs/15984-museveni-speech-in-full-at-5th-icglr-summit.html.
27 Interview with former child soldier, returnee from Australia (April 2009).
28 Interview with a programme manager with the American National Democratic Institute (February 2013).
29 Interviews SPLA press office Bilpham SPLA HQ.
30 Presidential address to parliament on the decision to go, Heglig/Panthou (March 2012).
31 Interview with an SPLM party official at the party national HQ (October 2012).
32 Interview with an SPLM member of parliament for Upper Nile (November 2012).
33 Interview NDI Programme Manager – NDI 5 (February 2013).

34 Interview with a consultant with the Ministry of Defence and SPLA Affairs (March 2011).
35 Informal chat with an SPLA colonel; proud of the army's achievements during the war, dismissive of the political process that resolved the conflict in 2005 and suspicious of the government which he says is run specifically by people who are returning from Khartoum and from exile and hence don't understand the sacrifices they made.
36 Interview SPLM organizer (July 2011).
37 Interview Deloitte consultant – state parliaments (October 2011).
38 Interview Louis Berger Group consultant on gender (September 2011).
39 Interview with IRI programme officer (February 2013).
40 Interview NDI programme assistant – NDI 3 (February 2013).
41 The Derg was a military council that governed Ethiopia under Mengistu Haile Mariam.
42 Interview Louis Berger Group consultant with the Ministry of Roads (September 2011).
43 Interview director South Sudanese think tank – Juba (February 2014).
44 Interview Louis Berger Group consultant with the Ministry of Roads (November 2012).
45 Interview Louis Berger Group consultant with the Ministry of Finance (May 2012).
46 Interviews with local businessmen, community leaders, local leaders and civilian population expresses a dissatisfaction with the government but acknowledged they were better than having war.
47 Interview Chief Imilai Boma (November 2010).
48 Interview with IRI programme officer (August 2011).
49 Interview with Irish Catholic missionary who has worked in Sudan (South) for 30 years – (November 2010).
50 See FGs data attached.
51 Interview with assistant administrator Catholic Diocese of Torit/Misereor Germany (November 2010).
52 Interview Country Director IRI – INGO working on governance, democracy and elections (August 2011).
53 Interview Country Director NDI – INGO working in governance, democracy and elections (October 2011) and the Sudanese Group for Democracy and Elections (SuGDE) and the Sudanese Network for Democratic Elections (SuNDE) elections report April 2010.
54 Interview with South Sudanese consultant for the Chinese government (November 2010).
55 In story carried by the newspaper the *Sudan Tribune* on Wednesday 1 July 2009, Sudan delays national elections for the second time.

56 Interview with IRI programme officer (November 2012).
57 Interview NDI programme manager – NDI 5 (February 2013).
58 Interview with the Catholic Bishop of Torit on the new Eastern Equatoria State government (November 2010).
59 Interviews with Ikotos County commissioner (July 2009), Gurtong reporter – Torit (November 2010), informal chats with participants of training for elections observers by NDI at hotel Torit (June 2009).
60 Telephone interview with the chairman of the South Sudan High Elections Committee (April 2010).
61 Interviews carried on BBC *Focus on Africa* programme with various candidates in western Equatoria State (15.00 hrs programme 17 April 2010).
62 Article from *Sudan Tribune* newspaper published on 19 April 2010.
63 Interview programme manager CDOT (November 2010).
64 Interview IRI country director (August 2011).
65 See timeline of Sudan's coups, elections and countercoups in the appendix.
66 Small Arms Survey – The Human Security Baseline Assessment (HSBA) for Sudan and South Sudan.
67 UN Secretary General Ban Ki-moon quoted by the UN News Centre – accessed on 9 April 2013.
68 See Appendix 2 for table of current armed rebellions in South Sudan.
69 Interview IRI programme officer (November 2012).
70 Ibid.
71 Interview Universal Strategy Group Inc. legal consultant with the Ministry of Defence (July 2011).
72 Interview SPLM Member of Upper House of Parliament – Council of States (December 2011).
73 Deloitte consultant working with state parliaments (October 2011).
74 Interview vice president for Africa Internews (August 2011).
75 Interview IRI country director (September 2012).
76 Interview IRI programme officer (November 2012).
77 Interview CEO MatMedia Ltd (April 2012); interview Universal Strategy Group Inc legal consultant with the Ministry of Defence (March 2011).
78 Focus Group 6 was held with South Sudanese senior staff of NDI (February 2013).
79 Interview NDI senior programme officer – NDI (February 2013).
80 See Appendix 6 ministers in post-CPA Government and their roles current and previous in the SPLA/M.
81 Interview with senior researcher South Sudan think tank – the Sudd Institute (February 2013).
82 Interview IRI programme officer (November 2012).

83 Interview SPLM Member of Upper House of Parliament – Council of States (April 2011).
84 Interview operations manager of Warrior Security, a private security company in South Sudan (February 2013).
85 Jok Madut Jok Nairobi Forum, accessed 15 January 2014: http://www.riftvalley.net/event/south-sudan-peace-possible.
86 UNOCHA – South Sudan statistics document: https://docs.unocha.org/sites/dms/SouthSudan/South_Sudan_Media_Briefing_Pack/South%20Sudan%20humanitarian%20and%20development%20statistics%20-%20December%202013.pdf. Accessed July 2018.
87 During the research I asked every person I spoke to what impact they thought illiteracy had on their work and very few had thought about it as an issue.
88 Interview with SSRC official (November 2010).
89 FG 6 with NDI senior staff involved in-depth discussions on patronage in South Sudan.
90 Interview SPLM Member of Upper House of Parliament – Council of States (December 2011).

7 Arms and livelihoods

1 South Sudan's man-made famine demands a response: *Washington Post* 22 February 2017 by Editorial Board accessed April 2017.
2 Interview with the Justice & Peace coordinator – Catholic Diocese of Torit (December 2011).
3 Interview with Swiss military official working on SSR (September 2011).
4 Interview with research director Sudd Institute (April 2013).
5 Interview with SRRC official Torit (March 2012).
6 Sudan's First Civil War (1955–72) went on for 17 years, the Second Civil War (1983–2005) lasted for 21 years.
7 Interview Bishop Paride Taban Kuron Peace Village (November 2009).
8 The periphery in the Sudan was said to include all areas in the country outside the two cities of Khartoum and Omdurman. These cities on the conference of the White and Blue Niles have been the seat of power throughout Sudan's civilizations. They have also received the lion's share of the country's resources while marginalizing the rest of the region. This has been the cause of all of Sudan's conflicts in recent history.
9 Interview with World Bank official working with the Multi Donor Trust Fund in January 2011.
10 World Bank classifications, accessed 5 April 2013: http://data.worldbank.org/about/country-classifications.

11 Extracted from South Sudan Development Plan 2011–13 from the Ministry of Finance and Economic Planning.
12 Interview professor of economics University of Juba (June 2012).
13 Interview with GIZ DDR coordinator (EES) (November 2010).
14 Interview with the executive director Sudd Institute (May 2013).
15 Interview with economics professor University of Juba (June 2012).
16 Interview with senior government official (February 2013).
17 Conflict trap a term used to refer to the high risk of civil war and / or recurrence of war in fragile and post-conflict countries (Paul Collier 2003).
18 Interview with project assistant agriculture GIZ (November 2010).
19 Interview with former commissioner western Equatoria State (March 2013).
20 Interview with Assistant Minister of Humanitarian Affairs (May 2012).
21 Interview with senior official Ministry of General Education Juba (May 2012).
22 Interview with coordinator skills South Sudan (August 2012).
23 Interview commissioner Magwi County (November 2012).
24 Interview with former state Minister of Labour (October 2012).
25 Interview with Assistant Minister of Humanitarian Affairs (May 2012).
26 World Bank report titled 'World Bank for results 2012' in the 'support to sector actions related Toposa-Crisis Directions' section, p. 9.
27 Interview with agriculture professor University of Juba (May 2011).
28 Interview with project assistant agriculture GIZ (November 2010).
29 A reflection of many reports by the government and donors i.e. World Bank, 2012; Agricultural Potential, Rural Roads, and Farm Competitiveness in South Sudan, USAID South Sudan, 2011; Maize Yield in South Sudan – Central, Eastern and Central Equatoria, Selassie, 2009; Southern Sudan: Non-Oil Revenue Study. Report for the African Development Bank, Sebit, 2011; Analysis of Farm Production Costs in Southern Sudan, GOSS, 2011a; South Sudan Development Strategy 2011–13, Government of Southern Sudan (GOSS), 2007; Agriculture and Forestry Sector Strategic Plan, 2007–11.
30 Interview with the senior researcher training the Sudd Institute (April 2013).
31 United States Institute of Peace – special report: Oil and State-Building in South Sudan; accessed May 2014: http://www.usip.org/sites/default/files/Oil_and_State_Building_South_Sudan.pdf.
32 South Sudan seeks food and farmland investments Thursday 22 December 2011, accessed 20 April 2013: http://english.alarabiya.net/articles/2011/12/22/184063.html.
33 South Sudan's literate population is about 27 per cent (South Sudan Development Plan 2011).
34 Interview with professor of agriculture University of Juba (May 2011).
35 Ibid.

36 Interview with food and security coordinator Catholic diocese of Torit (April 2011).
37 Blood compensation applies when, for example, someone has been killed and the family of the victim is compensated for their loss by the perpetrator and his family.
38 Interview with village elder Imuyalei (March 2011).
39 Interview with a former rebel soldier now farmer in Torit (June 2011).
40 Interviews with agriculture professor University of Juba and consultant for the Ministry of Agriculture on food security and food production potential in South Sudan (May 2011), WFP in Kapoeta (August 2011), food security coordinator CDOT (November 2012).
41 Interview with coordinator Akil Centre (June 2011).
42 Interview with professor of agriculture University of Juba (May 2011).
43 Ibid.
44 Interview senior government minister (May 2013).

8 Conclusion

1 See: http://www.bbc.co.uk/news/world-africa-12317927 accessed 17 January 2014.
2 The Rift Valley Institute (RVI) is an independent, non-profit organization, founded in Sudan in 2001, currently working in seven countries in Eastern and Central Africa.
3 See: Sudan Downhill – Under Omar al-Bashir, Sudan is in steepening decline (1 February 2014).
4 Interview with negotiator at South Sudan talks in Addis Ababa (February 2014).
5 Meeting of South Sudanese professionals in the capital Juba in February 2014.
6 Interview peacebuilding expert PACT South Sudan (May 2016).
7 Interview with professor of politics University of Juba (September 2013).
8 See: Western 'nation-building' system was as chaotic and dysfunctional as it was in Iraq, Afghanistan, Somalia, Yemen, Libya and East Timor.
9 See Riek Machar Voice of America interview 3 February 2014.
10 See: http://www.huffingtonpost.co.uk/paul-reynolds/south-sudan_b_4491066.html accessed 4 February 2014.
11 The 2009 national Baseline Household Survey also reveals that the country faces several human development challenges. Only 27 per cent of the population aged 15 years and above is literate, with significant gender disparities: the literacy rate for males is 40 per cent compared to 16 per cent for females. World Bank: accessed December 2016. https://siteresources.worldbank.org/SUDANEXTN/Resources/South-Sudan-Poverty-Profile.pdf. Accessed July 2018.

12 Interview with SPLA major general – Army SPLA training and transformation (June 2013).
13 Interview Country Director – International Republican Institute (IRI) (September 2012).
14 Interview director South Sudanese think tank – Juba (February 2014).
15 See: http://www.dailymaverick.co.za/article/2014-01-23-analysis-south-sudans-president-can-moan-but-the-un-will-keep-picking-up-his-slack/. Accessed February 2014.
16 Comments by: Nicola Pontarathe World Bank Representative in Juba http://www.riftvalley.net/event/south-sudan-peace-possible. Accessed February 2014.
17 Comments by Jok Madut Jok: former Undersecretary of Youth Culture and Sports GOSS http://www.riftvalley.net/event/south-sudan-peace-possible. Accessed February 2014.

Bibliography

Abbink, J. (2003) 'Ethiopia-Eritrea: Proxy wars and prospects of peace in the horn of Africa', *Journal of Contemporary African Studies*, 21(3), 407–26.

Abrahamsson, B. (1972) *Military Professionalization and Political Power*, Beverly Hills, CA: Sage Publications.

Adams, G. and Dzokoto, V. (1985) 'Doubts about the "Lost Pharaohs"', *Journal of Near Eastern Studies*, 44(3), 185–92.

Adams, G. and Dzokoto, V. (2010) 'Self and identity in African Studies', *Self and Identity*, 2(4), 345–59.

Adams, W. (1977) *Nubia: Corridor to Africa*, London: Princeton University Press.

ADB (2012) 'South Sudan Interim Country Strategy Paper 2012–2014', *Technical report*, African Development Bank Group.

Adler, E. (1997) 'Seizing the middle ground: Constructivism in world politics', *European Journal of International Relations*, 3(3), 319–63.

Africa Confidential (2010) 'Strategy of sabotage', 51(17).

Africa, S. (2011) 'The transformation of the South African security sector: Lessons and challenges', *Geneva Centre for the Democratic Control of Armed Forces (DCAF)*, Policy Paper 33.

Ahluwalia, P. (2001) *Politics and Post-colonial Theory: African Inflections*, Psychology Press.

Akol, J. (2007) *Dinka Folktales*, Nairobi: Paulines Publications Africa.

Akol, L. (2011), *SPLM-SPLA: Inside an African Revolution*, Khartoum University Printing Press.

Albrecht, P. and Jackson, P. (2011) *Reconstructing Security after Conflict: Security Sector Reform in Sierra Leone*, London.

Alden, C. (1995) 'Swords into ploughshares? The United Nations and demilitarisation in Mozambique', *International Peacekeeping*, 2, 175–93.

Alison, J. (2008) *Gramsci, Political Economy and International Relations Theory: Modern Princes and Naked Emperors*, London.

Alliance for a Green Revolution in Africa (AGRA) (2016) *Africa Agriculture Status Report 2016: Progress towards Agricultural Transformation in Africa*.

Andrews, M. (2008) 'The good governance agenda: Beyond indicators without theory', *Oxford Development Studies*, 36(4), 379–407.

Annor-Frempong, I. and Ojijo, N. (2012) 'Rebuilding Livelihoods in Post-Conflict and Protracted Crisis Countries: Results of the Kigali Workshop on Strengthening Capacity for Agricultural Innovation'. Workshop paper.

Apuuli, K. (2014) 'Explaining the (il)legality of Uganda's intervention in the current South Sudan conflict', *African Security Review*, 23(4), 352–69.

Apuuli, K. (2015) 'IGAD's mediation in the current South Sudan conflict: Prospects and challenges', *African Security*, 8(2), 120–45.

Arnold, M. and Alden, C. (2007) 'This gun is our food: Demilitarising the white army militias of South Sudan', *Security in Practice: Norwegian Institute of International Affairs*, 722(3), 1–26.

Ayangafac, C. (2009) 'An alternative policy option to post-conflict elections in Africa', *Technical report*, ISPI (Italian Institute for International Political Studies).

Baas, S. (2012) *From Civilians to Soldiers and from Soldiers to Civilians: Mobilization and Demobilization in Sudan*, Amsterdam University Press.

Babbie, E. (2010) *The Practice of Social Research*, Boston, MA.

Bader, V. (2001) 'Culture and identity: Contesting constructivism', *Ethnicities*, 1(2), 251–85.

Baker, B. (2007), 'Conflict and African police culture: The cases of Uganda, Rwanda and Sierra Leone'. In *Police Occupational Culture (Sociology of Crime, Law and Deviance, Volume 8)*. Edited by Megan O'Neill, Monique Marks, Anne-Marie Singh. Emerald Group, pp. 321–47.

Baldwin, D. A. (1997) 'The concept of security', *Review of International Studies*, 23(1) (January 1997): 5–26.

Banal, L, Rowe, I, and Berhe, M. G. (2009) *Sudan: Assessment of the Disarmament and Demobilisation Process*, Khartoum: United Nations Integrated DDR Unit Report.

Barakat, S. and Zyck, S. (2009) 'The evolution of post-conflict recovery', *Third World Quarterly*, 30(6), 1069–86.

Baral, L. (2006) *Nepal: Quest for Participatory Democracy*, New Delhi.

Barnes, J. (1979) *Who Should Know What? Social Science, Privacy and Ethics*, Cambridge.

Barnes, S. (2001) 'The contribution of democracy to rebuilding post-conflict societies', *American Journal of International Law*, 95(1), 86–101.

Bassil, N. (2013) *The Post-Colonial State and Civil War in Sudan: The Origins of Conflict in Darfur*, I.B. Tauris.

Bastian, S. and Luckham, R. (2003) *Can Democracy Be Designed? The Political Institutional Choice in Conflict-Torn Societies*, London.

Batchelor, P. and Lamb, K. (2004) *Demilitarisation and Peace-Building in Southern Africa*, Aldershot.

Bayart, J.-F. (2009) *The State in Africa*, Paris.

Beetham, D. (1992) 'Liberal democracy and the limits of democratization', *Political Studies*, Special issue, 40–53.

Belsey, C. (2002) *Poststructurism – A Very Short Introduction*, Oxford.

Berghof Foundation (2006) 'Sudan: Conflict Analysis and Options for Systemic Conflict Transformation – A Northern and a Southern View'. Report by Berghof Foundation for Peace Support.

Berman, B. (1998) 'Ethnicity, patronage and the African state: The politics of uncivil nationalism', *African Affairs*, 97(388), 305–41.

Berman, B. (2010) 'Ethnicity & democracy in Africa', *JICA Research Institute*, 22, 1–40.

Bernstein, H., Crow, B. and Johnson, H. (1992) *Rural Livelihoods: Crises and Responses*, Oxford.

Berridge, W. (2015) *Civil Uprisings in Modern Sudan: The 'Khartoum Springs' of 1964 and 1985*, Bloomsbury Publishing.

Berridge, W. (2013) 'Sudan's security agencies: Fragmentation, visibility and mimicry, 1908–89', *Intelligence and National Security*, 28(6), 845–67.

Birner, R., Cohen, M. J. and Ilukor, M. (2011) 'Rebuilding agricultural livelihoods in post-conflict situations: What are the governance challenges? The case of Northern Uganda', *Technical report, International Food Policy Research Institute, Oxfam America, Makerere University*.

Blair, S. (2012) *Switching Gears from Concepts to Implementation: Defence Transformation in South Sudan*, Ontario, Canada: The Centre for Security Governance.

Blanchard, L. P. (2012) *Sudan and South Sudan: Current Issues for Congress and U.S. Policy*, Washington, D.C.: Congressional Research Service.

Bland, D. (1999) 'A unified theory of civil–military relations', *Armed Forces and Society*, 26(1), 7–26.

Boas, M. and Dunn, K. (2007) *African Guerrillas: Raging against the Machine*, Boulder, CO.

Bogaards, M. (2013) 'Re-examining African elections', *Journal of Democracy*, 24(4), 151–60.

Boudreau, L. (2013) *Don't Call Me Out of My Name Spirituality for the 21st Century a Member of the Christian Left Speaks Out: Some Insights into Social Analysis for Ordinary People*, Bloomington, IA.

Branch, A. and Mampilly, Z. (2005) 'Winning the war, but losing the peace? The dilemma of SPLM/A civil administration and the tasks ahead', *The Journal of Modern African Studies*, 43(1), 1–20.

Branch, D. and Cheeseman, N. (2008) 'Democratization, sequencing, and state failure in Africa: Lessons from Kenya', *African Affairs*, 108, 1–26.

Breidlid, A. (2010) *A Concise History of South Sudan*, Kampala.

Breidlid, A. (2014) *A Concise History of South Sudan*, African Books Collective, 2010, East Africa, Revised edition.

Brinkerhoff, D. (2005) 'Rebuilding governance in failed states and post-conflict societies: Core concepts and cross-cutting themes', *Public Administration and Development*, 25, 3–14.

Bryden, M. and Brickhill, J. (2010) 'Disarming Somalia: Lessons in stabilisation from a collapsed state', *Conflict, Security & Development*, 10(2), 239–62.

Bryman, A. (1988) *Quantity and Quality in Social Research*, London.

Bryden, A. (2012) *Pushing Pieces around the Chessboard or Changing the Game? DDR, SSR and the Security-Development Nexus*, Geneva Centre For the democratic control of armed forces (DCAF), chapter 7, pp. 201–24.

Brzoska, M. (2000) 'The concept of security sector reform', *Security Sector Reform Briefing Paper, Technical report, Bonn International Centre for Conversion (BICC)*.

Brzoska, M. (2003) *Development Donors and the Concept of Security Sector Reform*. DCAF Occasional Paper No. 4. Geneva: DCAF, November 2003, p. 36.

Brzoska, M. (2006) 'Introduction: Criteria for evaluating post-conflict reconstruction and security sector reform in peace support operations', *International Peacekeeping*, 13(1), 1–13.

Brzoska, M. and Heinemann-Grüder, A. (2004), *Security Sector Reform and Post-Conflict Reconstruction under International*. Auspices, Genève, Geneva Centre for the Democratic Control of Armed Forces, chapter 6, pp. 121–41.

Bucholtz, M. (2001) 'Reflexivity and critique in discourse analysis', *Critique of Anthropolog*, 21, 165.

Bulmer, M. and Gilbert, N. (2004) *Researching Social Life*, London, 45–57.

Burchill, S., Devetak, R., Linklater, A., Donnelly, J., Nardin, T., Paterson, M., Reus-Smit, C. and True, J. (2009) *Theories in International Relations*, London: Palgrave Macmillan.

Burk, J. (2002) 'Theories of civil-military relations', *Armed Forces and Society*, 29(1), 7–29.

Burnham, P., Lutz, K., Grant, W. and Layton-Henry, Z. (2008) *Research Methods in Politics*, Basingstoke.

Butler, C. (2002) *Postmodernism: A Very Short Introduction*, Oxford.

Buxton, J. (2006) 'Securing democracy in complex environments', *Democratization*, 13(5), 709–23.

Buzan, B. (2008) *People, States and Fear: An Agenda for International Security Studies in the Post-Cold War Era*. 1st edition 1981, 2nd Edition. Hertfordshire: Harvester Wheatsheaf, 1991 and 2008 with a new preface from the author.

Buzan, B. (1991) 'New patterns of global security in the twenty-first century', *International Affairs*, 67(3) (1 July 1991), 431–51.

Buzan, B. and Hansen, L. (2009) *The Evolution of International Security Studies*, Cambridge.

Buzan, B., Wæever, O. and de Wilde, J. (1998) *Security: A New Framework for Analysis*, Boulder, CO.

Cain, M. (1979) 'Trends in the sociology of police work', *International Journal of the Sociology of Law*, 7, 143–67.

Call, C. and Cook, S. (2003) 'On democratization and peace-building', *Global Governance*, 9, 2.

Call, C. and Cousens, E. (2008) 'Ending wars and building peace: International responses to war-torn societies', *International Studies Perspectives*, 9(1), 1–21.

Call, C. and Wyeth, V. (2008) *Building States to Build Peace*, Boulder, CO.

Campbell, D., Dunne, T., Kurki, M. and Smith, S. (2007) *International Relations Theories: Discipline and Diversity*, Oxford.

Campbell, D. and Campbell, K. M. (2010) 'Soldiers as police officers / police officers as soldiers: Role evolution and revolution in the United States', *Armed Forces and Society*, 36(2), 327–50.

Carney, D. (1998) *Sustainable Rural Livelihoods: What Contribution Can We Make?*, Department for International Development.

Carothers, T. (2011) *Aiding Democracy Abroad: The Learning Curve*, Carnegie Endowment.

Carr, C. (2008) *Kalashnikov Culture: Small Arms Proliferation and Irregular Warfare*, Santa Barbara, CA.

Carrier, N. and Kochore, H. (2003) *Sustainable Livelihoods Approaches: Progress and Possibilities for Change*, Department for International Development.

Carrier, N. and Kochore, H. (2014) 'Navigating ethnicity and electoral politics in northern Kenya: The case of the 2013 election', *Journal of Eastern African Studies*, 8(1), 135–52.

Carter Center, The (2010) 'Observing Sudan's 2010 National Elections – Final Report', *The Carter Center Technical report*.

Castells, M. (1983) *The City and the Grassroots: A Cross-Cultural Theory of Urban Social Movements*, London.

Castillejo, C. (2011) 'Building a state that works for women: Integrating gender into post-conflict state-building', *Technical report, FRIDE – A European Think Tank for Global Action*.

Cervantes-Godoy, D. and Dewbre, J. (2010) 'Economic importance of agriculture for sustainable development and poverty reduction: Findings from a case study of Indonesia', *OECD, Technical report, Policies for Agricultural Development, Poverty Reduction and Food Security*.

Chabal, P. (2002) 'The quest for good government and development in Africa: Is NEPAD the answer?', *International Affairs*, 78(3), 447–62.

Chabal, P. and Daloz, J.-P. (1999) *Africa Works: Disorder as Political Instrument*, Oxford: James Currey Publishers.

Chachiua, M. (2000) 'Demilitarisation of post-conflict societies: The case of demobilisation of youth in Mozambique', www.katu-network.fi/Artikkelit/kirja01b/Martinho.htm.

Chadda, M. (2000) *Building Democracy in South Asia: India, Nepal, Pakistan*, Lynne Rienner Publishers.

Chaliand, G. (1977) *Revolutions in the Third World*, Vol. Translation from French – Mythes Revolutionnaires du Tiers Monde (1976), Hassocks.

Chanaa, J. (2002) 'Security sector reform: Issues, challenges, and prospects', *Adelphi Paper*, no. 344, Oxford University Press for the International Institute for Strategic Studies.

Chandler, D. (2004) 'The responsibility to protect? Imposing the "Liberal Peace"', *International Peacekeeping*, 11(1), 59–81.

Cheeseman, N. (2008) 'The Kenyan Elections of 2007: An introduction', *Journal of Eastern African Studies*, 2(2), 166–84.
Cheeseman, N., Lynch, G. and Willis, J. (2014) 'Democracy and its discontents: Understanding Kenya's 2013 elections', *Journal of Eastern African Studies*, 8(1), 2–24.
Chesterman, S. (2005) *You, the People: The United Nations, Transitional Administration, and State-Building*, Oxford.
Chuter, D. (2006) 'Understanding security sector reform', *Journal of Security Sector Management*, 4(2): 1–22.
Chuter, D. (2011) *Governing and Managing the Defence Sector*, Pretoria: Institute for Security Studies.
Clapham, C. (1996) *Africa and the International System. The Politics of State* Survival, Cambridge: Cambridge University Press.
Clapham, C. (1998) *African Guerrillas*. 17 September 1998. Bloomington: Indiana University Press.
Clapham, C. (2000) *War and State Formation in Ethiopia and Eritrea*, Brighton.
Clapham, C. and Currey, J. (1998) *African Guerrillas*, Oxford.
Clark, H. (2001) *Demilitarising Minds and Societies*, London: Committee for Conflict Transformation Support.
Clarke, S. (2008) 'Culture and Identity'. In *The SAGE Handbook of Cultural Analysis*, edited by Tony Bennett and John Frow. London: Sage, pp. 510–29.
Cliffe, L. (1999) 'Regional dimensions of conflict in the horn of Africa', *Third World Quarterly*, 20(1), 89–111.
Cock, J. (1997) 'The cultural and social challenge of demilitarization'. In *Defensive Restructuring of the Armed Forces in Southern Africa*, edited by G. Cawthra and B. Møller. Ashgate: Aldershot, pp. 117–44.
Cock, J. and Nathan, L. (1989) *War and Society: The Militarisation of South Africa*, Cape Town.
Colletta, N., Kastner, M. and Wiederhofer, I. (1996) *The Transition from War to Peace in Sub-Saharan Africa*, World Bank Publications, Washington, DC.
Collier, P. and Hoeffler, A. (2004) 'Greed and grievance in civil war', *Oxford Economic Papers*, 56(4), 563–95.
Collier, P., Hoeffler, A., and Söderbom, M. (2008) 'Post-conflict risks', *Journal of Peace Research*, 45(4), 461–78.
Collier, P., Elliott, V., Hegre, H., Hoeffler, A., Reynal-Querol, M. and Sambanis, N. (2003) 'Breaking the Conflict Trap: Civil War and Development Policy', *Technical report*, World Bank, Washington, DC.
Collins, R. O. (2005) *Civil Wars and Revolution in the Sudan: Essays on the Sudan, Southern Sudan and Darfur, 1962–2004*, Tsehai Publishers.
Collins, R. O. (2008) *A History of Modern Sudan*, Cambridge University Press.
Coons, S. (2012) 'The Nexus of Security, Development and Governance – Reflections from a Recent Trip to East Africa', *Center for Strategic and International Studies (CSIS)*.

Cooper, R. (2000) *Post-Modern State and the World Order*, London.
Cooper, N. (2006), 'Putting disarmament back in the frame', *Review of International Studies* 32(2), 353–76.
Cordesman, A. (1993) 'The Military Balance in Yemen and the Red Sea States 1986–1992', *Center for Strategic and International Studies*.
Costa, A. and Medeiros, M. (2002) 'Police demilitarisation: Cops, soldiers and democracy', *Journal of Conflict & Development*, 2(2), 25–45.
Cramer, C. (2006) *Civil War Is Not a Stupid Thing: Accounting for Violence in Developing Countries*, Hurst & Company.
Crocker, C., Hampson, F. and Aall, P. (2007) *Leashing the Dogs of War: Conflict Management in a Divided World*, Washington, DC.
Crook, R. and Manor, J. (1998) *Democracy and Decentralisation in South Asia and West Africa: Participation, Accountability and Performance*, Cambridge.
Curless, G. (2010) 'Sudan's 2010 National Elections', *Ethnopolitics Papers: University of Exeter* 3, 1–15.
Curless, G. (2011) 'Sudan's 2011 Referendum on Southern Secession', *Ethnopolitics Papers: University of Exeter* 7.
Curtis, D. (2012) 'The international peacebuilding paradox: Power sharing and post-conflict governance in Burundi', *African Affairs*, 112(446) (1 January 2012), 72–91.
Dargatz, A. (2011) 'Elections and Conflict in Sudan', Friedrich-Ebert-Stiftung Publications.
Davies, L. (2014) 'Conflicting identities? The role of identities in conflicts and in citizenship education', *European Conference 2014, Vienna*.
Davies, S. (1996) *Adaptable Livelihoods: Coping with Food Insecurity in the Malian Sahel*, London.
D'Cruz, C. (2008) *Identity Politics in Deconstruction – Calculating with the Incalculable*, Abingdon.
de Alcántara C. (2002) 'Uses and abuses of the concept of governance', *International Social Science Journal*, 50(155) (March 1998), 105–13.
Deng, F. (1995) *War of Visions: Conflicts of Identities in the Sudan*, Washington, DC.
Deng, F. (2006) 'A nation in turbulent search of itself', *American Academy of Political and Social Science*, 603, 155–162.
Department for International Development (1999) 'Policy Statement on Security Sector Reform'. London, UK.
Department for International Development (2000) 'Security Sector Reform and the Management of Military Expenditure. High Risks for Donors, High Returns for Development'. London, UK.
Department for International Development (2002) 'Understanding and Supporting Security Sector Reform'. London, UK.
de Waal, A. (2009) 'Vernacular politics in Africa', *Monthly Review*.
de Waal, A. (2010a) 'Sudan's choices: Scenarios beyond the CPA', *Heinrich Boll Stiftung Publication Series on Democracy*, 18, 9–30.

de Waal, A. (2010b) 'Dollarised', *London Review of Books*, 32(12), 38–41.
de Zeeuw, J. (2008) *From Soldiers to Politicians – Transforming Rebel Movements after Civil War*, Boulder, CO.
Diamond, L. (2006) 'Promoting democracy in post-conflict and failed states; lessons and challenges', *Taiwan Journal of Democracy*, 2(2), 93–116.
Diao, X., You, L., Alpuerto V. and Folledo, R. (2012) 'Assessing agricultural potential in South Sudan – a spatial analysis method', *International Food Policy Research Institute (IFPRI)*, Washington, DC, Chapter 8.
Diao, X., Alpuerto, V., Folledo, R., Guvele, C. and You, L. (2009) Assessing Food Security and Development Opportunities in Southern Sudan. Paper prepared by Development Strategy and Governance Division of IFPRI for US Agency for International Development. IFPRI, Washington, DC.
Diehl, K., Arol, R. and Malz, S. (2015) 'South Sudan: Linking the Chiefs' Judicial Authority and the Statutory Court System', *Non-State Justice Institutions and the Law*. London: Palgrave Macmillan, 55–79.
Donais, T. (2009) 'Empowerment or imposition? Dilemmas of local ownership in post-conflict peacebuilding processes', *Peace & Change*, 34(1), 1–24.
Dorosh, P. A., Dradri, S. Haggblade, S. (2009) 'Regional trade, government policy and food security: Recent evidence from Zambia', *Journal Food Policy*, 34(4) (August 2009), 350–66.
Duffield, M. (2001) *Global Governance and the New Wars – the Merging of Development and Security*, London.
Duffield, M. (2007) *Development, Security and Unending War*, Cambridge.
Ebohon, S. (2009) 'Post-militarism: Provenance of praetorian democracy in Nigeria, 1999–2007', *Global Journal of Social Sciences*, 8(2), 129–38.
Edkins, J. and Vaughan-Williams, N. (2009) *Critical Theorists and International Relations*, London.
Eichler, M. (2012) *Militarizing Men: Gender, Conscription and War in Post-Soviet Russia*, Stanford CA.
Eisman, A. (2011) *Peace Deserves a Chance – Bishop Paride Taban, a Sudanese Shepherd*, Nairobi.
el Battahani, A. (2006) 'A complex web: Politics and conflict in Sudan', *Accord*. Technical report by Accord.
Emberling, G. (2011) *Nubia: Ancient Kingdoms of Africa*, Princeton, NJ.
Encarnacion, O. (2000) 'Beyond transitions: The politics of democratic consolidation', *Comparative Politics*, 32(4), 479–98.
Englebert, P. and Tull, D. M. (2008) 'Post-conflict reconstruction in Africa: Flawed ideas about failed states', *International Security*, 32, 106–39.
Enloe, C. (2000) *Maneuvers: The International Politics of Militarizing Women's Lives*, Oakland, CA.
Eribon, D. (1991) *Michel Foucault*, Cambridge, MA.

Erikson, K. (1967) 'A comment on disguised observation in sociology', *Social Problems*, 14, 366–73.
Esteban, J., Mayoral, L. and Ray, D. (2012) 'Ethnicity and conflict: An empirical study', *American Economic Review*, 102, 1310–42.
Etzioni, A. (2007) 'Reconstruction: An agenda', *Journal of Intervention and Statebuilding*, 1(1), 27–45.
Feaver, P. (1998) 'Crisis as shirking: An agency theory evolution of the sourcing of American civil–military relations', *Armed Forces and Society*, 24, 407–34.
Feaver, P. (2003) *Armed Servants: Agency, Oversight and Civil–Military Relations*, Cambridge, MA.
Feyami, J. (1998) 'The future of demilitarisation and civil–military relations in West Africa: Challenges and prospects for democratic consolidation', *African Association of Political Science*, 3(1), 82–103.
Fierke K. (2007) *Critical Approaches to International Security*, Cambridge.
Finer, S. (1976) *The Man on Horseback: The Role of Military in Politics*, Harmondsworth.
Fisher, M., Lacovara, P., D'Auria, S. and Ikram, S. (2012) *Ancient Nubia: African Kingdoms on the Nile*, Cairo.
Fitzgerald, M. (2002) *Throwing the Stick Forward: The Impact of War on Southern Sudanese Women*, United Nations Development Fund for Women (UNIFEM) and United Nations Childrens Fund.
Fitzgerald, M. (2004) 'Addressing the security-development Nexus: Implications for joined-up government', *Policy Matters*, 5(5), 5–24.
Flores, T. and Nooruddin, I. (2009) 'Democracy under the gun: Understanding postconflict economic recovery', *The Journal of Conflict Resolution*, 53(1), 3–29.
Fluri, P. (2003) 'Oversight and guidance: The relevance of parliamentary oversight for the security sector and its reform'. In *Handbook for Parliamentarians No 5, Oversight of the Security Sector: Principles, Mechanisms and Practices, IPU/DCAF*, edited by Hans Born, Philipp Fluri, Anders Johnsson. Geneva: Belgrade.
Foran, J. (1997) *Theorizing Revolutions*, London.
Fuli, S. and Ga'le, B. (2002) *Shaping a Free Southern Sudan: Memoirs of Our Struggle 1934–1985*, Nairobi.
Garfield, R. (2007) 'Violence and victimisation after civilian disarmament: The case of Jonglei', Small Arms Survey Working Paper No. 11 December 2007.
Garner, R., Ferdinand, P. and Lawson, S. (2009) *Introduction to Politics*, Oxford.
Gbla, O. (2006) 'Security sector reform under international tutelage in Sierra Leone', *International Peacekeeping*, 13(1), 78–93.
Gibia, R. (2008) *John Garang and the Vision of New Sudan*, Toronto.
Ginty, R. and Richmond, O. (2007) 'Myth or reality: Opposing views on the liberal peace and post-war reconstruction', *Global Society*, 21(4), 491–97.
Ginty, R. and Richmond, O. (2013) 'The local turn in peacebuilding: A critical agenda for peace', *Third World Quarterly*, 34(5), 763–83.

Giordano, T. (2011) 'Agriculture and economic recovery in post-conflict countries: Lessons we never learnt', *Development Bank of Southern Africa, Technical report, Development Planning Division*.

Glaeser, E. (2007) 'Why does democracy need education?', *Journal of Economic Growth*, 12(2), 77–99.

Goldsmith, B. (2005) 'Out-of-country voting in post-conflict elections', 1(4), *Technical Report, Democracy Fellowships, Elections Today*.

Goldstone, J. (2003) *Revolutions – Theoretical, Comparative and Historical Studies*, 3rd edn, Hassocks.

Goldstone, J. A., Bates, R. H., Epstein, D. L., Gurr, T. R., Lustik, M. B., Marshall, M. G., Ulfelder, J., Woodward, M. (2010) 'A global model for forecasting political instability', *American Journal of Political Science*, 54(1), 190–208.

Goold, B. J. (2004) *CCTV and Policing: Public Area Surveillance and Police Practices in Britain*, Oxford University Press.

GOSS (2011) 'South Sudan Development Plan 2011–2013: Realising Freedom. Equality, Justice, Peace and Prosperity for All', *Government of South Sudan, Technical report, Ministry of Finance and Economic Planning*.

Grbich, C. (1999) *Qualitative Research in Health*, London.

Griffiths, M. (2007) *International Relations Theory for the Twenty-First Century*, London.

Grimm, S. (2008) 'External democratization after war: Success and failure', *Democratization*, 15(3), 525–49.

Grimm, S. and Merkel, W. (2008) 'War and democratization: Legality, legitimacy and effectiveness', *Democratization*, 15(3), 457–71.

Grinker, R., Lubkemann, S. and Steine, C. (2010) *Perspectives on Africa: A Reader in Culture, History and Representation*, Hoboken, NJ.

Grugel, J. (2001) *Democratization: A Critical Introduction*, Basingstoke: Palgrave.

Guarak, M. (2011) *Integration and Fragmentation of the Sudan: An African Renaissance*, Bloomington, IA.

Guibernau, M. and Hutchinson, J. (2001) *Understanding Nationalism*, Oxford, 207–241.

Gunther, R., Diamandouros, N. and Puhle, H.-J. (1995) *The Politics of Democratic Consolidation: Southern Europe in Comparative Perspective*, Baltimore, MD.

Guo, S. (1999) 'Democratic transition: A critical overview (research note)', *Issues & Studies*, 35(4), 133–48.

Gutteridge, W. (1969) *The Military in African Politics*, London.

Guzzini, S. (2000) 'A reconstruction of constructivism in international relations', *European Journal of International Relations*, 6, 147–82.

Gyimah-Boadi, E., Stedman, S. and Lyons, T. (2004) *Democratic Reform in Africa*, 'Conflict in Africa', Chapter 6, Boulder, CO, 141–58.

Hagmann, T. and Péclard, D. (2010) 'Negotiating statehood: Dynamics of power and domination in Africa', *Development & Change*, 41(4), 539–62.

Haken, N. and Taft, P. (2013) 'The Dark Side of State-Building: South Sudan', *Failed States Index*. Published by Fund for Peace as report.

Hanggi, H. and Scherrer, V. (2008a) *Security Sector Reform and UN Integrated Missions: Experience from Burundi, the Democratic Republic of the Congo, Haiti and Kosovo*, Genève, Geneva Centre for the Democratic Control of Armed Forces.

Hanggi, H. and Scherrer, V. (2008b) 'Towards an integrated security sector reform approach in UN peace operations', *International Peacekeeping*, 15(4), 486–500.

Hansen, H. B. and Twaddle, M. (1991) *Changing Uganda: The Dilemmas of Structural Adjustment and Revolutionary Change*, London, 178–86.

Harir, S. and Tvedt, T. (1994) *Short-Cut to Decay: The Case of the Sudan*, Uppsala.

Harris, G. (2003) *The case for demilitarisation in sub-Saharan Africa*, Institute for Security Studies, Pretoria, 3–14.

Harris, G. (2004a) *Epilogue: Some Necessary Conditions for Demilitarisation – Demilitarising Sub-Saharan Africa*, Institute for Security Studies, Pretoria, 199–212.

Harris, G. (2004b) *Achieving Security in Sub-Saharan Africa: Cost Effective Alternatives to the Military*, Institute for Security Studies, Pretoria.

Hartmann, G. and Crawford, G., Hartmann, C. (2008) *Decentralisation in Africa: A Pathway Out of Poverty*, Amsterdam.

Hay, C. (2002) *Political Analysis: A Critical Introduction*, Basingstoke.

Haynes, J. (1992) *Nubia: Ancient Kingdoms of Africa*, Museum of Fine Arts Boston.

Hazen, J. M. (2007) 'Can peacekeepers be peacebuilders?', *International Peacekeeping*, 14(3), 323–38.

HBSA (2010) 'Symptoms and causes Insecurity and underdevelopment in Eastern Equatoria', *Small Arms Survey*, Technical report, Sudan Human Security Baseline Assessment.

Hehir, A. (2007) 'The myth of the failed state and the war on terror: A challenge to the conventional wisdom', *Journal of Intervention and State-Building*, 1(3), 307–32.

Held, D. (1996) *Models of Democracy*, Stanford, CA.

Hegre, H., Ellingsen, T., Gates, S., Gleditsch, N. P. (2001) 'Toward a democratic civil peace? Democracy, political change, and civil war, 1816–1992', *The American Political Science Association*, 95(1), 33–48.

Hill, R. (1965) *Slatin Pasha*, Oxford University Press.

Holt, P. M. (1961), *A Modern History of the Sudan, from the Funj Sultanate to the Present Day*, Worcester and London: The Trinity Press.

Holt, P. M. and Daly, M. W. (1988) *A History of the Sudan: From the Coming of Islam to the Present Day*. London and New York: Longman, 1988 (4th edition), 2000 (5th edition).

Hood, L. (2006) 'Security sector reform in East Timor, 1999–2004', *International Peacekeeping*, 13(1), 60–77.

Hoy, D. (1986) *Foucault: A Critical Reader*, Oxford.

HSBA (2011) 'Fighting for spoils: Armed insurgencies in Greater Upper Nile', *Small Arms Survey*.

Humphreys, M. and Weinstein, J. (2006) 'Handling and manhandling civilians in civil war', *American Political Science Review*, 100(3), 429–47.

Huntington, S. (1957) *The Soldier and the State: The Theory and Politics of Civil-Military Relations*, Cambridge, MA.

Hunwick, J. (1999) *Timbuktu and the Songhay Empire: Al-Sa'Di's Ta'Rikh Al–Sudan Down to 1613 and Other Contemporary Documents*, Leiden.

Hutchful, E. (1997) 'Demilitarising the political process in Africa: Some basic issues', *African Security Review*, 6(2), 2–16.

Hutchful, E. (1998) 'The leadership challenges of demilitarisation in Africa', Arusha, Tanzania, July 22–4.

Hutchful, E. and Bathily, A. (1998) *The Military and Militarism in Africa*, Codesria Book Series.

Hutchinson, S. (2000) 'Nuer ethnicity militarised', *Anthropology Today*, 16(3), 6–13.

Hutchinson, S. (2001) 'A curse from god? Religious and political dimensions of the post-1991 rise of ethnic violence in South Sudan', *The Journal of Modern African Studies*, 39(2), 307–31.

ICG (2002) *God, Oil and Country: Changing the Logic of War in Sudan*, International Crisis Group.

ICG (2011) 'Politics and transition in the New South Sudan', *International Crisis Group Africa*, Africa Report no. 172.

Idris, A. (2005) *Conflict and Politics of Identity in Sudan*, Springer.

Ikejiaku, B.-V. (2009) 'The relationship between poverty, conflict and development', *Journal of Sustainable Development*, 2(1), 15–28.

Ingham, B. (1995) *Economics & Development*, New York.

Isima, J. (2004) 'Demilitarisation, non-state actors and public security in Africa: A preliminary survey of the literature', *Journal of Security Sector Management*, 2(4), 1–15.

Janowitz, M. (1971) *The Professional Soldier: A Social and Political Portrait*, Newport.

Janowitz, M. (1983) 'Civic consciousness and military performance', in *Janowitz and Stephen D Westbrook, The Political Education of Soldiers*, edited by Morris Janowitz and Stephen D. Westbrook. Beverly Hills, CA: Sage.

Jarstad, A. and Sisk, T. (2008) *From War to Democracy: Dilemmas of Peacebuilding*, Cambridge.

Jenkins, C. (1983) 'Resource mobilisation theory and the study of social movements', *Annual Review of Sociology*, 9, 527–53.

Jha, B. (2006) 'Employment, Wages and Productivity in Indian Agriculture', *Institute of Economic Growth – University of Delhi Enclave*.

Jok, J. (1999) 'Militarism, gender and reproductive suffering: The case of abortion in Western Dinka', *International African Institute*, 69(2), 194–212.

Jok, J. (2012) 'Insecurity and Ethnic Violence in South Sudan: Existential Threats to the State?', *Technical report, the Sudd Institute*.

Jok, J. and Hutchinson, S. (1999) 'Sudan's prolonged second civil war and the militarization of Nuer and Dinka ethnic identities', *African Studies Review*, 42(2), 125-45.

Johnson, D. H. (2003) *The Root Causes of Sudan's Civil Wars*, Indiana University Press.

Johnson, D. (1998) 'The Sudan People's Liberation Army and the Problem of Factionalism'. In *African Guerrillas*, edited by Christopher Clapham. Oxford: James Currey.

Jones, J. S. and Watt, S. (2010) *Ethnography in Social Science Practice*, Abingdon.

Jooma, M. (2005) 'Feeding the peace: Challenges facing human security in post-Garang South Sudan', *Technical report, Institute of Security Studies*.

Jooma, M. (2011) 'Dual Realities: Peace and War in the Sudan – An Update on the Implementation of the CPA', *Technical report, Institute for Security Studies (ISS)*.

Joseph, R. (1999) *State, Conflict & Democracy in Africa*, Boulder, CO, 299-317, 319-37.

Junne, G. and Verkoren, W. (2005) *Post-Conflict Development: Meeting New Challenges*, Boulder, CO.

Kalyvas, S. (2003) 'The ontology of "political violence": Action and identity in civil wars', *Perspectives on Politics*, 1, 475-94.

Karabelias, D. (1998) 'Civil–military relations: A comparative analysis of the role of the military in the political transformation of Post-War Turkey and Greece: 1980-1995', *Technical report, NATO – Final Report*.

Kasara, K. (2007) 'Tax me if you can: Ethnic geography, democracy and the taxation of agriculture in Africa', *American Political Science Review*, 101(1), 159-72.

Kevlihan, R. (2013) *Aid, Insurgencies and Conflict Transformation: When Greed Is Good*, London.

Khadiagala, G. (2014) 'Road maps in resolving African conflicts: Pathways to peace or Cul de Sacs?', *African Security*, 7(3), 163-80.

Kibreab, G. (1990) *The Sudan, from Subsistence to Wage Labour: Refugee Settlements in the Central and Eastern Regions*, Trenton, NJ.

Kingma, K. (1997) 'Demobilization of combatants after civil war in Africa and their reintegration into civilian life', *Policy Science*, 30, 151-65.

Kingma, K. (2000) *Demobilisation in Sub-Saharan Africa, The Development and Security Impacts*, Basingstoke.

Kingma, K. (2002) 'Demobilisation, reintegration & peacebuilding in Africa', *International Peacekeeping*, 9(2), 181-201.

Kingston, P. and Spears, I. (2004) *States-within-States: Incipient Political Entities in the Post-Cold War Era*, London, 15-34.

Kjaer, A. M. (2004) *Governance*, Wiley.

Klingebiel, S. (2007) *The New Peace and Security Architecture in Africa: G8 and EU Interests and Approaches*. Discussion Paper / Deutsches Institut für Entwicklungspolitik.

Klingebiel, S. (2009) *New Interfaces between Security and Development: Changing Concepts and Approaches*, German Development Institute (DIE).

Klockars, C. B. (1985) *The Idea of Police*, Sage Publications.

Knaus, G. and Martin, F. (2003) 'Travails of the European Raj', *Journal of Democracy*, 14(3), 61.

Knight, M. (2008) 'Expanding the DDR model: Politics and organisations', *Journal of Security Sector Management*, 6(1), 1–19.

Knight, W. A. (2010) 'Linking DDR and SSR in post-conflict peacebuilding in Africa: An overview', *African Journal of Political Science and International Relations*, 4(1), 29–54.

Kozul-Wright, R. and Fortunato, P. (2011) *Securing Peace: State-building and Economic Development in Post-conflict Countries*, London.

Krause, K. and Jütersonke, O. (2005) 'Peace, security and development in post-conflict environments', *Security Dialogue*, 36(4), 447–62.

Kuhne, W. (2010) 'The Role of Elections in Emerging Democracies and Post-Conflict Countries: Key issues, Lessons Learned and Dilemmas', *Technical report, Friedrich-Ebert-Stiftung*.

Kushner, S. (1996) 'The limits of constructivism in evaluation', *Evaluation*, 2, 189–200.

Kusow, A. (2003) 'Beyond indigenous authenticity: Reflections on the insider/outsider Debate in immigration research', *Symbolic Interaction*, 26(4), 591–9.

Kusow, A. (2004) *Putting the Cart before the Horse: Contested Narratives and the Crisis of the Nation-State in Somalia*, Trenton, NJ, 1–14.

Lamb, G. (1997) 'Demilitarisation and Peacebuilding in Southern Africa – A Survey of the Literature', *Centre for Conflict resolution – University of Cape Town*.

Lamb, G. (1999) 'Demilitarization: A Review of the Concept and Observations from the Southern African Experience', *SACDI Defence Digest* working paper 7.

Lanjouw, P. and Murgai, R. (2009) 'Poverty Decline, Agricultural Wages, and Non-Farm Employment In Rural India', *World Bank*.

Lareau, A. and Shultz, J. (1996) *Journeys through Ethnography: Realistic Accounts in Fieldwork*, Boulder, CO.

Le Vacher, Fr. J. (Self-publication, 2000), 'Anguish and Joys in Southern Sudan'. This is the Journal of Fr. Le Vacher, a French Catholic priest from the missionaries of Africa. He arrived in North Sudan in 1975 and moved to Torit – Southern Sudan in 1984. This book is a journal of his life at the height of the SPLA split and violence from 31 December 1989 to 31 December 1996.

Leonardi, C. and Jalil, M. (2012) *Traditional Authority, Local Government and Justice*. Rift Valley Institute, 108–21.

Leonardi, C., Isser, D., Moro, L. and Santschi, M. (2011) 'The politics of customary law ascertainment in South Sudan', *Journal of Legal Pluralism and Unofficial Law*, 63, 111–42.

Leopold, M. (2003) 'Slavery in Sudan, past and present', *African Affairs*, 102(409). Oxford University Press on behalf of The Royal African Society.

Leopold, M. (2006) 'Legacies of slavery in North-West Uganda: The story of the "one-elevens"', *Cambridge International African Institute*, 76(2) (May 2006), 180–99.

Leonardi, C. and Abdul Jalil, M. (2011) 'Traditional authority, local government and justice'. In *The Sudan Handbook*. Ryle, John, Willis, Justin, Baldo, Suliman and Jok Madut Jok. Woodbridge: James Currey. 108–21.

Leonardi, C. and Jalil, M. (2012) *Traditional Authority, Local Government and Justice*, 108–121.

LeRiche, M. (2007) 'Guerrilla government: Political changes in the Southern Sudan during the 1990s', *Canadian Journal of African Studies; Toronto*, 41(1), 165–7.

LeRiche, M. and Arnold, M. (2012) *South Sudan: From Revolution to Independence*, Columbia University Press.

Lewarne, S. and Snelbecker, D. (2004) 'Economic Governance in War Torn Economies: Lessons Learned from the Marshall Plan to the Reconstruction of Iraq', *Technical Report, USAID*.

Lindberg, S. (2006) *Democracy and Elections in Africa*, Baltimore, MD.

Linz, J. and Stepan, A. (2011) *Problems of Democratic Transition and Consolidation*, Baltimore, MD.

Little, P. (2003) *Somalia: Economy without State*, Hargeisa.

Little, R. and Smith, M. (2006) *Perspectives on World Politics*, London; New York: Routledge.

Loader, I. and Walker, N. (2007), *Civilizing Security*, Cambridge University Press.

Lokosang, L. B. (2010) *South Sudan: The Case for Independence & Learning from Mistakes*, Xlibris.

Lokuji, A. Abatneh, A. and Wani, K. (2009) 'Police reform in Southern Sudan', *The North-South Institute (NSI)*, 1–40.

Luckham, R. (2001) 'Conflict and poverty in sub-Saharan Africa: An assessment of the issues and evidence', *IDS Working Paper*, no. 128, Brighton.

Luckham, R., Hutchful, E. and Bathily, A. (1998) *The Military Militarism and Democratization in Africa: A Survey of Literature and Issues*, Codesria Book Series, 1–45.

Luckham, R., Goetz, A. and Kaldor, M. (2003) 'Democratic institutions and democratic politics'. In *Can Democracy be Designed? The Politics of Institutional Choice in Conflict-Torn Societies*, edited by Bastian and Luckham. London: Zed Books.

Luengo-Cabrera, J. (2016) 'South Sudan: The cost of conflict', *Technical report, European Union Institute for Security Studies (EUISS)*.

Lynch, G., Cheeseman, N. and Willis, J. (2014) 'Kenya's 2013 Election: Lessons for Democracy Promotion'. In *Commonwealth Governance Handbook 2013–2014*, edited by A. Robertson and R. Jones-Parry. Cambridge: Nexus/Commonwealth Secretariat, pp. 22–5.

Lyons, T. (1995) 'Closing the transition: The May 1995 Elections in Ethiopia, *Journal of Modern African Studies*, 34(1), 121–42.

Lyons, T. (2002) 'Post-conflict Elections: War Termination, Democratization, and Demilitarizing Politics', *Institute for Conflict Analysis and Resolution – George Mason University*.

Lyons, T. (2004) 'Post-conflict elections and the process of demilitarizing politics: The role of electoral administration', *Democratization*, 11(3), 1–27.

Lyons, T. (2009) 'The Ethiopia–Eritrea conflict and the search for peace in the horn of Africa', *Review of African Political Economy*, 36(120), 167–80.

Mamdani, M. (1996) *Citizen and Subject: Contemporary Africa and the Legacy of Late Colonialism*, Princeton University Press.

Mamdani, M. (1998) *When Does a Settler Become a Native? Reflections on the Colonial Roots of Citizenship in Equatorial and South Africa*, University of Cape Town.

Mamdani, M. (2001) *When Victims Become Killers: Colonialism, Nativism and the Genocide in Rwanda*, Princeton, NJ.

Mamdani, M. (2005), 'Political Identity, Citizenship and Ethnicity in Post-Colonial Africa', Arusha Conference, 'New Frontiers of Social Policy', Technical report, Columbia University.

Mampilly, Z. (2011) *Rebel Rulers: Insurgent Governance and Civilian Life during War*, New York.

Mansfield, E. and Snyder, J. (2008) 'Democratisation and civil war', Saltzman Institute of War and Peace. Technical/conference report.

Marsh, D. and Stoker, G. (2002) *Theory and Methods in Political Science*, London.

Mashike, L. (2000) 'Standing down or standing out? Demobilising and reintegrating former soldiers', *African Security Review*, 9(5/6), 64–71.

Madut Jok, J. (2001) *War and Slavery in Sudan (The Ethnography of Political Violence)*, University of Pennsylvania Press.

Madut Jok, J. (2011) *Diversity, Unity and Nation Building in South Sudan*. Washington, DC: United States Institute of Peace.

Madut Jok, J. (2013) *Police Service and Law Enforcement in South Sudan*, Jube: The Sudd Institute.

Madut Jok, J. and Hutchinson, S. E. (2002) 'Gender violence and the militarisation of ethnicity: A case study from South Sudan'. In *Postcolonial Subjectivities in Africa*, edited by R. Werbner. London: Zed Books.

Manning, C. (2004) 'Elections and political change in post-war Bosnia and Herzegovina', *Journal Democratization*, 11(2), 60–86.

Mansfield, E. D. and Snyder, J. (2005) 'Electing to fight: Why emerging democracies go to war', 47(2), 354–55.

Maputo Declaration (2003) AU 2003 Maputo Declaration on Agriculture and Food Security. African Union. https://www.nepad.org/publication/au-2003-maputo-declaration-agriculture-and-food-security. Accessed July 2018.

Maxwell, A. M. (2004), 'The role of education in demilitarising Sub-Saharan Africa', *Institute for Security Studies*, Pretoria, 123–36.

Mayai, A. (2012) 'Mapping Social Accountability: An Appraisal of Policy Influence on Service Delivery in South Sudan', Technical report, the Sudd Institute.

McCaskie, T. (2008) 'Gun culture in Kumasi', *Journal of the International African Institute*, 78(3), 433–54.

McDonough, D. (2008) 'From Guerrillas to government: Post-conflict stability in Liberia, Uganda and Rwanda', *Third World Quarterly*, 29(2), 357–74.

McKenna, T. (1998) *Muslim Rulers and Rebels. Everyday Politics & Armed Separatism*, Berkeley, CA.

McLauchlin, T. (2008) 'Civil war and state-building in Uganda', *McGill University, University Paper prepared for presentation at the Annual Meeting of the International Studies Association*, San Francisco.

McNally, M. and Schwarzmantel, J. (2009) *Gramsci and Global Politics: Hegemony and Resistance*, London.

Mendelson-Forman, J. (2006) 'Security sector reform in Haiti', *International Peacekeeping*, 13(1), 14–27.

Menocal, A. (2011) 'State-building for peace: A new paradigm for international engagement in post-conflict fragile states?', *Third World Quarterly*, 32(10), 1715–36.

Metelits, C. (2004) 'Reformed rebels? Democratization, global norms, and the Sudan People's Liberation Army', *Africa Today*, 51(1), 65–82.

Metelits, C. (2009) 'The logic of change: Pushing the boundaries of insurgent behavior theory', *Defense and Security Analysis*, 25(2), 105–18.

Metelits, C. (2010) *Inside Insurgency: Violence, Civilians, and Revolutionary Group Behavior*, New York.

Michael, K., Kellen, D. and Ben-Ari, E. (2009) *The Transformation of the World of War and Peace Support Operations*, Westport, CT.

Miller, J. (1993) *The Passion of Michel Foucault*, London.

Mirzeler, M. and Young, C. (2000) 'Pastoral politics in the northeast periphery in Uganda: AK-47 as change agent', *The Journal of Modern African Studies*, 38(3), 407–29.

Mkandawire, T. (2007) '"Good governance": The itinerary of an idea', *Journal Development in Practice*, 17(4–5).

Moore, B. (1966) *Social Origins of Dictatorship and Democracy: Lord and Peasant in the Making of the Modern World*, Boston.

Moskowitz, J. (1997) 'Involvement in Politics: A Content Analysis of Civilian and Military Journals in Pakistan, France and Israel, p. 14, cited in Kotera M Bhimaya, Civil–Military Relations: A Comparative study of India and Pakistan', PhD thesis, *RAND Graduate School* – Published Dissertation.

Moug, P. (2007) 'Non-participative observation in political research: The "poor" relation?', *Politics*, 27(2), 108–14.

Mueller, S. (2011) 'Dying to win: Elections, political violence, and institutional decay in Kenya', *Journal of Contemporary African Studies*, 29(1), 99–117.

Muggah, R. (2005) 'No magic bullet: A critical perspective on disarmament, demobilization and reintegration and weapons reduction during post-conflict', *Commonwealth Journal of International Affairs*, 94(379), 239–52.

Muggah, R. (2009) *Security and Post-conflict Reconstruction: Dealing with Fighters in the Aftermath of War*, New York.

Murray, T. (2007) 'Police-building in Afghanistan: A case study of civil security reform', *International Peacekeeping*, 14(1), 108–26.

Mwanika, P. A. N. (2012) *Transition and Transformation of the South Sudan National Defence and Security*, International Peace Support Training Centre.

Nathan, L. (1998) 'The 1996 Defence White Paper: An agenda for state demilitarisation?' In *From Defence to Development: Redirecting Military Resources in South Africa*, edited by J. Cock and P. McKenzie. Cape Town: David Philip, pp. 41–59.

Ndlovu-Gatsheni, S. J. (2013) *Coloniality of Power in Postcolonial Africa: Myths of Decolonization*. African Books Collective.

Newman, E. (2009), 'Failed states and international order: constructing a post-Westphalian World', *Journal of Contemporary Security Policy*, 30(3), 421–43.

Newman, E. (2011), 'A human security peace-building agenda', *Third World Quarterly*, 32(10), 1737–56.

Newman, E. Roland Paris, R. and Richmond, O. (2009) *New Perspectives on Liberal Peacebuilding*, United Nations University Press.

Nordlinger, E. (1971) *Soldiers in Politics: Military Coups and Governments*, Upper Saddle River NJ.

Norris, C. and Armstrong, G. (1999) *The Maximum Surveillance Society: The Rise of CCTV*, Berg.

Norris, P. (2012) *Making Democratic Governance Work: How Regimes Shape Prosperity, Welfare, and Peace*, Cambridge.

Nyaba, P. (1997) *The Politics of Liberation in South Sudan; An Insider's View*, Kampala.

O'Brien, A. (2009) 'Sudan's election paradox', *The Enough Project*.

Oduho, J. and Deng, W. (1963) *The Problem of the Southern Sudan*, Oxford University Press.

Ogbaharya, D. (2008) '(Re-)building governance in post-conflict Africa: The role of the state and informal institutions', *Development in Practice*, 18(3), 395–402.

Ojielo, O. (2010) 'Critical lessons in post-conflict security in Africa: The case of Liberia's Truth and Reconciliation Commission', *Institute for Justice and Reconciliation*.

Omotola, J. (2006) 'Beyond transition: Challenges of security sector reform and reconstruction in Liberia', *Journal of Security Sector Management*, 4(4), 1–9.

Organisation for Economic Co-operation and Development (2001) DAC Guidelines on Helping Prevent Violent Conflict, Paris: OECD.

Ottaway, M. (1999), 'Ethnic Politics in Africa: Change and Continuity'. In *State, Conflict & Democracy in Africa*, edited by Richard Joseph. London: Lynne Rienner Publishers, pp. 299–317.

Ottaway, M. (2003) *Democracy Challenged: The Rise of Semi-Authoritarianism*, Washington, DC: Carnegie Endowment for International Peace.

Ottaway, M. (2007), *Leashing the Dogs of War: Conflict Management in a Divided World*, US Institute of Peace Press.

Pantuliano, S. (2009) *Uncharted Territory: Land, Conflict and Humanitarian Action*, Rugby.

Paris, R. and Sisk, T. (2009), *The Dilemmas of Statebuilding: Confronting the Contradictions of Postwar Peace Operations*, London and New York: Routledge.

Payne, L. (1996) *Rebuilding Communities in a Refugee Settlement: A Casebook from Uganda*, Oxfam GB.

Pieterse, J. (1996) 'Varieties of ethnic politics and ethnicity discourse'. In *The Politics of Difference: Ethnic Premises in a World of Power*, edited by Edwin Wilmsen and Patrick McAllister, Chicago.

Pillora, S. (2011) 'Local government and community governance: A literature review' (2), Technical report, Australian Centre of Excellence for Local Government.

Porto, J., Parsons, I. and Alden, C. (2007) *From Soldiers to Citizens – The Social, Economic and Political Reintegration of UNITA Ex-Combatants*, ISS Monography Series.

Powers, N. (2001) *Grassroots Expectations of Democracy and Economy: Argentina in Comparative Perspective*, Pittsburgh, PA.

Price, R. and Reus, C. (1998) 'Dangerous liaisons? Critical international theory and constructivism', *European Journal of International Relations*, 4(3), 259–94.

Prozorov, S. (2007) *Foucault, Freedom and Sovereignty*, Abingdon.

Przeworski, A. (1991) *Democracy and the Market: Political and Economic Reforms in Eastern Europe and Latin America*, Cambridge.

Pur, M. (2012) *The Scholars' Wisdom: Students' Wisdom*, Xlibris Corporation.

Radu, M. (1990) *The New Insurgencies*, London.

Rands, R. (2010) 'In Need of Review: SPLA Transformation in 2006–10 and Beyond', *Small Arms Survey*, Graduate Institute of International and Development Studies, Geneva.

Rehfisch, F. (1964) 'Sketch of the early history of Omdurman'. Sudan Notes and Records, 45, 35–47. University of Khartoum. JSTOR, www.jstor.org/stable/41716857.

Reiner, R. (2010) *The Politics of the Police*, Oxford University Press.

Renders, M. and Terlinden, U. (2010) 'Negotiating statehood in a hybrid political order: The case of Somaliland', *Development & Change*, 41(4), 723–46.

Rennie, J. and Singh, N. (1996) *Participatory Research for Sustainable Livelihoods*, Winnipeg.

Reno, W. (1998) *Warlord Politics and African States*, Boulder, CO.

Reinton, Per Olav (1971) *Imperialism and the Southern Sudan*. Makerere Institute for Social Research. Oslo: Kampala International Peace Research Institute.

Richards, P. (1995), 'Rebellion in Liberia and Sierra Leone: A crisis of youth?' In *Conflict in Africa*. London: I.B. Tauris, pp. 134–70.

Richmond, O. (2006) 'The problem of peace: Understanding the "liberal peace"', *Conflict, Security & Development*, 6(3), 291–314.

Richmond, O. (2009) 'Becoming liberal, unbecoming liberalism: Liberal-local hybridity via the everyday as a response to the paradoxes of liberal peacebuilding', *Journal of Intervention and State-building*, 3(3), 324–44.

Richmond, O. P. and Franks, J. (2009), *Liberal Peace Transitions: Between Statebuilding and Peacebuilding*, Edinburgh: Edinburgh University Press.

Roberts, D. (2008) 'Post-conflict state-building and state legitimacy: From negative to positive peace?', *Development & Change*, 39(4), 537–55.

Roberts, D. (2010), 'From liberal to popular peace?', *Open Democracy*, 29 October.

Roberts, D. (2011) 'Post-conflict peacebuilding, liberal irrelevance and the locus of legitimacy', *International Peacekeeping*, 18(4), 410–24.

Roberts, D. (2012), 'Saving liberal peacebuilding from itself', *Peace Review: A Journal of Social Justice*, 24(3), 366–73.

Roberts, P. (2007) *Political Constructivism*, London.

Robinson, C. D. and Richard Scaglion, R. (1987) 'The origin and evolution of the police function in society: Notes toward a theory', *Law & Society Review*, 21(1), 109–54.

Rolandsen, Ø. (2005) *Guerrilla Government: Political Changes in the Southern Sudan in the 1990s*, Nordic Africa Institute.

Rolandsen, Ø. (2007) 'Sudan: The Janjawiid and government militias'. In *African Guerrillas: Raging Against the Machine*, edited by Bøås, Morten and Kevin C. Dunn. Boulder, CO: Lynne Rienner Publishers, pp. 151–71.

Rolandsen, Ø. (2015) 'Another civil war in South Sudan: The failure of Guerrilla Government?', *Journal of Eastern African Studies*, 9(1), 163–74.

Rone, J. (1996) *Behind the Red Line: Political Repression in Sudan*, Human Rights Watch, Africa.

Rone, J. (1999) *Famine in Sudan, 1998: The Human Rights Causes*, New York: Human Rights Watch.

Rone, J., Prendergast, J. and Sorensen, K. (1994) *Civilian Devastation: Abuses by All Parties in the War in Southern Sudan*, New York: Human Rights Watch.

Rose, G. (1982) *Deciphering Sociological Research*, London.

Ross, A. (1987) 'Dimensions of militarisation in the third world', *Armed Forces and Society*, 13, 562–64.

Saferworld (2008), 'Developing integrated approaches to post-conflict security and recovery: A case study of integrated DDR in Sudan', *Technical Report*, SaferWorld.

Salahub, J. (2012) 'Police reform in an independent South Sudan', *Technical Report, The North–South Institute*.

Salehyan, I. (2007) 'Transnational rebels: Neighboring states as sanctuary for rebel groups', *World Politics*, 59(2), 217–42.

Sambanis, N. (2000) 'Partition as a solution to ethnic civil war: An empirical critique of the theoretical literature', *World Politics*, 52(4), 437–83.

Sambanis, N. (2004) 'What is civil war? Conceptual and empirical complexities of an operational definition', *Journal of Conflict Resolution*, 48(6), 814–58.

Santiso, C. (2002) 'Promoting democratic governance & preventing the recurrence of conflict: The role of the United Nations development programme in post-conflict peacebuilding', *Journal of Latin American Studies*, 34(3), 555–86.
Sarup, M. (1993) *An Introductory Guide to: Post-Structuralism & Postmodernism*, 2nd edn, Hemel Hempstead.
Saunders, B. (2010) 'Political equality and majority rule', *Chicago Journals*, 121(1), 148–77.
Sawyer, E. (2008) 'Remove or reform? A case for (restructuring) chiefdom governance in post-conflict in Sierra Leone', *African Affairs*, 107(428), 387–403.
Schatz, E. (2013) *Political Ethnography: What Immersion Contributes to the Study of Power*, Chicago.
Schensul, S., Schensul, J. and LeCompte, M. (2012) *Initiating Ethnographic Research: A Mixed Methods Approach*, Lanham, MD.
Schiff, R. (2009) *The Military & Domestic Politics – A Concordance Theory of Civil-military Relations*, London.
Schirmer, J. (1998) *A Violence called Democracy: The Guatemala Military Project 1982–92*, Philadelphia.
Schlichte, K. (2009) *In the Shadow of Violence: The Politics of Armed Groups*, Chicago.
Schmidt, V. (2002) *The Futures of European Capitalism*, Oxford.
Schmidt, V. and Radaelli, C. (2004) 'Policy change and discourse in Europe, conceptual and methodological issues', *West European Politics*, 27(2), 183–210.
Schnabel, A. and Ehrhart, H.-G. (2005) *Security Sector Reform and Post-conflict Peacebuilding*, Tokyo.
Schöpflin, G. (2001). *The Construction of Identity*. Österreichischer Wissenschaftstag, Austria, 1–10.
Schumpeter, J. (1976) *Capitalism, Socialism, and Democracy*, Abingdon.
Scroggins, D. (2004) *Emma's War: Love, Betrayal and Death in the Sudan*, New York.
Seale, C. (2004) *Social Research Methods – A Reader*, London.
Sedra, M. (2004) 'Security sector transformation in Afghanistan', *Geneva Centre for the Democratic Control of Armed Forces (DCAF)*, 1–36.
Sedra, M. (2009), 'Security sector reform monitor: Southern Sudan', Centre for International Governance Innovation.
Shaw, M. (1991) *Post-Military Society*, Cambridge.
Shaw, M. (2003) *War and Genocide*, Oxford.
Shaw, T. and Mbabazi, P. (2007) 'Two Ugandas and a "liberal peace"? Lessons from Uganda about conflict and development at the start of a new century', *Global Society*, 21(4), 567–78.
Sheptycki, J. (2000) *Issues in Transnational Policing*, London: Routledge.
Sidahmed, A. S. and Alsir Sidahmed, A. (2005) *Sudan: The Contemporary Middle East*, London: Routledge.
Skedsmo, A., Danhier, K. and Luak, H. (2003) 'The changing meaning of small arms in Nuer society', *African Security Review*, 12(4), 57–67.

Skocpol, T. (1979) *States and Social Revolution*, Cambridge.
Smith, C. (2001) 'Security-sector reform: Development breakthrough or institutional engineering?', *Conflict, Security & Development*, 1(01), 5–20.
Snowden, J. A. (2012) *Work in Progress: Security Force Development in South Sudan through February 2012.* Working paper no. 27. Switzerland: Small Arms Survey, p. 10.
Snyder, J. (2010) *Elections as Milestones and Stumbling Blocks for Peaceful Democratic Consolidation*, Washington, DC.
Soderlund, W. (2008) *Humanitarian Crises and Intervention: Reassessing the Impact of Mass Media*, West Hartford, CT.
Soussan, J. (2000) 'Understanding livelihood processes and dynamics', *Technical report, DFID – the UK Department for International Development.*
Southall, A. (1974) 'State formation in Africa', *Annual Review of Anthropology*, 3, 153–65.
South Sudan Development Plan 2011–13. Government of Southern Sudan (GoSS). Juba: Ministry of Legal Affairs and Constitutional Development. 2011.
Spence, R. (2004) 'Befriending the neighbours – demilitarising sub-saharan Africa', *Institute for Security Studies*, Pretoria, 59–73.
SPLA White Paper on Defence (2008) *Government of Southern Sudan (GoSS)*, Juba: Ministry of Legal Affairs and Constitutional Development.
Stavrianakis, A., Selby, J. (2012) *Militarism and International Relations: Political Economy, Security and Theory*, Routledge.
Steinert, J. and Grimm, S. (2015) 'Too good to be true? United Nations peacebuilding and the democratization of war-torn states', *Conflict Management and Peace Science*, 32(5), 513–35.
Sterling-Folker, J. (2006) *Making Sense of International Relations Theory*, Boulder, CO.
Stearns, Peter N. (2013) *Demilitarization in the Contemporary*, University of Illinois Press.
Stewart, F. (2004) 'Development and security', *Conflict, Security & Development*, 4(3), 261–88.
Stokes, S. (1995) *Cultures in Conflict: Social Movements and the State in Peru*, Oakland, CA.
Stones, R. (1998) *Key Sociological Thinkers*, London.
Stone, Marianne (2009) *Security According to Buzan: A Comprehensive Security Analysis.* Security discussion papers series, 2009. Columbia University, School of International and Public Affairs – New York, USA.
SuGDE and SuNDE (2010), 'Elections Statement – 24 April 2010', *The Sudanese Group for Democracy and Elections (SuGDE) and the Sudanese Network for Democratic Elections (SuNDE), Technical report.*
Suhrke, A., Tjønneland, E. and Wang, V. (2005) 'Governance interventions in post-war situations: Lessons learned', *Technical report, Chr. Michelsen Institute.*
Šulović, V. (2010) 'Meaning of security and theory of securitization', *Belgrade Centre for Security Policy.*

Sumner, Andy and Tribe, Michael (2008) 'Development studies and cross disciplinarity: Research at the social science–physical science interface', *Journal of International Development*, 20(6), 751–67.

Suter, K., 'National ministries for peace'. In *Achieving Security in Sub- Saharan Africa: Cost Effective Alternatives to the Military*, edited by Geoff Haris. Institute for Security Studies, Pretoria, pp. 173–5.

Tadjbakhsh, S. (2011), *Rethinking the Liberal Peace: External Models and Local Alternatives*, London, UK: Routledge.

Taeb, M. (2004) *Agriculture for Peace: Promoting Agricultural Development in Support of Peace in Support of Peace*. Institute of Advanced Studies. United Nations University (UNU-IAS).

Tagarev, T. (1957) 'The role of military education in harmonizing civil–military relations (the Bulgarian case)', *Technical report, NATO – Democratic Institutions Individual Fellowship Project, Final Report*.

Tanja, R. (2006) 'State making in the horn of Africa: Notes on eritrea and prospects for the end of violent conflict in the horn', *Conflict, Security and Development*, 6(4), 503–30.

Tansey, O. (2007) 'The concept and practice of democratic regime-building', *International Peacekeeping*, 14(5), 633–46.

Tarrow, S. (1994) *Power in Movement: Social Movements, Collective Action and Politics*, Cambridge.

Tarrow, S. (2007) 'Inside insurgencies: Politics and violence in an age of civil war', *Perspectives on Politics*, 5(3), 587–600.

Taylor, I. (2007) 'What fit for the liberal peace in Africa?', *Global Society*, 21(4), 553–66.

Thies, C. (2007) 'The political economy of state-building in sub-saharan Africa', *Journal of Politics*, 69(3), 716–31.

Thomas, C. (2001) 'Global governance, development and human security: Exploring the links', *Third World Quarterly*, 22(2), 159–75.

Thomas, E. (2009) 'Against the gathering storm: Securing Sudan's comprehensive peace agreement', *Technical Report, Chatham House*.

Thomas, E. (2010) 'Decisions and deadlines: A critical year for Sudan', *A Chatham House Report*.

Thompson, W. (2009) *Systemic Transitions: Past, Present and Future*, Basingstoke.

Tilly, C. (1978) *From Mobilization to Revolution*, Reading, MA.

Tizikara, C. and Lugor, L. (2012) 'Post-conflict development of agriculture in South Sudan: Perspective on approaches to capacity strengthening', *Technical report, Ministry of Agriculture, Forestry, Cooperatives and Rural Development*.

Tschirgi, N. (2005) 'Security and development policies: Untangling the relationship', *Technical Report, the European Association of Development Research and Training Institutes (EADI)*.

Tziarras, Z. (2012) 'Liberal peace and peace-building: Another critique', *The Globalized World Post-Research Paper*.

UK Parliament (2006) 'Conflict and development: Peacebuilding and post–conflict reconstruction', *House of Commons – UK, Technical report, International Development Committee*.
United Nations (2006) 'Integrated disarmament demobilisation and reintegration standards', *United Nations, Technical Report, Inter Agency Working Group on Disarmament Demobilisation and Reintegration*.
UN Secretary-General (2005) United Nations, Fifty-ninth session. Agenda items 45 and 55. A/59/2005.
USAID (2009a) 'Patterns of post-conflict economic recovery', *Technical Report, United States Agency for International Development – Nathan Associates Inc*.
USAID (2009b) 'A guide to economic growth in post-conflict countries', *Technical Report, U.S. Agency for International Development – Office of Economic Growth Bureau for Economic Growth, Agriculture and Trade*.
USIP and PKSOI (2009) *Guiding Principles for Stabilization and Reconstruction*. United States Institute of Peace (USIP) and US Army Peacekeeping and Stability Operations Institute (PKSOI).
Valters, C., Rabinowitz, G. and Denney, L. (2014) 'Security in post-conflict contexts. What counts as progress and what drives it?', ODI Technical Report.
Vansina, J. (1956) *Kingdoms of the Savanna*, Oxford.
Vansina, J. (1962) 'A comparison of African kingdoms', *Journal of the International African Institute*, 32(4), 324–35.
Vansina, J. (1972) *The Tio Kingdom of the Middle Congo, 1880–92*, New York.
Various, 'Demilitarising sub-saharan Africa', *Institute of Security Studies (Africa)*.
Vondracek, H. (2014) 'A single raised hand: Prospects for peace in the Sudanese rivalry', *African Security*, 7(4), 251–76.
Waihenya, W. (2006) *The Mediator: Gen. Lazaro Sumbeiywo and the Southern Sudan Press Process*, Nairobi.
Wakason, E. N. (1993) 'The politics of Southern Sudan 1972–83'. In *Civil War in the Sudan*, edited by M.W. Daly and Ahmad Alawad Sikainha. London: British Academic Press.
Warner, L. (2012), 'Force reduction key to South Sudan's military transformation', *Technical Report, World Politics Review*.
War-Torn Societies Project (2005) *Rebuilding Somaliland: Issues and Possibilities*, Trenton, NJ.
Weinstein, J. (2007) *Inside Rebellion: The Politics of Insurgent Violence*, Cambridge.
Weiss, T. (2000) 'Governance, good governance and global governance: Conceptual and actual challenges', *Third World Quarterly*, 21(5), 795–814.
Welch, C. E. and Forman, J. M. (1998) Civil–military Relations: USAID's Role, USAID: Center for Democracy and Governance, United States. Bureau for Democracy, Conflict, and Humanitarian Assistance.
Wendt, A. and Barnett, M. (1993) 'Dependent state formation and third world militarisation', *Review of International Studies*, 19, 321–47.

Willett, S. (1998), 'Demilitarisation, disarmament & development in Southern Africa', *Review of African Political Economy*, 25(77), 409–30.

Willis, J. (2003) 'Authority, and the state in the Nuba mountains of condominium Sudan', *The Historical Journal*, 46(1), 89–114.

Willis, J. and El-Battahani, A. (2010) '"We changed the law": Electoral practice and malpractice in sudan since 1953', *African Affairs*, 109(435), 191–212.

Wily, L. A. and Pantuliano, S., ed. (2009) *Tackling Land Tenure in the Emergency to Development Transition in Post-Conflict States: From Restitution to Reform*, Practical Action Publishing, Chapter 2, 27–50.

Wood, E. (2003) *Insurgent Collective Action and Civil War in El Salvador*, Cambridge.

Woodward, P. (1990) *Sudan, 1898–1989: The Unstable State*. Boulder, CO: Rienner.

Woodward, P. (2003) *The Horn of Africa: Politics and International Relations*, London.

World Bank (2008) *World Development Report 2008: Agriculture for Development*, Washington, DC.

World Bank (2012) *Agricultural Potential, Rural Roads, and Farm Competitiveness in South Sudan*. Report No. 68399-SS (May 23, 2012). Agriculture and Rural Development Unit.

Wulf, H. (2004) 'Security-sector reform in developing and transitional countries', Berghof Handbook Series, The Berghof Center for Constructive Conflict Management, Berlin, Germany.

Ylönen, A. (2005) 'Grievances and the roots of insurgencies: Southern Sudan and Darfur', *Peace, Conflict and Development: An Interdisciplinary Journal*, 7, 99–134.

Young, C. (2004) 'The end of the postcolonial state in Africa? Reflections on changing African political dynamics', *African Affairs*, 103, 23–49.

Young, J. (2006), 'The South Sudan defence forces in the wake of the Juba declaration', Small Arms Survey, Technical report, The Sudan Human Security Baseline Assessment (HSBA), Electronic – HSBA Working Paper 1.

Young, J. (2007) *The White Army: An Introduction and Overview*. Working Paper 5. Small Arms Survey.

Youngs, R. (2008) 'Fusing security and development: Just another Euro-platitude?', *Journal of European Integration*, 30, Issue 3 – Special Issue: Policy Coherence and EU Development Policy, 419–37.

Zehfuss, M. (2001) 'Constructivism and identity: A dangerous liaison', *European Journal of International Relations*, 7, 315.

Index

Abboud, Ibrahim 46
Abdul, Jalil, Musa 192
Addis Ababa Agreement (1972) 51, 52
affordability issues 92–3
Africa 27
    ethnicity and conflict 34–6
    police and policing in 105–6
    post-colonial experience 23–4, 25, 29
    strongman politics 34–5
African Development Bank 169, 170
African identities 22, 28–9, 32–3, 36–7
Africanism 26, 31
African Union 61, 63
African Union Maputo Declaration of 2003 185, 200
Afro-Arab identities 25
Agar, Malik 62
Agreement on the Resolution of the Conflict in the Republic of South Sudan (ARCRSS) 2–3
agriculture 176–7, 180–4, 184–5, 200
    and post-conflict recovery 177–9
Akol, Lam 55, 57
Akot, Daniel Awet 151
Alden, C. 171
Ali, Mohammed 27, 30
Alliance for a Green Revolution in Africa (AGRA) 178
ancient Sudan 26–7, 39
Angola, UNITA 137
Annan, Kofi 166
Anyanya wars *see* civil wars
Apedemak 45
Arab-African 37
Arab identity 28, 38
Arabisation 25
Arabism 26, 31
Arab League 26
Arabs 31
    as superior and master 30
Arnold, M. 171
Arusha Conference (1998) 17

Athor, George 207
Awan, Paul Malong 151

Balkans War 150
Bany, William Nyuon 52
Barnett, M. 43–4
Barre, Siad 34
al-Bashir, Omar Hassan Ahmad 46, 56, 58, 139
Bastian, S. 149
Bayart, J.-F. 158–9
Berlin Conference (1884–5) 26
Bilad al-Sudan (the land of the blacks) 30
bilateral donors 12
black southerners, oppression of *see* slavery and slave trade
Blair, Stephanie 100–1, 102
Blue Nile, rebellions in 62
Boas, M. 35–6
Bol, Kerubino Kuanyin 52
bottom-up 136, 200
Brzoska, M. 70
Bureau for Community Security and Small Arms Control (BCSSAC) 82, 83
Bureau of Community Security 75
Buzan, B. 221 n.2

capacity building programmes 174–5
capital-intensive militarization 44
Catholic Diocese of Torit (CDOT) 47, 163, 179, 180, 181–2
cattle-keeping community 173, 180–1, 183
central government structure 47, 120, 126
Chan, Gabriel Tang Gatwich (aka Tang-Ginye (Long Pipe)) 208
child soldiers 110, 112–15, 120
Chol, Gordon Koang 55, 59, 60
Chuter, D. 72
civilians
    arming of 55, 56, 57
    disarmament of 81, 82–3, 87

and soldiers, distinction between 87–8
civil–military relations restructuring 7
civil wars 24, 26, 30, 34, 36, 67, 87, 91, 94, 168, 172, 187, 190, 201
   Anyanya 2 52, 54
   and elections 147–9
   First Civil War 24, 26, 28, 39, 46–50
   Jesh Ahmr 112–15, 120
   post-independence 1–2
   Second Civil War 33, 39, 51–2, 119
clanism 29, 34
Closed District Order 48
Collins, Robert 31
colonial state legacies 23, 25, 26, 27–8, 29, 33 *see also* Condominium era (1899–1955)
communities
   and firearms 173, 181
   isolated communities 193
compensation programme, First Civil War 95
competitive politics 148
comprehension capacity 191–2
Comprehensive Peace Agreement (CPA) (2005) 1, 31, 58, 61, 65, 67, 70, 75, 94, 96, 131, 134, 187
   and DDR 82
   disarmament 82
   and elections 143
   and institutional and structural changes in security 92–3
   militarization after 58–61
   policing constructions and formulations 103
   SSPS provisions 103–4
concordance theory of civil–military relations 7
Condominium era (1899–1955) 45–6, 48
conflicts *see also* civil wars; war legacies
   and ethnicity, links between 34–6
   motivations for 35–6
   in Sudan's Blue Nile and South Kordofan states 34
constructed identities 33, 34, 38
   and conflicts 37
coups 24, 36, 54
Cramer, Christopher 165
Crowley, P. J. 145–6
cultural identities 33, 115

Dahab, Abdel Rahman Seward 46
Darfur 99
Dargatz, Anja 145
DDR *see* Disarmament Demobilisation and Reintegration (DDR)
December 2013 conflict 66, 99, 188–9, 197, 201
decentralized police system 106
Declaration of Principles (IGAD) 57
demilitarization 5, 7, 9, 10, 13–19, 33, 36, 39–40, 42, 63, 119–20, 123, 136–7, 144, 152, 155, 160, 171, 193, 195, 201
   as a concept 15
   definitions of 15
   dynamics of 19
   and elections 148
   history of 15–16
   of India by emperor Ashoka 16
   institutional 19
   of livelihoods 173–7, 179, 185
   as a multi-track process 19
   perceived success and real changes 137
   as a phenomenon 15
   in the pre-Cold War periods 16
   as a process 15, 16–17
   qualitative versus quantitative 19
   societal 19
   of the state and of the society 18–19
   structural 19
demobilization 87, 88
democracy 10
   democratic consolidation 157
   democratic governance, 149–51, 197
   democratic institutions 157–8
   and elections 149–51
   public forums on 131
Deng, Francis 22, 26, 27, 29, 33, 46
Department of Peacekeeping Operations (DPKO) 83
depopulisation for oil 56, 223 n.12
Derg (Ethiopia) 53, 138
development 10
   and security, convergence of 14
Development Plan 169–71
de Waal, Alex 150
Diamandouros, N. 157
Diehl, K. 192
diplomacy 167

Disarmament Demobilisation and
    Reintegration (DDR) 75–6, 88–9,
    92, 94, 103, 194
  addressing local conflict dynamics
    versus applying as an all-
    encompassing process 78–9
  ambiguity in definitions of 195
  challenges of 78–88
  commission on 75
  and CPA 82
  and force resizing 96
  implementation of 76–7
  integrated' approaches to 76–7, 80–1
  local agency challenges 77
  primary purpose 78
  process phases 88
  resolutions of fourth meeting 84–6
  and SSR 84, 86
  structural and procedural challenges 77
  structure and design of the process 78
donor interventions 12, 70–1, 176
donors and international practitioners and
    local elite, relationship between 70–1
Duffield, Mark 166
Dunn, K. 35–6

Eastern Africa Police Chiefs Cooperation
    Organisation (EAPCCO) 111
Eastern Equatoria 4, 56, 61
  militarized livelihood 172–3
education, limited access to 120 see also
    illiteracy
egalitarian systems 192
Egypt, Egyptians 45, 222 n.2
  independence of 27–8
  role in colonial administrators of Sudan
    48
Eichler, M. 42–3, 44
Eisman, A. 46
elections 123–4, 125, 131, 140–4, 187
  flaws in 144–7
  fraud observed among SPLM
    candidates 145
  limitations of 147–8
  and re-emergence of war 147–9
Emor, Aloisio 151
Enough Project 143
Equatoria 46, 49
Ethiopia 53

ethnicity 33
  and conflict 34–6
  marginalization based on 35
  patronage 159
  and politics 35
  rivalries 186
exercise of power 130–1

factionalism 158–9
firearms
  civilian disarmament 8, 81, 82–3
  and communities 173, 181
  DDR (see Disarmament Demobilisation
    and Reintegration (DDR))
  and livelihoods 163, 198–200
  and livelihoods, in Eastern Equatoria 183
  ownership and use 81
  proliferation of small arms 186
First Sudanese Civil War see civil wars
Fluri, P. 72
food security 185

Gai, Gatluak 208
Gai, Taban Deng 2, 151
Garang, Galuak Deng 151
Garang, John 52, 53, 54, 55, 58, 98
Gatdet, Peter 207
al-Ghazouly, Dafallah 53
Giordano, T. 175
Good Friday Agreement in Northern
    Ireland 107
governance 195–7
  building of 125–9
  and democracy 123, 124–5
  during the war 127–9
  organization of 5
  public forums on 131
  restructuring 124–5, 129–32, 160
  and rules 124
  by the SPLA/M 130, 132–7
Government of South Sudan (GOSS) 127,
    135, 140, 185–6, 199
  semi-autonomous 141
  and SPLA/M-IO forces, fighting
    between 2
Government of Sudan (GOS) 44, 143
  and SPLA, peace negotiations between
    57, 58
  and SPLA-United 57

Greater Upper Nile region 57, 63, 189
greed thesis 37
Gunther, R. 157

Haken, N. 101
Heinemann-Grüder, A. 70
High Executive Council (Southern Sudan Autonomous Region) 51
humanitarianism 10, 15, 126, 176
Hutchful, Eboe 16–17, 201

Iboni 192
identities 26, 28
  African identities 22, 28–9, 32–3, 36–7
  Afro-Arab identities 25
  Arab identity 28, 38
  conflict identities 36–8
  constructed identities 33, 34, 37, 38
  cultural identities 33
  identity complex 31–2
  impact of the colonial legacy on 28–9
  influence in post-conflict planning 36–8
  politicization of 29
  politics 32–4
ideology, shifts in 138–9
Igga, Wani 121
illiteracy 120–1, 161, 191, 192, 193
  and democracy 152–8
Imuyalei, Ikotos County 180–1
insecurity, and underdevelopment 167–8
institutionalization
  of democracy 158
  reform by 101–2
  of security 66
  of SPLA 99
institutional organization 27–8
institutions
  building of 159–60
  establishment 131
  and governance restructuring 158–60
  involvement in internal and external security 75
  issue of building 156–7
  and post-conflict governance restructuring 157
inter-communal fighting see conflicts
Intergovernmental Authority on Development (IGAD) 2, 57, 58, 221 n.4

Interim Constitution of Southern Sudan 96, 103
Interim Disarmament, Demobilisation and Reintegration Programme (IDDRP) 76
Interim National Constitution 96, 103
internal conflict (2013–14), South Sudan 13
International Conference on the Great Lakes Region (ICGLR) 132–3
international engagement in South Sudan 12, 69
International Republican Institute (IRI) 138, 149
international stability 190
Islam 45, 47, 48, 51–2
Islamisation 25, 30, 56

Jesh Ahmr (Red Army) 112–15, 120
  cattle raider story 115, 116–18
  an NGO worker's story 114–15
  an SPLA soldier's story 114
Joint Monitoring and Evaluation Commission (JMEC) 2
Jointness' of action 175
Jok, Jok Madut 57, 213–15
Jonglei 83
Juba Declaration (2006) 59–61, 93, 98, 99, 178
Juluk, Kuol Manyang 151
Justice and Equality Movement (JEM) 99

Kapoeta 143
Kenya, ethnicity in 35
Kevlihan, R. 126
Khartoum 25, 99, 230 n.8
  Arab elites 26
  national government in 139
Khartoum Peace Agreement (KPA) 57–8, 59
Kiyala 95
Kjaer, Anne Mette 124, 157
Konga, Clement Wani 151
Kumba, Jemma Nunu 151

labour-intensive militarization 44
Lagu, Joseph 49
law and order 108, 111
Leonardi, C. 192

liberal peacebuilding 1, 3, 5, 11–13, 40, 67, 75, 77, 108, 160, 187–8, 191, 194, 200
-based security sector reforms 100
challenges facing the pursuit 161
contextualization of experience of 189–93
DDR (*see* Disarmament Demobilisation and Reintegration (DDR))
failings of 67–8
SSR (*see* Security Sector Reforms (SSR))
livestock 180–1
local agency 7, 66, 77, 188
local government 24, 198
locally led post-conflict approach 82
Lost Boys 112–14
Lowoi 46, 47, 50
Luckham, R. 149

Machar, Riek 2, 55, 57, 58, 63, 151, 152, 187, 190
exit from Juba 2–3
Magwi County 173, 179, 180
al-Mahdī, Muammad Amad ibn Abd Allāh 222 n.3(Ch. 3)
Mahdist state 27, 45, 222 n.3
Mamdani, Mahmood 192
Manning, Carrie 125
Mariam, Mengistu Haile 53, 138
Marxist-Leninist socialist 138
Matip, Paulino 59, 60
Mawien, Toor Deng 151
Mayardit, Salva Kiir 6, 59, 134, 187, 198–9
militarism 41–2
definition of 42–3
and demilitarization 15, 16
militarization 41, 62–3
Arab indoctrination 47
Arab north and African south, relationships between 46, 47, 48–9
border disputes 60
capital-intensive 44
colonial administration 48
contextualization of 41–3
definition of 42–3
and deterioration of community relations 57
First Civil War (1955–72) 46–9
Juba Declaration of 8 January 2006 59–61

labour-intensive 44
of livelihoods 171–4, 184
Nasir Declaration 54–6
of policing 109
politics of oil and war 56–8
post-colonial administration 48–9
post-CPA 58–61
post-election insurrections 60, 61
post-independence 46–56
pre-independence (before 1955) 44–6
Second Civil War (1983–2005) 51–2
southern mutinies 52–4
third-world 44
Torit Mutiny 49–51
of youth 119–20, 121
military
and civil society 7
and police 106
and politics 129
structures and attitudes 151–2
militias 44, 56, 59, 60, 62
Ministry of Agriculture 185–6
Ministry of Defence 75, 100
Ministry of Interior 75
Monituel, Bapiny 208
multilateral donors 12, 144
multi-party political system 10, 139
Munyumiji 181–3
Museveni, Yoweri 132–3
Muslim Brotherhood 24
mutinies
southern 52–4
Torit Mutiny 47, 49–51
Mwanika, P. A. N. 101–2

Nasir Declaration 54–6
national census 131
National Congress Party (NCP) 139–40, 143, 145
National DDR Commission 77, 82, 84
National DDR Coordination Council 82
National Defence Forces of South Sudan (NDFSS) 100
National Democratic Institute (NDI) 138, 149
national elections *see* elections
National Elections Commission (NEC) 145
National Intelligence and Security Service 100–1

National Intelligence and Security Service (NISS) 100–1
National Intelligence Service 100
National Islamic Front (NIF) 46, 55–6, 57–8
National Strategic Plan 77
national symbolism 26
Ndlovu-Gatsheni, S. J. 29
neocolonialism 23
neoliberalism 10, 24, 40
Newman, E. 190, 221 n.1
new security, emergence of 14
New South Sudan Administrative Divisions 203
Nile
  basin 45
  riverine kingdoms legacies 27
Nkrumah, Kwame 26
non-urban population 136, 142, 153, 155, 160–1, 191–3
Northern Sudan National DDR Commission 82
north-south civil wars *see* civil wars
Nuba mountains, rebellions in 62
Numeiri, Gaafar Mohamed 46, 50, 51, 52, 56
Nyerere, Julius 26
Nyipuoch, Mark 151

oil
  control over revenues 189
  depopulisation for 56, 223 n.12
  politics of 56–7
Omdurman 230 n.8
Ottaway, Marina 35, 150

party officials 135
patriarchal politics 34–5, 159
patronages 158–9, 188, 198
peace agreement (2015) 72, 74, 76, 93, 103, 189
policing, police service 102–4
  contextual challenges associated with 105
  contextualization of 111
  contextualizing the challenges to 105–8
  decentralized police system 106
  encroachment by SPLA 92
  hierarchical inequalities 109
  needs-driven versus dogma-based 108–12
  perception of societal expectations 110
  in post-conflict restructuring of security 107
  reform plan 106–7
  roles of 106–7
  specialized policing 108–9
  and technology 111
  training school 106
  weaknesses of 106–7
political parties 133, 138
political process 124
post-Cold War period 16
post-colonial identities
  identity complex 31–2
  politics 32–4
post-colonial state 23–8
post-conflict development 175
post-conflict reconstruction
  SSR (*see* Security Sector Reforms (SSR))
post-conflict security 5 *see also* security
  programmes and working groups 71
  spaces 11
post-December 2013 conflict 3, 83, 131, 163
post-election insurrections 147
power, centralization of 24
Przeworski, Adam 157
public forums on democracy and governance 131, 132
public investments 185
public–stakeholders disparities 71
Puhle, H.-J. 157
Pur, M. 113

referendum on independence 131, 187
regional bodies 12
regional government 67
Reiner, R. 110
rent-seeking systems 188
reorganization, and conflicts 98–9
Report to the Fabian Colonial Bureau 31–2
Republic of South Sudan 1
reskilling programmes 174–5
restructuring and reform of
  restructuring 97–100
  restructuring and reform of 66

retirement policy 96
rules and regulations 96
and SPLM 132–7, 190
Revolutionary United Front Party (RUFP) in Sierra Leone 137
Rift Valley Institute forum 187–8
Rolandsen, Ø. 129–30, 136
rule of law 108, 111

Saferworld 83
Salah, al-Tayeb 26
Savimbi, Jonas 124, 148
security 193–5
    ambiguity of 91
    development nexus, gaps in 185
    and development policies 184
    institutions, perception of societal expectations 110
    national security 75, 100, 101, 102
    prioritization 67–8
security reconstruction 7, 91–4 *see also* Disarmament Demobilisation and Reintegration (DDR); Security Sector Reforms (SSR)
    and former rebel army 97–8
Security Sector Reforms (SSR) 68–9, 84, 92, 194
    ambiguity in definitions of 195
    complexities of 71–2
    and DDR 86, 92
    definitions of 72–3
    and development 69–76
    donor-driven 70
    extent and intent in South Sudan 70
    intended outcomes and goals as 73–4
    trajectory of after 2005 CPA 74
Security Sector Transformation (SST) 71, 72, 74
Selby, J. 41–2
September Laws 52, 56
Sharia law 52, 56
Shilluk 45
Sierra Leone, DDR process 79
slavery and slave trade 28–31, 45, 222 n.2, 222 n.3(Ch. 3)
    slave raiding 56
small arms, proliferation of 57, 62
Snyder, J. 159
social economic development 164–5, 200

and demilitarization 165–8
social organization 27–8
socio-economic crisis 163
Soderlund 138
soldier and civilian, distinction between 87–8
Somalia 34
South Africa, post-apartheid 107
South America 16
Southern Equatoria Corps (SEC) 50
Southern Sudan Defence Council 101–2
Southern Sudan National DDR Commission 82
South Sudan 1, 21 *see also individual entries*
    ARCRSS agreement 2–3
    independence of 37–8
    post-colonialism 23–4
    post-conflict security in 23
    secession of 37
    state-building 24, 25–8
South Sudan Armed Rebellions 207–8
South Sudan Defence Forces (SSDF)
    disintegration of 60
    integration into SPLA 59, 60
South Sudan Disarmament Demobilisation and Reintegration Commission (SSDDRC) 88
South Sudan Liberation Movement (SSLM) 49
South Sudan National Disarmament Demobilisation and Reintegration Commission (SSNDDRC) 83
South Sudan Police Service (SSPS) 66, 102–4
    challenges of 104
    domination by SPLA 109–10
    From the shadows of the SPLA 104–5
South Sudan Security Committee 101–2
South Sudan's National Bureau of Statistics (SSNBS) 169
Soviet Union, arms deal with 50
Special Needs Groups (SNG) 79–80
SPLA *see* Sudan People's Liberation Army (SPLA)
SPLA Act 96
SPLA-drawn police
    civilian police 105

soldiers passed on to the SSPS after the CPA 105
SPLA-IO 97
SPLA-Torit 58
SPLA-United 56, 57–8
SPLA White Paper on Defence (2008) 96
SPLM *see* Sudan People's Liberation Movement (SPLM)
SPLM-North (SPLM-N) 62–3
state-building 13, 68
statehood 1, 10, 24, 26–7, 39
Stavrianakis, A. 41–2
strongman politics 34–5
sub-Saharan Africa 16, 185
Sudan 21–2, 62, 170
  borders 26
  Closed District Order 48
  colonial administration of 48
  colonial state legacies 23
  countercoups 24
  democratic front 24
  Egyptian military officials and civil servants removal from 27–8
  First Sudanese Civil War (1955–72) 46–9
  imperialist state 25
  Second Sudanese Civil War (1983–2005) 51–2
  sovereignty 21
  state formation 23–5
  statehood, journey to 26–7
  timeline 22
  Torit Mutiny 49–51
  underdevelopment 24–5
Sudan Administrative Conference (SAC) of 1946 48
Sudan Armed Forces (SAF) 59, 61
Sudan Army 54, 55, 56
Sudanese Communist Party 24
Sudan Liberation Army
  Abdul Wahid faction (SLA-AW) 99
  Minni Minawi faction (SLA-MM) 99
Sudan People's Liberation Army (SPLA) 54–5, 61, 66, 91, 92
  active service soldiers 95
  administrative structures 126
  and arming of civilians 55, 56
  civilian disarmament 83
  and civil war 94
  communications department of 135
  complexity of professionalizing 66
  day-to-day law and order matters 92
  divisions and locations 98–9
  dominance, post-CPA 98
  domination of the SSPS by 109–10
  downsizing of 93–4
  encroachment into police service functions 92
  Ethiopia's support to 53
  force reduction 93, 94–7
  formation of 52
  inclusivity issue 95
  integration of SSDF into 59, 60
  mandatory decommissioning[reduction] 93
  monopoly and hold over security 92
  and National Islamic Front (NIF) 55–6
  as peacetime force 96–7
  post-CPA 2005 80, 97
  professionalization, 94
  reform frameworks 96
  reorganization into peacetime force 96–7
  resentment of local communities against 56
  retirement issue 95–6
  split in 55, 56
  and SSPS, distinguishing between 110
  trajectory of 52–3
Sudan People's Liberation Army/Movement (SPLA/M) 44, 53, 54, 59, 60, 67, 87, 133
  and governance 127–9
  interpretation of democracy by leadership of 134
  peace agreement 1
  split in 1991 33
  visas and travel permits 127–8
  war 33, 39
Sudan People's Liberation Army/Movement In Opposition (SPLA/M-IO) 2, 94
Sudan People's Liberation Movement (SPLM) 99, 188
  dominance of 137–40
  inexperience of 139
  power struggle within 1, 188
  as a proper political party 134
Sudan Political Service 28

Sudan Recovery Fund (SRF) 176
Sudan Relief and Rehabilitation Association (SRRA) 126
Sudan Revolutionary Front (SRF) 99

Taban, Paride 47
Taft, P. 101
third-world militarization 44
top-down approach 200
Torit Mutiny 47, 49–51, 143, 178, 190
Touré, Ahmed Sékou 26
traditional government 192
Transitional Government of National Unity (TGoNU) 2, 3, 65, 70, 196
Transitional Military Council (TMC) 53–4
Tribe, Michael 222 n.5 (Ch. 3)
Tschirgi, Necla 184, 185
Turco-Egyptian state 27, 30, 37
Turks 45, 222 n.2

underdevelopment
  history of 168–9
  and militarism 198
unemployment 73, 186, 200
United Kingdom 25
  House of Commons Committee on International Development 166
United Nations 13
  agencies 12, 83–4
  Development Programme 83, 226 n.2
  Food Agriculture Organisation (FAO) 178
  Human Development Index (HDI) 169
  Integrated Disarmament, Demobilisation and Reintegration Standards (IDDRS) 75–6, 81, 83
  Mission in South Sudan (UNMISS) 69, 194
  Mission in Sudan (UNMIS) 69, 77 (*see also* Disarmament Demobilisation and Reintegration (DDR))
  Security Council, resolution 2046 61, 63
United States
  Agency for International Development (USAID) 149, 175–6
  guide to economic development 175

violence experts 81
visas and travel permits 127–8
'Voices of the Poor' 166
voter registration 131 *see also* elections

war legacies 112–15, 120
  and underdevelopment 168
Wassara, Samson 216–19
Wendt, A. 43–4
White Army 55
Wolfensohn, James 165
Woodward, Peter 26
World Bank 169, 176, 178
World Food Programme 183
world wars 16
Wulf, H. 73–4, 75

Yau Yau, David 60, 63, 207
youth, militarization of 173

Zande Scheme 49

www.ingramcontent.com/pod-product-compliance
Lightning Source LLC
Chambersburg PA
CBHW070021010526
44117CB00011B/1658